PROTECTING CHILDREN AND SUPPORTING FAMILIES

MODERN APPLICATIONS OF SOCIAL WORK

An Aldine de Gruyter Series of Texts and Monographs

Series Editor

James K. Whittaker

Paul Adams and Kristine E. Nelson (eds.), **Reinventing Human Services: Community and Family Centered Practice**

Ralph E. Anderson and Irl Carter, **Human Behavior in the Social Environment: A Social Systems Approach** (Fourth Edition)

Richard P. Barth, Mark Courtney, Jill Duerr Berrick, and Vicky Albert, **From Child Abuse to Permanency Planning: Child Welfare Services Pathways and Placements**

Gary Cameron and Jim Vanderwoerd, **Protecting Children and Supporting Families: Promising Programs and Organizational Realities**

Kathleen Ell and Helen Northen, **Families and Health Care: Psychosocial Practice**

Marian Fatout, **Models for Change in Social Group Work**

Mark W. Fraser, Peter J. Pecora, and David A. Haapala, **Families in Crisis: The Impact of Intensive Family Preservation Services**

James Garbarino, **Children and Families in the Social Environment** (Second Edition)

James Garbarino, and Associates, **Special Children—Special Risks: The Maltreatment of Children with Disabilities**

James Garbarino, and Associates, **Troubled Youth, Troubled Families: Understanding Families At-Risk for Adolescent Maltreatment**

Roberta R. Greene, **Social Work with the Aged and Their Families**

Roberta R. Greene, **Human Behavior Theory: A Diversity Framework**

Roberta R. Greene and Paul H. Ephross, **Human Behavior Theory and Social Work Practice**

André Ivanoff, Betty J. Blythe, and Tony Tripodi, **Involuntary Clients in Social Work Practice: A Research-Based Approach**

Susan Kemp, James K. Whittaker, and Elizabeth M. Tracy, **Person-Environment Practice: The Social Ecology of Interpersonal Helping**

Paul K. H. Kim (ed.), **Serving the Elderly: Skills for Practice**

Jill Kinney, David A. Haapala, and Charlotte Booth, **Keeping Families Together: The Homebuilders Model**

Robert M. Moroney, **Social Policy and Social Work: Critical Essays on the Welfare State**

Peter J. Pecora, Mark W. Fraser, Kristine Nelson, Jacqueline McCroskey, and William Meezan, **Evaluating Family-Based Services**

Peter J. Pecora, James K. Whittaker, Anthony N. Maluccio, Richard P. Barth, and Robert D. Plotnick, **The Child Welfare Challenge: Policy, Practice, and Research**

Robert L. Selman, Lynn Hickey Schultz, and Caroline L. Watts (eds.) **Fostering Friendship: Pair Therapy for Treatment and Prevention**

John R. Schuerman, Tina L. Rzepnicki, and Julia H. Littell, **Putting Families First: An Experiment in Family Preservation**

Madeline R. Stoner, **The Civil Rights of Homeless People: Law, Social Policy, and Social Work Practice**

Betsy S. Vourlekis and Roberta R. Greene (eds). **Social Work Case Management**

James K. Whittaker, and Associates, **Reaching High-Risk Families: Intensive Family Preservation in Human Services**

PROTECTING CHILDREN AND SUPPORTING FAMILIES

Promising Programs and Organizational Realities

Gary Cameron and Jim Vanderwoerd
with the assistance of Leslea Peirson

ALDINE DE GRUYTER
New York

About the Authors

Gary Cameron is the Director of the Centre for Social Welfare Studies and associate professor in the Faculty of Social Work, Wilfrid Laurier University, Waterloo, Ontario, Canada.

Jim Vanderwoerd (MSW) is a Research Coordinator with the Centre for Social Welfare Studies, Faculty of Social Work, Wilfrid Laurier University, Waterloo, Ontario, Canada

Leslea Peirson has a Master's degree in Community Psychology from Wilfrid Laurier University, Waterloo, Ontario, Canada

Copyright © 1997 by Walter de Gruyter, Inc., New York

All rights reserved. No part of this publication may be reproduced or transmitted in any form or by any means, electronic or mechanical, including photocopying, recording, or any information storage or retrieval system, without prior permission in writing from the publisher.

ALDINE DE GRUYTER
A division of Walter de Gruyter, Inc.
200 Saw Mill River Road
Hawthorne, New York 10532

This publication is printed on acid free paper ∞

Library of Congress Cataloging-in-Publication Data
Cameron, Gary.
  Protecting children and supporting families : promising programs
and organizational realities / Gary Cameron and Jim Vanderwoerd ;
with the assistance of Leslea Peirson.
    p.   cm. — (Modern applications of social work)
  Includes bibliographical references and index.
  ISBN 0-202-36105-5 (alk. paper). — ISBN 0-202-36106-3 (pbk. :
alk. paper)
    1. Social work with children—Canada.   2. Socially handicapped children—
Services for—Canada.   3. Child welfare—Canada.   4. Family social work—
Canada.   I. Vanderwoerd, Jim.   II. Peirson, Leslea.   III. Title.   IV. Series.
  IIV745.A6C2   1997
  362.7'0971—dc20   96-33570
                                                                          CIP

Manufactured in the United States of America

10   9   8   7   6   5   4   3   2   1

To Diane Cameron
for the magic and the inspiration

Contents

Acknowledgments

Funding for the research required to complete this volume was provided by the Waterloo Area Office, Ontario Ministry of Community and Social Services, and by National Welfare Grants, Health and Welfare Canada. We also want to express our appreciation for the financial support for several research and continuing education projects, which allowed us to formulate some of the ideas expressed in this book, provided by the Laidlaw Foundation, Toronto; National Welfare Grants, Health and Welfare Canada; Social Sciences and Humanities Research Council, Ottawa; and, Ontario Ministry of Community and Social Services.

The presence of the Centre for Social Welfare Studies at the Faculty of Social Work, Wilfrid Laurier University permitted the work required for this book to be undertaken. Staff at the centre have been instrumental in allowing this and many other related projects to be completed successfully. Thanks for the contributions of Lyne Renaud, Karen Hayward, and Marilyn Jacobs. The centre was the inspiration of Dean Shankar Yelaja, and we want to thank him for his vision and unwavering support for our efforts.

Michael Rothery at the Faculty of Social Work, University of Calgary, worked with Gary Cameron on several earlier family support projects, and his contributions are reflected in this book.

Special thanks to Lyne Renaud, who is responsible for the word processing and graphics required in this project.

Finally, the members of the three parent mutual aid organizations with which we worked (WISH, HOPES, MAPP) showed us how enthusiastic and effective parents can be in helping themselves and each other. In addition, Pam Kipp and Roy Walsh of the Children's Aid Society at Brant were particularly helpful in enabling us to better understand the nature and potential of informal helping in child welfare.

An Overview of Support Programs

Child welfare service providers and administrators face daunting challenges in improving their work with children and families. They are increasingly under pressure to demonstrate greater efficiency in their operations and often express the concern that they have been asked to "do more with less." More and more, child welfare personnel are seeking better ways to help the people they serve. There is a growing awareness of new and promising ways of working with various child welfare populations—interventions that seem to bring greater benefits to clients and to reduce costs for the host organizations. Yet how to choose? How can these approaches be adapted to their realities?

There is currently no well-defined way for child welfare personnel interested in promising programs to decide in an informed fashion between competing approaches—some of which are being sold in a very assertive fashion. It is also clear that no one knows how their organizations would have to change to accommodate these new approaches to helping. There is also no guidance available about how these new approaches fit within the legal mandates of child welfare organizations or how these mandates would have to change. Finally, child welfare personnel find themselves in a double bind as financial resources become scarcer. On the one hand, there is pressure to be more conservative and to concentrate resources on traditional, mandated services. On the other hand, there are expectations to be more effective and to incorporate better ways of helping children and families. It is not clear how these contradictory demands can be brought into balance.

This volume is intended to begin sorting out these issues in a constructive fashion. While our attention will focus upon child welfare, much of the information presented will be relevant to working with other disadvantaged populations. The volume has several purposes: (a) to present an up-to-date review and interpretation of the research evidence about the effectiveness of various popular and/or promising program models for working with disadvantaged children and families; (b) to develop a program impact framework that will be useful for understanding and developing a range of program approaches and for seeing their relationship to each other; and (c) to begin a systematic discussion of the issues that need to be faced in incorporating the more promising ways of helping as everyday ways of working in child welfare and other settings.

In creating our arguments, we have drawn on information from various knowledge bases: (a) information about the nature and effectiveness of formal programs designed to support families with children at risk of abuse and neglect and out-of-home placements; (b) evidence about the nature of promising prevention approaches with disadvantaged children and families; (c) social support theory and research describing its relevance and effectiveness in high-stress situations; and (d) information about the nature and effectiveness of mutual aid/self-help organizations with disadvantaged populations. Our emphasis has been on the synthesis of information from these various sources in order to inform social service practice and organization. Finally, we have given priority to understanding approaches designed to prevent child abuse and neglect and to minimize out-of-home placements of children. We do not address directly issues of placement, protection, and treatment of children and families after serious trauma or breakdown has occurred. Nor do we discuss the investigative or legal monitoring requirements of child welfare. However, many of the principles and methods discussed have relevance to working with children and families in these unfortunate circumstances since they share numerous challenges with the rest of the child welfare population.

This project builds upon a number of research and demonstration projects in which the principal author has participated over the past ten years. Between 1983 and 1986, we carried out an investigation of the nature and effectiveness of family support services in sixteen Ontario child welfare agencies—including a review of 547 cases and an assessment of eight different family support programs (Rothery & Cameron, 1985). From 1988 to 1992, we were involved in a demonstration project creating and assessing parent mutual aid organizations in three child welfare settings (Cameron, Hayward, & Mamatis, 1992). Currently, we are investigating the nature and effectiveness of intensive family preservation services (IFPS) in five child welfare and children's mental health settings in Ontario (Hayward & Cameron, 1993). Finally, we are completing an action research project with four child welfare agencies and local government officials focused on the challenges of translating innovative program ideas into every day ways of working in child welfare agencies. In addition to these research and demonstration projects, we have hosted two conferences focusing on interventions with high-risk populations and have edited two volumes comprised of selected papers from these conferences (Pressman, Cameron, & Rothery, 1989; Rothery & Cameron, 1990).

This work over the past decade was the crucible within which the principles and ideas in this volume were forged. These principles and ideas have been shared with many graduate students and community professionals across Canada during this period, greatly helping to clarify our thinking. In addition, for this volume, we have supplemented this previous work with a comprehensive review of the research evidence on the effectiveness of the program approaches discussed later.

Our overall objective has been to translate disparate research findings and general theoretical formulations into practical ways of thinking for those wishing to help disadvantaged children and families. In the end, it seemed most important to try to help people to be able to make their own sense of the claims made by proponents of different programs and to help them to choose and to combine program elements that are appropriate for their particular settings. Finally, there was an interest in assisting people to grapple with the unaddressed challenges of reorganizing child welfare agencies to take advantage of what we have learned about helping children and families over the past decades.

Our ambition in reviewing theory and research on social support and formal support programs has been to interpret, as a guide to creating interventions, what is already known, rather than to break new ground theoretically or to resolve outstanding research issues. Nonetheless, our effort to construct a general framework that can be used to understand a broad range of formal and informal ways of helping does represent an original contribution. While the effort is far from complete, the conceptual framework outlined in this volume can be used to comprehend the potential of quite different approaches to helping disadvantaged families and to understand how these approaches can be used to complement each other. Eventually, we want to contribute to an "expanded concept of helping" (Rothery & Cameron, 1990) in child welfare and other jurisdictions. In addition, the extensive literature and research review in this volume should be of interest to practitioners, administrators, policymakers and others who are curious about finding better ways to help children and families.

Our work has suggested the need for and the potential for creating a sense-making framework for "supportive" interventions. On the one hand, a variety of program approaches with very different parameters or characteristics are being used indiscriminately and interchangeably. It is common to find programs that differ on almost every important program parameter (e.g., frequency of contact, duration of involvement, functional content of interventions, types of helpers) that are described as producing identical outcomes (e.g., preventing child abuse and neglect, reducing out-of-home placements, improving parenting, improving child-parent relations, augmenting parental self-esteem, increasing parental life skills, etc.). Most programs are justified on the basis of very general rationales with very little explicit attention paid to how actual program content, parameters, and participant characteristics relate to predicted program impacts. On the other hand, there is reason to believe that it is possible to use available evidence about program characteristics and their relationships to outcome patterns to construct a generic impact framework to understand the potential of various approaches to helping children and families.

The repertoire of helping strategies being tried in almost all programs in child welfare is very limited: basically adaptations of familiar formal helping methods such as individual and group counselling, behavior modification, and educational strategies that focus on specific areas of personal and family functioning (Cameron & Rothery, 1985; Rothery & Cameron, 1990). More recently, formal crisis intervention strategies have become quite popular. Much less frequently, paraprofessional helpers are being used. What is striking, despite the powerful theoretical and empirical support for the importance of positive social connections for coping with problems, for a positive sense of self, and for ongoing well-being, and the accessibility of practical program models based on these informal processes, is the almost total lack of attention paid to informal ways of helping and to positive social integration.

In addition, most programs and interventions in child welfare focus on a narrow range of individual and family concerns—those considered to be proper for child welfare—for example, parenting, child-parental interactions, basic life skills, and selected child development issues. This continues despite good theoretical and empirical reasons for believing that a much broader range of factors are important contributors to child abuse and neglect and to family breakdown—factors such as social isolation of children and parents, inadequate diets, poor physical health, school difficulties, lack of meaningful social roles, unsafe neighborhoods, bad housing, delinquent peer relations, substance abuse, and lack of money. It is sensible to anticipate that helping strategies that help to remove or to reduce a greater number of these sources of stress will produce superior outcomes within multiple-problem situations. There is a need to look at much more holistic and flexible ways of helping in child welfare. It is our contention that a support perspective in child welfare can be useful in expanding our concepts of helping in appropriate fashions.

Support is a term that is poorly understood and is used to refer to a confusing array of activities. Some of this ambiguity can be attributed to the fact that a variety of formal and informal relationships and helping strategies can legitimately be considered supportive of families and children. For example, consider the following scenarios:

- A man trains on the job as a mechanic after two years of unemployment.
- A young multiply challenged woman has just successfully completed her academic training and faces the intimidating challenge of finding work in order to continue living independently in the community. Her

counselor calls a meeting of fifteen members of her social network to help her through this difficult period.

- A single mother cannot cope with the responsibilities of caring for her children this week. Her friend in a single mothers' self-help group takes her kids for a few days.
- A middle-aged woman finds herself actively involved in planning for the local multicultural center after recently being elected to its board of directors.
- A "stay-at-home" mother plays the heroine in an amateur theatre production.
- A crisis intervention worker works in a family's home for many hours a day during a time of high stress.
- A team of homemakers, public health nurses, and pediatricians reaches out and establishes ongoing contact with young mothers identified in the hospital as being potentially at high risk for child maltreatment.
- Teenagers having difficulty in school and at home are provided with a house to go to four days a week after school where they can join their peers in social, recreational, and educational activities.
- A judo instructor shows special interest in one of his young protégés.
- A child management worker spends time regularly with a lonely mother to improve her social skills.

It will become clear in the following chapters that useful support may be anticipated from each of the above situations and that the types of benefits that can be reasonably expected are not identical across all of these scenarios. One implication for service providers is that the adoption of a support perspective requires rejection of a preferred way of helping and a preferred type of helper. There are times when it is more worthwhile to participate in an amateur theatre production than to be involved with a professional counselor or treatment group. In order to exploit the potential of support interventions, we have to become more able to differentiate the potential of various types of supportive relationships and to comprehend how these various approaches might be combined to complement each other. In particular, because they have been so neglected, we have to resurrect informal and social ways of helping that are fundamental to people's well-being yet usually do not place the professional at the center of the helping nexus.

Although many of the principles and methods underpinning a support approach to disadvantaged families are not new to the social services (Specht, 1986), our contention is that these ideas can be used provide a useful integrating perspective. For example, it is our experience that the theory and language of support bridges the traditional gaps between those focusing on personal and family functioning and those emphasizing the importance of environmental context in determining outcomes. As social workers, we have found two clear benefits to using a support perspective: (a) it offers a vocabulary that bridges both clinical and community intervention realities, that is, it helps people to talk to each other and appreciate the potential contributions of the other orientation; and (b) it identifies a powerful, yet neglected, middle range of program options or approaches to helping between the traditional "micro" and "macro" emphases. A support perspective provides concepts and guides to interventions that, sadly, seem absent from the training of most social workers and other professional helpers.

PARAMETERS FOR SUPPORT PROGRAMS

Because of the potentially open-ended nature of the support concept, it is necessary to define what will be considered in these discussions. The phrase *support programs* has been chosen to refer to the types of helping approaches examined here. The term *support* is appropriate for two reasons:

(1) This volume looks at helping approaches that are typically classified under a variety of categories such as social support, family support, family preservation, prevention, child management, parent education, and self-help/mutual aid. It was useful to have a generic label within which critical elements from these different approaches to helping disadvantaged populations could be synthesized.

(2) The focus is on supporting children and parents to prevent serious occurrences of child abuse and neglect as well as unnecessary out-of-home child placements and to help children and families to prosper.

The term *programs* is useful because we will be comparing types of helping strategies that are identifiable and coherent wholes, that is, they have describable program rationales, content, and structural parameters and there is some history of evaluation research for them. Even though we will eventually make an argument for the need to move beyond thinking in terms of discrete program approaches and to seek more flexibility in how we create organizations to work with children and families, initially it will be helpful to investigate the potential and the complementarity of specific types of programs.

As mentioned, there are a few helping interventions or environmental manipulations that cannot be considered in some way to be supportive of children and families. However, when the support construct is defined this expansively, it loses its practical relevance. On the other hand, some defini-

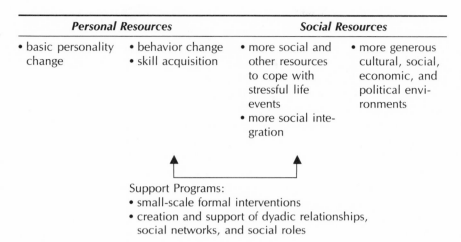

Personal Resources		*Social Resources*	
• basic personality change	• behavior change • skill acquisition	• more social and other resources to cope with stressful life events • more social integration	• more generous cultural, social, economic, and political environments

Support Programs:
• small-scale formal interventions
• creation and support of dyadic relationships, social networks, and social roles

Figure 1.1   Parameters of support programs.

tions of support include only a narrow range of informal relationships such as friendships, peer networks, and family relations. As a guide to understanding a variety of promising approaches to helping families, this focused definition is too restrictive. It is important to be able to look at a range of informal and formal helping strategies and how they potentially can relate to each other. The parameters of the definition of support programs for this volume are described in Figure 1.1.

Support will refer to the benefits received from the immediate environment within which the majority of the person's activities take place. Our definition includes support received from both formal and informal helpers. The focus will be upon the web of interpersonal contacts that are important, or can become so, to a person's success at everyday living.

Our conception of support programs is deliberately restricted. For example, while it is evident that economic and social policies have a great influence over the problems that individuals and families confront, and over the resources they have available to manage these difficulties, the type of work required to bring about such policy changes falls outside our definition of support programs. Support programs are conceived of as relatively small-scale efforts that provide individuals, families, or small groups of people with direct access to the personal and/or social resources that they require in order to be able to cope with problems and/or to maintain their ongoing well-being. While a complete conception of psychological or social well-being would have to pay attention to the characteristics of the broader economic, political, and social environments (Bronfenbrenner, 1979;

Brown, 1986; Rappaport, 1977), such general concerns will not be addressed by our discussion of support programs.

In a similar view, many researchers have demonstrated that basic personality characteristics and the early life experiences that contribute to the development of these traits strongly influence people's access to supportive relationships and their ability to personally benefit from such relationships (Kessler, McLeod, & Wethington, 1985; Hobfoll, 1985; W. H. Jones, 1985; Lefcourt, 1985; Mitchell, 1982; Monroe, 1983; Pepleau, 1985; Thoits, 1982). However, our conception of support programs does not include the intensive therapies designed to bring about fundamental changes in personality or to manage serious emotional or psychiatric disorders. To the extent that this definition of support programs focuses upon personal or family change, it concentrates upon specific behavior changes, or upon the acquisition of knowledge or skills, that are directly relevant to people's capacity to cope with stressful life events or to their ability to access and benefit from supportive relationships and social roles. Without in any way negating the value of more intensive therapies, a consideration of their nature and effectiveness is beyond the scope of this volume.

In summary, in order to render the idea of support programs manageable, the definition concentrates upon those formal and informal exchanges and interpersonal relationships that help people directly to cope with stressful events or that foster positive social identities and feelings of belonging. Support programs are those which bring about relevant changes in personal and family behaviors or abilities or that constructively modify the person's or family's immediate environment. Considerations of fostering basic personality changes or coping with serious psychological problems or of modifying macroenvironmental circumstances are not covered by this definition of support programs.

ORGANIZATION OF THE VOLUME

In Chapters 2 and 3, social support theory and research are reviewed and linked to the construction of support programs. Following this discussion, Chapter 4 reviews the lessons from earlier assessments of the effectiveness of various formal and informal support programs. This discussion is purposively brief because subsequent chapters include more in-depth examinations of the nature and effectiveness of selected types of formal and informal support programs. Chapter 5 develops a generic support program impact framework building upon the discussion in the previous chapters. In Part II, Chapters 6 through 10 examine the rationales and the evidence for the effectiveness of a range of promising formal and informal support program types. In Part III, Chapter 12 looks at incentives and obstacles in adopting a support perspective in child welfare. Chapter 13 discusses organization design and administrative issues emanating from a support perspective in child welfare.

A Framework For Understanding Programs to Protect Children and Support Families

The main purpose of this volume is to develop a way to understand diverse support programs, which will allow us to describe and to differentiate these programs' potential as well as their limitations. We believe that our most useful contribution is a way of thinking—a more systematic and informed basis for creating and assessing programs for disadvantaged children and families. The Support Program Impact Assessment Framework elaborated in Chapters 2 through 5 is presented for this purpose.

Chapter 5 provides an overview of the impact principles, methods, and questions constituting our Support Program Impact Assessment Framework. However, this Framework relies directly on the ideas and evidence highlighted in Chapters 2, 3, and 4. A careful reading of these chapters is required in order to understand the Support Program Impact Assessment Framework and to use it in an informed fashion. In addition, the Framework provides the structure used to review the five general categories of support programs discussed in Chapters 6 to 10.

The Support Program Impact Assessment Framework synthesizes a substantial amount of conceptual and empirical information about informal and formal helping strategies. It requires some diligence to absorb this material, but, in our experience, the benefit of this exercise is greater clarity in our efforts to create promising programs for struggling children and families.

What Is Social Support? 2

This chapter and the next examine social support theory and research in some detail. There are several reasons for paying this much attention to the social support construct. First, understanding the nature and the potential of social support focuses our attention on an important range of helping approaches that essentially have been ignored by helping professionals in child welfare and in most other settings. Second, we will become oriented to helping processes that complement professional methods, which typically focus on personal and family change. Indeed, a basic thesis in this volume is that, unless we find ways to construct packages of a broader range of formal and informal ways of helping as a regular part of our work with disadvantaged children and families, we will not see superior outcomes. Finally, social support theory and research allow us insights into challenges of general interest in social services such as the development of positive self-esteem and the reconstruction of shattered identities. These insights are different than those embedded in our preferred helping paradigms. We learn both the limits of what we can contribute directly as paid helpers and therapists and the importance of using our auspices to open up different kinds of helping relationships for both children and their parents.

FUNCTIONAL CONTENT OF SOCIAL SUPPORT

In the research on social support, the construct has been defined and operationalized in a disconcertingly large variety of ways; nonetheless, there are some general areas of agreement about the nature of social support provisions. It is clear that social support should be viewed as a multidimensional construct with various functional and structural components (Gottlieb, 1983; Vaux, 1988; Wilcox & Vernberg, 1985). Social support is not a single thing; it cannot be represented by one sort of assistance, or by one type of relationship. Rather, nearly all definitions of the functional content of social support—the types of assistance that are helpful—indicate that there are various kinds of social support assistance, and most would agree that any consideration of the value of social support should be specific about the functional content available. For example, a particular supportive relationship might provide friendly encouragement and empathy, instruction in useful life skills, or concrete assistance such as child care, or confirmation of one's social position and worth, or any combination of these supports.

It also is clear that the various functional components of social support—or the different types of social support assistance—are not equally relevant to each problem situation. Access to emotional support or appropriate information and guidance may be helpful in a variety of stressful situations, whereas concrete supports—such as child care—may only be relevant to coping with particular stressors (Cohen & Wills, 1985; Kessler & McLeod, 1985; Vaux, 1988). When considering the relevance of the social support received or offered, especially when the interest is in helping people to manage specific life difficulties, it is important to consider the appropriateness of the match between the functional content of the support and the problems confronting the individual or family.

In addition, while most research operationalizes social support in terms of general categories of assistance such as emotional support or informational support, greater specificity about the actual content of the assistance provided will be required when assessing specific support program models. While some types of social support are considered generally relevant to many problem situations, which may help to explain why social support research has repeatedly shown positive benefits across many problems and populations (Vaux, 1988), with our interest in the creation of viable support program models for disadvantaged families, more detailed attention will have to be paid to the content and to the delivery mechanisms underpinning these helping strategies. These issues will be discussed in some detail later.

Valuable social support can be provided by different types of people under a variety of arrangements. Social support can come from a relationship with a family member, with a friend, from working on a project with colleagues, from neighbors, from volunteering to help others, from peers in a created support or mutual aid group, from formal classroom or in-home instruction about relevant skills or coping strategies, from professional or peer counseling, and so on. A focus on the functional content of supportive relationships indicates that formal helpers as well as informal helpers can be useful sources of social support.

A basic tenet in our concept of support programs is that these various types of helpers, and the intervention strategies developed around them, are generally not substitutable for each other. As will be elaborated later, many formal and informal helpers have almost opposite strengths and weaknesses and, even within these two categories, various helpers can be differentiated in terms of the benefits that they can be expected to provide. For example, a professional social worker may be particularly well suited to provide short-term emotional support and problem-relevant advice to a family, but singularly unable to use her/his personal relationship with family members to foster in them a more positive social identity. An in-home worker may be an excellent source of high levels of crisis support, but quite inappropriate as a long-term support for a family. Similarly, immediate family members often can be excellent sources of long-term emotional support and substantial concrete support when coping with serious life difficulties; however, ongoing, reciprocal relationships with friends and co-workers may make a more substantial contribution to positive feelings of self-worth and affiliation (Hall & Wellman, 1985; Litwak, 1985; Schulz & Rau, 1985; Shumaker & Brownell, 1984). Hall and Wellman (1985) reinforce the perception of the differential contributions of various kinds of helpers:

> Our East York study has found that ties are quite specialized in the supportive resources they convey with clear distinction between many of those ties that provide emotional aid, companionship, services, information, and financial aid. (p. 37)

An understanding of the structural dimensions of helping relationships can be used to illustrate the potential contributions of various types of helping relationships and helping strategies in multiple problem situations. Eugene Litwak (1985) utilized this basic idea in differentiating various types of helpers in his study of the elderly (see Table 2.1 and Table 2.2).

From the perspective of developing useful helping strategies, acceptance of this functional conception of social support, and the structured advantages and disadvantages of various types of helpers, requires a rejection of the idea of a preferred way of helping or a preferred type of helper. In particular, for social service providers, creativity in support provision lies in developing an ability to link users of services with a variety of formal and informal helpers and in expanding the repertoire of helping strategies that we are willing and able to use to support those who come to us for assistance.

Typologies of the functional content of social support provisions abound in the social support literature (see Table 2.3 for a representative selection). The functional typology adopted for this volume has been synthesized from the literature with two objectives in mind:

1. to incorporate those functional components of social support that are most commonly identified;
2. to accommodate the basic distinction made in the social support literature between social support provision intended to increase abilities to cope with particular stressful circumstances (the buffering effect) and provisions that foster a sense of well-being independently of the presence of stressors (the main effect).

However, the decision to adapt the typology to incorporate both the buffering- and the main-effect models of social support is somewhat awkward in that it involves classifying two basically different helping processes within a

Table 2.1. Forms of Differentiation in Primary-Group Structure That Have Evolved in Modern Industrial Society

Dimensions of Group and Task Structure	Some Typical Types of Primary Groups				
	Marital Dyad	Modified Extended Family	Friends	Neighbors	Formal Organizations
Face-to-face continual contact of group	Highest	Low	Low	High	Low
Long-term commitments	High	Highest	Moderate	Low	Lowest
Size	Smallest	Large	Large	Large	Very Large
Affection	High	High	High	Moderate	Lowest
Duty to group survival	High	Highest	Moderate	Low	Lowest
Common life style (age homogeneity)	High	Low	High	Moderate	Lowest
Peer ties	High	High	Highest	High	Low
Membership eligibility—everyday socialization	High	High	High	High	Low
Division of labor	Low	Low	Low	Low	High
Illustrations of Services That Match Dimensions of Groups in Columns Above					
	Daily cooking, shopping, housecleaning, laundry	Care for bedridden for 2 to 3 weeks; emotional support in death of spouse	Companions for free-time activities; advice on daily living for widows	Reporting "break-ins" while out; helping with daily chores; emergency loans of small household items	Major surgery; 24-hour permanent care of older person; selling food; arresting criminals

(Source: Litwak, 1985, p. 37)

Table 2.2. Percentage of Older Persons Saying They Received Services, by Relation to Helper and Type of Service

Percentage of Respondents Choosing Each Group

Helper's Relation to Respondent	Neighborhood Services		Friendship Services		Kinship Services		Individual or Marital Household Services	
	Watch House while Shopping	Borrow Small Things in Hurry	Join as Companion for Free Time	Check Daily	Provide Home Nursing Care	Provide Emotional Succor when Upset	Store Clothes and Do Laundry	Manage Money, Bills, Bank Account, Social Security
Neighbors	73.0	69.0	29.0	32.0	18.0	25.7	1.0	1.0
Friends	11.0	14.0	42.0	26.0	19.0	27.0	1.9	1.9
Relatives (and children)	9.6	11.0	31.0	52.0	44.0	55.0	22.0	22.5
Spouse or respondent	10.1	4.0	27.0	24.0	32.0	27.3	20.0	19.5
Formal organization	8.1	1.0	0.0	2.0	8.0	3.7	1.8	2.4
No one	13.0	18.0	14.0	17.0	12.0	14.2	59.0	58.0
n	(1396)	(1406)	(1402)	(1419)	(1411)	(1414)	(1403)	(1371)

Source: Litwak (1985, p. 44).

Table 2.3.   A Sample of Typologies of the Functional Components of Social Support

Barrera et al. (1981)	
Material Aid	Money and other objects
Physical Assistance	Sharing of tasks
Intimate Interaction	Nondirective interactions such that feelings and personal concerns are expressed
Guidance	Offering advice and guidance
Feedback	Providing individuals with information about themselves
Social Participation	Engaging in social interaction for fun, relaxation, and diversion from demand conditions
Cobb (1976)	
Emotional Support	Information that one is cared for and loved
Esteem Support	Information that one is valued and esteemed
network Support	Information that one belongs to a network of mutual obligation
Thoits (1985)	
Socioemotional Aid	Assertions or demonstrations of love, caring, esteem, value, empathy, sympathy, and/or group belonging
Cohen et al. (1985)	
Tangible Support	Instrumental aid
Appraisal Support	Availability of someone to talk to about one's problems
Self-Esteem Support	Availability of a positive comparison when comparing oneself with others
Belonging Support	Availability of people one can do things with
Wills (1985)	
Esteem Support	Information that a person is esteemed and accepted
Information Support	Help in defining, understanding, and coping with problematic events
Social Companionship	Spending time with others in leisure and recreational activities
Instrumental Support	Provision of financial, material resources and needed services
Hirsch (1980)	
Cognitive Guidance	Provision of information or advice, or an explanation of something troubling
Social Reinforcement	Provision of either praise or criticism regarding specific actions
Tangible Assistance	Such as helping with chores or child care
Socializing	Going to the movies or to dinner with others
Emotional Support	An interaction that makes one feel better or worse when one had already been feeling upset or under pressure

single typology. Yet, both from the point of view of accurately reflecting the consensus about the nature of social support provisions and in light of our objective of providing guidance for the development of support programs, this choice seems reasonable. With these objectives in mind, the following typology of the functional content of social support provisions is offered:

TYPOLOGY OF THE FUNCTIONAL COMPONENTS
OF SOCIAL SUPPORT

Concrete support:	providing some form of material aid such as money, clothing, accommodation and/or assistance with carrying out everyday tasks such as parent relief, homemaking services, transportation
Educational support:	providing the information or knowledge or developing the skills required so that the person will be more able to cope effectively with specific problems and/or so that the person will be more capable of accessing and benefiting from available supportive relationships
Emotional support:	providing intimate interpersonal connections that serve to meet the person's need for acceptance, or encouragement and understanding when coping with particular stressful events and the challenges of everyday living
Social integration:	providing positive contacts with members of an enduring social network and/or providing access to valued and stable social roles that foster the person's sense of affiliation and personal validation.

As indicated, this typology of the functional content of social support incorporates two quite different types of helping processes. Concrete, educational and emotional supports are presented as specific benefits received by people that are directly relevant to managing stressful situations and/or to increasing their ability to access and to benefit from available supportive relationships. However, social integration support refers to augmenting someone's sense of affiliation or belonging, and their social valuation, by increasing their positive social connectedness or integration. Positive social integration is more clearly related to the challenges of creating and maintaining a positive sense of identity and well-being than to coping with particular problems. Clearly, there is some relationship between these two general types of social support provisions in that people who have more diverse and valued social connections are also likely to have greater access to the personal and social resources germane to coping with stressful circumstances.

What is relevant to understanding support programs is that they can draw upon two quite distinct helping processes within the general social support construct: (a) access to adequate and appropriate personal and social resources to manage specific circumstances (the buffering effect of social support) and (b) the positive impact of stable, reciprocal, and valued social connectedness on social and psychological well-being independent of the levels of stress being experienced (the main effect of social support) (Cohen & Wills, 1985; Gottlieb, 1983; Kessler & McLeod, 1985, Thoits, 1982; Vaux 1988).

For formal social service providers, this distinction between the buffering effect and the main effect of social support is of primordial importance. While the buffering-effect model of social support points to a need to recognize the value of informal helping and a broader repertoire of helping strategies, it also indicates that many of the traditional modes of working in social services can be used to directly provide useful combinations and levels of assistance. However, the main-effect model of social support highlights that essential ingredients in the development, maintenance, and reconstruction of identify and well-being have been substantially ignored in traditional helping paradigms. In addition, the personal relationship between a service user and a professional helper makes much less of a direct contribution to the ongoing psychological well-being of the service user than many professionals would like to believe. Professional contributions to positive social integration for children and parents, while not insignificant, only occur through facilitating access to positive social involvements and valued social roles.

This typology of the functional content of social support is a classification of the benefits received by people; it is not a classification of types of supportive relationships or types of support programs. Indeed, it would be expected that a particular relationship or program would involve elements from several functional categories of social support. From the point of view of understanding and developing support programs, the typology focuses attention on the importance of being specific about the benefits received, or the benefits potentially available, from a particular type of involvement.

STRUCTURAL DIMENSIONS FOR ASSESSING SOCIAL SUPPORT

Social support has been described in the previous section as a multidimensional construct incorporating various functional and structural components. Besides being specific about the functional content of social support provisions, it is also necessary to give explicit attention to a range of structural dimensions in order to properly understand the nature and potential of supportive relationships. While these structural considerations are important for social support research and theory development in general (Vaux, 1988), they are particularly important considerations for developing support programs.

Unfortunately, with the current state of knowledge, it is not possible to be precise about the relative importance of each of these structural considerations or how they might interact with each other. Nonetheless, it is essential to consider these structural dimensions when trying to assess or to create support programs.

In the final analysis, the most important contribution of these discussions of the functional and structural components of social support may be their potential to improve our way of thinking and dialoguing about interventions and programs. If these deliberations are helpful in fostering a more systematic consideration and informed debate about the rationales, content, parameters, and reasonable expectations of various helping strategies, and in enabling us to broaden our concept of helping disadvantaged populations, this would be a significant contribution (Cameron & Rothery, 1985; Rothery & Cameron, 1990).

The following structural dimensions are useful in considering the potential benefits of a particular relationship or support program:

1. Range of Supports Available. In considering the potential of any support strategy, it is important to be realistic about the functional content (concrete, educational, emotional, social integration) of the supports that are or potentially can be provided in this way. It is also important to consider the match between these support provisions and the stressors of the situation (Unger & L. P. Wandersman, 1985). As an example, while emotional support may be a broadly useful coping resource, it will not be sufficient in a situation where the basic problems are chronic loneliness and a negative social identity. Explicit consideration of the range of supports available and their appropriateness will help to guard against a common pattern in social services of proposing focused service or support strategies as general solutions in situations where the problems of the individual, family or group are multiple (Cameron & Rothery, 1985; Rothery & Cameron, 1985).

2. Levels of Support Available. Are the resources available from the relationships or programs adequate to permit the person(s) to cope with the presenting problems or stressors? While it is not possible to quantify the relationship between levels of support and the ability to cope with stress, it must at least be possible to make a reasoned case that the levels of support available or proposed are likely to be adequate for the circumstances. It remains too common in social service programming for proponents of a particular support or treatment strategy to make claims that sweeping improvements will result from very modest levels of support. From an ecological perspective, the underlying assumption is that access to adequate levels of appropriate personal and social resources is necessary to cope successfully with daily living challenges (Rappaport, 1977).

3. Length of Commitment. People's needs for support are not only responses to particular crises or events, but are ongoing requirements in normal lives (Pearlin, 1985). It is especially evident that many users of social services suffer from serious deficiencies in personal and family capabilities as well as long-term access to useful social resources, to supportive personal relationships, and to productive social roles. Traditional social service interventions are time-limited and structurally they are particularly poor at responding to ongoing needs for access to buffering social resources or for positive social integration. Certainly, one of the most difficult and serious challenges for social service workers is responding to enduring support requirements among their clientele.

4. Reciprocity. Relationships that endure over time tend to be governed by norms of reciprocity (Brown, 1986; Huston & Burgess; 1979). That is, they are characterized by exchanges that are perceived to be roughly equal in value by the various parties involved. There are also good theoretical and empirical reasons to believe that our sense of self-worth and our experiences of positive social identity depend on our having access to one or more valued, reciprocal relationships, as well as upon our successful social role performances (Allen, Wilder, & Atkinson, 1983; Bronfenbrenner, 1979; Brown, 1986; Gartner & Riessman, 1984; McCall & Simmons, 1966; Pearlin, 1985; Thoits, 1983; Weigert, Smith Teitge, & Teitge, 1986; Wills, 1985). Discovering ways of accessing or creating positive reciprocal relationships for users of social services and opportunities for them to occupy valued social roles remains fundamentally unexplored territory in most social services settings. Given the importance of social integration support in the development, maintenance, and reconstruction of a positive social identity and self-esteem, these structural requirements for reciprocity in relationships— to be a giver as well as a receiver—raise serious questions about how these issues are being addressed by social service providers.

5. Technical Expertise. Effective responses to some problems clearly require assistance from people with specialized knowledge and training in appropriate methods of helping. For example, dealing with a violent spouse, a previously or currently abusive family environment, or a drug/alcohol addiction usually calls for access to formal or informal helpers knowledgeable about these problems and experienced in responding to them. Providing focused technical expertise is an area of helping where formal helpers often have structural advantages over informal helpers; indeed, some problem-specific support or mutual aid groups use professionals in this way to complement, but not replace the groups' efforts (for example, Parent's Anonymous, support groups for sexual abuse survivors, independent living organizations for the physically handicapped). On the other hand, some mutual aid groups themselves acquire a good deal of expertise in dealing with specific problems (for example, Alcoholics Anonymous, Overeaters Anonymous).

6. Openness to All in Need. Many users of social services have to confront problems or to live with social identities that have a social stigma attached to them (Rappaport, 1977; Sarabin & Scheibe, 1983; Weigert et al., 1986; Withorn, 1984). In such situations, assistance from paid helpers or from support networks or groups created specifically for these circumstances may be more acceptable than asking for help from family, friends, or colleagues—both in terms of the user's willingness to ask for help and the potential helper's judgment of the appropriateness of the request. Similarly, people with impoverished or dysfunctional informal support networks are more likely to turn to formal helpers for assistance—particularly with stigmatized problems or problems that would be too threatening or difficult to members of their networks. Formal helpers and specialized networks or groups may have structural advantages in such situations, at least as points of initial contact, over many existing sources of informal support in the community.

7. Availability in a Crisis. Most people look first to family, friends, and colleagues for assistance with a broad range of everyday problems. Families are often major sources of emergency and longer-term concrete assistance when confronting major difficulties such as unemployment or illness (Hall & Wellman, 1985; Litwak, 1985). However, when dealing with crisis situations involving stigmatizing problems, or emergencies requiring technical expertise, formal organizations and specialized networks or groups often provide more accessible and appropriate initial sources of assistance.

8. Motivation and Skills Requirements. Access to the benefits of reciprocal relationships and social roles or to formal programs that incorporate these social support strategies presumes basic levels of ability and motivation. There is a great deal of research establishing the reciprocal link between personal behaviors or social skills and social isolation (Hobfoll, 1985; W. H. Jones, 1985; Mitchell, 1982; Monroe, 1983; Peplau, 1985; Thoits, 1982). In the absence of these abilities, less demanding modes of providing support may be more appropriate—at least as a precursor to more enduring support strategies.

The prime motivation behind considering these functional and structural dimensions of support is to facilitate our understanding of a broader range of helping strategies with individuals and families in multiple-problem situations. There are patterned differences in the *potential* functional contributions as well as the structural advantages of various types of helpers and helping strategies. It can be helpful to use these considerations as a framework to consider what can be reasonably expected under the best of circumstances from promising support programs (see the discussion in Chapter 5). What is required is a sense-making framework, or a way of thinking, that facilitates an understanding of the potential and complementarity of important helping options.

STRUCTURAL PROPERTIES OF SOCIAL NETWORKS

In a related area of investigation, many researchers have studied the structural characteristics of social networks, or the web of interpersonal relations within which daily living occurs, in order to better understand the relationships between these structural properties and the provision of social support and their connections, if any, to personal well-being. At this point in time, no universally valid or superior network structural properties can be identified. Rather, there is some evidence that the advantages of particular network configurations depend upon the personal benefits that are being sought:

> [A]ny given network characteristics can have contradictory implications for access to social support and for health (e.g., strong ties may provide a good deal of direct emotional and material aid but they may restrict access to new information and exert greater pressure for conformity). (Hall & Wellman, 1985, p. 35)

Also, given our prime interest in understanding support programs and helping strategies, it is important to stress that network theory and research do not easily yield clear principles that can be used to guide support interventions in the social services. Nonetheless, some general patterns have been identified with some relevance to support programming.

Many different social network structural properties have been identified and investigated (Hall & Wellman, 1985; House & Kahn, 1985; Mitchell & Trickett, 1980; Saulnier, 1982). Among the more important are:

Size:	the number of persons with whom the focal person in the network has direct regular contact
Density:	the number of actual direct ties between all of the members of a network as a proportion of the total potential number of direct ties between the members of the network
Stability:	the durability over time of the focal person's contacts with others in the network
Multidimensionality:	the number of functions served by the relationships between the focal person and others in the network (e.g., concrete, educational, emotional, social integration supports)
Dispersion:	the ease with which the focal person can make contact with other members of the network
Intimacy/intensity:	the strength of the ties between the focal person and others in the network, usually measured by the reciprocity of the tie, or the emotional importance of the tie, as perceived by the focal person
Homogeneity:	the social, economic, demographic and cultural similarity of the members of the network
Frequency:	the frequency the focal person can make contact with others in the network
Reciprocity:	the extent to which resources are both given and received between the focal person and others in the network.

Simple social connectedness, as measured by the size of the focal person's social network, has not been consistently associated with the positive buffering effect of social support, that is, with improved coping with stressful events. However, a consistent buffering effect has been found when the focal person is involved in one or more intimate, reciprocal, dyadic relationships, and when the focal person has frequent and easy access to these relationships (Cohen & Syme, 1985; Cohen & Wills, 1985; Hobfoll, 1985). Some of this research suggests that a threshold effect may exist in that a buffering effect can be found when the focal person has access to a few such intimate and reciprocal relationships, but that additional contacts of this nature have diminishing returns in terms of an increased positive buffering effect for the focal person. On the other hand, there is evidence that network size, as an indirect measure of social integration, may be related to the main effect of social support:

These findings are especially impressive because they consistently show effects of social relationships on health, including "hard" outcomes such as mortality, in well-designed and well-controlled, prospective studies of large and broad-based samples. The results on human populations are reinforced by experimental studies showing the health-protective effects of social relationships in a variety of animal species. They are reinforced by the frequent findings . . . that the size of social networks is predictive of health. All of these effects are, however, main or additive effects. (House & Kahn, 1985, p. 90)

Smaller, dense, intimate, and homogeneous networks may have advantages in providing intense emotional support and crisis supports, and in maintaining a specific social identity. Larger, less dense networks, with a more heterogeneous membership, and which incorporate several intimate, reciprocal, dyadic relationships for the focal person, may be more appropriate for supporting transitions from one social identity to another (Saulnier, 1982). In addition, large and heterogeneous social networks that facilitate the focal person's involvement in various "enduring, reciprocal, multi-faceted relationships [and social roles] that emphasize playing, working and loving" (Garbarino, 1983, p. 12) have been associated with increased ongoing psychological well-being and a positive social identity. These patterns have been noted by several reviewers of social network research:

> Granovetter (1973) has noted the importance of weak ties in linking the person to more diverse input. Lin (1982, 1986a) has elaborated this view, arguing that weak ties to diverse resources may be especially helpful in instrumental action whereas strong ties serve important expressive functions. (Vaux, 1988, p. 60)

> [T]here is some evidence that support satisfaction and more complex appraisals are associated with large low-density networks, comprising close friends, and involving close, reciprocal, and complex relationships. Our understanding of these links is far from complete. (p. 66)

> Studies by Hirsh (1979, 1980) found that women with sparsely knit, multi-stranded networks adjusted better to stressful events. Such networks may provide a greater range of access to non-family roles and activities, allowing a drastic reorganization of life style when changes are required—see also Fisher, 1982; Kaduskin et al., 1980; Wellman, 1979. (Hall & Wellman, 1985, p. 34)

> Walker, McBride and Vachon (1977), among others, have argued that networks of small size, strong ties, high density and homogeneity, and low dispersion are helpful in maintaining social identity and hence well-being to the extent that well-being relies on maintenance of [a specific] social identity. (House & Kahn, 1985, p. 92)

In summary, there are several identifiable patterns from research into the structural properties of social networks that may be useful for the design of support interventions. Having access to a small number of intimate, reciprocal relationships (i.e., friendships) seems to be related both to a greater ability to cope with particular stressful interactions and to increasing an ongoing sense of well-being. Specialized networks with intense connections between members can be helpful in coping with particularly difficult challenges. Increasing social connectedness through augmenting the size and diversity of social networks, as well as fostering intimate, multidimensional, dyadic relationships and, in particular, valued social roles, can be important strategies for bolstering social and psychological well-being and increasing adaptiveness for users of social services—if practical methods can be found to create and support these types of social involvements.

DEFINITIONS OF BASIC SOCIAL SUPPORT TERMINOLOGY

There is a large lexicon of terms in the social support literature. If our thinking is not to become convoluted, it is necessary to work from a clear understanding of the terminology of social support and to recognize that terms such as social support, social network, social resources, and informal helping are not properly substitutable for each other. The following definitions of basic social support terms are provided from a broader dictionary of relevant concepts in order to provide guidance to support interventions.

Social support: the instrumental, educational, social and psychological assistance *actually received* by a focal person

Social resources: the instrumental, educational, social, and psychological assistance *potentially available* to a focal person

Social network: the actual, reoccurring linkages between a focal person and significant others in her or his environment

Formal support: social support provided to a focal person by someone paid to provide that assistance

Informal support: social support provided to a focal person by unpaid people such as kin, friends, neighbors, and peers as part of their evolving relationship

Created supports: social support that comes from relationships with informal and formal helpers that did not previously exist, but were specifically developed to assist a focal person (Froland, Pancoast, Chapman, & Kimboko 1981, p. 51)

Embedded support: social support that comes from the existing informal relationships of the focal person or from existing relationships with formal helpers (p. 52).

THE IMPORTANCE OF ACCESS TO INFORMAL SOCIAL SUPPORT

There is little doubt that having access to the resources of a positive social network, to intimate reciprocal relationships, or to valued social roles can have a powerful influence on a person's well-being, and upon her or his ability to manage stressful situations. While a number of important issues remain unresolved in social support theory and research, there is little justification for continuing to question the relevance of augmenting informal support strategies for the social services. It is time to shift our energies to uncovering practical methods of exploiting the potential of various informal support strategies.

What strikes the new reader of the social support literature is the impressive variety of research evidence demonstrating the benefits of access to informal support and social connectedness. Much of this research analysis was correlational and could not legitimately define causal relationships, and actual causal dynamics remain unclear. While many important theoretical and research issues remain unresolved; nevertheless, there are excellent empirical as well as theoretical reasons to believe in the importance of informal supportive relationships and their relevance to improving social service helping strategies (Bronfenbrenner, 1979; Cohen & Syme, 1985; Cohen & Wills, 1985; Garbarino, 1983; Gottlieb, 1983, 1985; Hobfoll, 1985; Hurd, Pattison, & Llamas, 1981; Kessler & McLeod, 1985; Mitchell & Trickett, 1980; Monroe, 1983; Thoits, 1982, 1983, 1985; Vaux 1988; Wilcox & Vernberg, 1985). What follows is a selection from a much broader universe of social support research in order to highlight the relevance of informal support strategies to helping in the social services. Social support, typically operationalized as perceived satisfaction with, or actual positive, relations with family, friends, peers, and colleagues, or as active social participation, has been empirically associated with many positive benefits:

- Social support has frequently been shown to have a significant positive correlation with physical health (e.g., less heart disease, fewer pregnancy complications, fewer asthma attacks, recovery from surgery, and so on) [Berkman & Syme, 1979; Finlayson, 1976; Lynch, 1977; Medalie & Goldbourt, 1976; Nuckolls et al., 1972; De Araujo et al., 1973], as reported in Berkman, 1985; Cohen & Syme, 1985; House & Kahn, 1985; Turner, Frankel, & Levin, 1982; Wortman & Conway, 1985).
- Two evaluations of mutual aid groups for child welfare clients revealed a sizable reduction in the use of child care placements and an increased independence from formal service providers for members (Cameron et al., 1992; Cameron & Rothery, 1985).

- A study of Parents Anonymous members reported a substantial and immediate decrease in the frequency and severity of both physical abuse and verbal abuse as well as increases in participants' self-esteem and sense of competence (Lieber & Baker, 1977).

- Access to positive intimate relationships or to a positive social network has been associated with psychological well-being and the absence of depression [Brown et al., 1975; Davidson et al., 1981; Dean et al., 1980; Dimond, 1979; Jamison et al., 1979; Lesser & Watt, 1978; Lowenthal & Haven, 1968; Miller & Ingham, 1976; Porritt, 1979; Roy, 1978], as reported in Cohen & Wills, 1985; Schulz & Rau, 1985; Turner, Frankel, & Levin, 1982).

- Social support reportedly moderates the negative effects of job stress and unemployment [La Rocco et al., 1980; Gore, 1978], as reported in Wilcox, 1981).

- "These factors have been found to be significantly correlated with post-divorce adjustment. That is, the fewer the economic problems (Spanier & Casto, 1979), the greater the amount of social participation (Raschke, 1977; Spanier & Casto, 1979) and the more family and peer support received (Berman & Turk, 1981; Hunt & Hunt, 1977; Spanier & Casto, 1979) the better the adjustment. . . . [L]abor force participation has also been found to be positively related to adjustment to divorce (Raschke, 1977)" (Richardson & Pfeiffenberger, 1983, p. 228).

- Social isolation has been repeatedly identified as a correlate of child maltreatment and child placement. Along with a lack of access to economic resources, single parenthood is one of the best predictors of an open child welfare case and of family breakdown [Bakan, 1971; Bryant et al., 1963; Elmer, 1967; Helfer & Kempe, 1976; Lauer et al., 1974; Polansky et al., 1979; Smith et al., 1974; Smith, 1977; Stoch, 1974], as reported in Garbarino & Stocking, 1980; Snider & Skoretz, 1983).

- Skill training has been demonstrated to be relatively ineffectual in influencing long-term behaviors with low-income mothers and mental hospital patients, unless joined to a strategy that links participants into a network of positive social contacts (Edmunson, Bedell, Archer, & Gordon, 1982; Hawkins & Fraser, 1983; Wahler & Moore, 1975; Wahler, 1980a; see also Chapter 8 in this volume).

- "It appears that when young people are not attached and committed to their families, schools and communities, they are more likely to engage in delinquent behaviors. . . . Involvement with delinquent peers is one of the strongest correlates of delinquent behavior" (Hawkins & Fraser, 1983, p. 334).

- A controlled evaluation study of a community network created for ex-psychiatric patients revealed that members had fewer days in hospital after their initial discharge and fewer returns to the hospital and were more independent from formal services (Edmunson et al., 1982; Edmunson, Bedell, & Gordon, 1984).

- "A study of people who had been abused as children suggested that those who had strong and active social networks were much less likely to repeat the abusive patterns in their own child rearing than those without such a support system (Hunter & Kilstrom, 1979)" (Garbarino, 1983, p. 24).
- "[A] survey on domestic violence report[ed] that when family comprise the *only* social contacts, stress produces greater violence than when family is augmented by social relationships beyond kin (Strauss, 1980)" (Garbarino, 1983, p. 24).
- "The availability to a widow or a widower of a social network of others who have successfully weathered this loss provides both strength and a model for mastery when personal resources are close to depletion" (Walker, MacBride, & Vachon, 1977, cited in D'Augelli, 1983, pp. 90–91).
- "Among older people not tied into informal supports, use of formal services tend to be higher . . . instances of personally reported well-being tend to decline (and) the likelihood of institutionalization tends to increase" (Hooyman, 1983, p. 139).
- "The existence and quantity of contacts with friends and relatives have also been found to relate cross-sectionally, retrospectively, and prospectively to lower rates of psychological and physical disorders and mortality. Membership and attendance in church and participation in other voluntary organizations show positive relationships to well-being. These results are somewhat more sparse and variable than in the case of marital status, but still relatively consistent" (House & Kahn, 1985, p. 89).
- "[P]erceived support, social network resources, and support interventions were related to better postpartum adjustment for young mothers and improved health and development for their babies" (Unger & L. P. Wandersman, 1985, p. 29).
- "Relationships with kin, siblings and grandchildren are not consistently associated with life satisfaction in studies of the elderly; however, interactions with friends do appear to be beneficial" (Schulz & Rau, 1985, pp. 138–139).
- "There is now mounting evidence that support interventions can help young mothers more effectively cope with the transition to parenthood (cf. Family Resource Coalition, 1983)" (Unger & L. P. Wandersman, 1985, p. 42).

The above selection of research was chosen to demonstrate the relevance of social support principles and support interventions to helping in the social services; as such, the choice of examples is biased to make a point. In fact, there have been thousands of empirical investigations of social support over the past twenty years. Not surprisingly, given the complexity of the social support construct, the range of potential intervening variables, and the diversity of research methods employed, there have been substantial variations, even contradictions, in reported outcomes—leading some authors to question the usefulness of social support or to posit that other personal or situational factors may be mainly responsible for the observed changes. Fortunately, there have been several extensive reviews of the research evidence on the buffering-effect and the main-effect models of social support that add clarity to the topic (Cohen & Wills, 1985; Cohen & Syme, 1985; Kessler & Mcleod, 1985). Even more fortunate, Alan Vaux (1988) has provided a review of the reviews of the research on the relevance of social support as well as his own summary of this evidence and his conclusions are presented in detail below:

> Leavy (1983) includes ten epidemiological surveys of community residents. . . . [H]e concludes that evidence of the buffer hypothesis is mixed, probably because of weak measures, inappropriate data analysis, differences in how support is conceptualized, and variation in sample characteristics. On the other hand, he writes, regardless of research methods used one finding is consistently reported: the absence of social supports is associated with increased psychological disasters. . . . In short, Leavy would seem to conclude that evidence for a direct effect of social support on well-being is considerable whereas evidence for a stress buffering effect is mixed, in part because of inadequate tests of the hypothesis to date. (p. 105)

> Mitchell, Billings & Moos (1982) present tabular information on seventeen studies [and] conclude that a buffer effect was observed in thirteen of the studies though in some cases only for particular support variables. . . . [A]lso they cite nineteen relevant [to the direct effect of social support] studies [and] conclude that sixteen of these studies show evidence for a direct effect of support on functioning, although in several cases the effect is evident only for some support measures. [They] point out the association between support and well-being was observed for several populations including college students, psychiatric populations, and a range of at-risk groups. . . . Evidence consistent with a direct effect is provided by a number of longitudinal studies . . . even when previous levels of support and distress were controlled statistically. [They] conclude that evidence for a direct effect of support on well-being is fairly evident whereas that for a stress buffering effort is mixed. (p. 106)

> Lin (1986a) . . . includes thirteen cross-sectional and seven panel studies relevant to the buffer effect and concludes that only two provide confirmation

. . . whereas several others provide partial confirmation. . . . In contrast [he] concludes that of eleven cross-sectional and six panel studies relevant to a direct effect model, nine and three respectively provide evidence consistent with the model, and several others provide partial confirmation... [He] concludes that the buffer effect has tenuous credibility while there is sufficient evidence for the direct effect. (pp. 106–107)

Cohen and Wills (1985) provide a careful and thorough review of studies that tested the buffer hypothesis. [T]hey proposed that support buffers stress effects only when it matches the functional coping requirements posed by the particular stressful encounter.. [They] take the important step of organizing findings in terms of whether the support measure was structural, functional and global or specific. . . . Some nine studies involved specific structural support measures (for example, marital status and number of friends and relatives nearby). In general, these showed neither main nor interaction effects, except when they involved intimate relationships such as marriage. (This) may reflect the general reliability of intimate relationships as a source of functional support. Ten studies employed global structural support measures (for example, social integration, participation, and networks). As expected, these measures rarely yielded evidence of buffer effects, but they more often showed main effects. . . . Thirteen studies employed measures of confidant relationships, and these quite consistently show interaction [buffering] effects and often marginal main effects. . . . Eight studies employed compound functional measures . . . and eight employed global functional measures. . . . Results for both sets of studies are mixed, with many failing to show a buffer effect. . . . Finally three studies of occupational stress using global functional support measures were reviewed. Two of these yielded considerable evidence for a buffer model. (p. 107)

The review by Kessler and McLeod (1985) . . . apart from being one of the most recent, . . . is arguably the most systematic. . . . [I]t has a more distinct focus, survey studies of normal populations that examined support in relation to stressful life experiences and psychological distress. . . . Twenty-three studies were examined. . . . Tests were then classified as providing clear evidence for the buffer hypothesis or not, with flawed tests as unclear. Thus, of the twelve tests involving affiliative networks, six failed to show a significant buffer effect, four were unclear due to methodological flaws, and only two showed a significant effect. . . . In contrast, of the eight studies involving emotional support, seven yielded clear results, and four of these showed a significant buffer effect (the exception used a single item measure). . . . Kessler and McLeod concluded that strong and consistent evidence for a stress-buffering effect was found for emotional support and perceived availability of support but not for memberships in affiliative methods. . . . A clear buffer effect was observed in five studies for social support and in four studies for perceived availability of support, yet a marginal effect for support was observed in only one of each set. Thus, it appears that emotional support and perceived availability of support do not influence distress at low levels of stress. . . . Of eight relevant studies, a main effect for support was observed in three. Because the studies showing an effect were methodologically strong, and those failing to do so, weak, Kessler and McLeod conclude that affiliative network involvement does have a direct effect on distress. . . . In conclusion, the Kessler and McLeod (1985) review provides considerable evidence of a stress-buffering effect for emotional support and perceived availability of support and of a direct effect for membership in affiliative networks. These conclusions hold for longitudinal as well as cross-sectional studies. (pp 108–110)

[And Vaux (1988) concludes] From this perspective, five conclusions may be drawn. There is a good deal of evidence that social support can have a direct and positive effect on well-being, both generally (where stressors remain un-measured) and independently of life stressors. There is also convincing evidence that social support can buffer the effects of stressors. Direct and buffer effects, respectively, tend to occur with measures that focus on affiliation and resources or on appraisals of availability or quality of support. The effects remain unpredictable, being shaped by personal, social, and contextual factors in ways that are still unclear. Research to date has told us almost nothing about the process whereby support has its effects. (p. 130)

SUMMARY

This chapter has presented an overview of what is known about the functional and structural components of the social support construct. In addition, a selected review of the research evidence for the value of access to informal social support as well as for the buffering effect and main-effect models of social support was provided. From this discussion, it is possible to abstract a number of key themes that will be germane to understanding and to developing interventions drawing upon social support principles:

1. Social support should be viewed as a multidimensional concept with various functional and structural components. Social support is not a single thing and cannot be represented by a specific type of assistance or a particular type of relationship.

2. The functional content of social support provisions can be profitably grouped into concrete, educational, emotional, and social integration categories.

3. Concrete, educational, and emotional supports can be understood as specific benefits received by people that are directly relevant to managing stressful situations (the buffering-effect model of social support) and/or to increasing their ability to access and to benefit from available supportive relationships.

4. Social integration support provisions refer to augmenting people's sense of positive affiliation and valuation by increasing their stable social

connectedness. Social integration is more clearly related to the challenges of creating, maintaining or reconstructing a positive identity and a sense of well-being (the main-effect model of social support) than to coping with particular problems.

5.   Any assessment of the impacts of social support provisions has to be specific about the functional content of the support provided.

6.   Generally, different types of social support cannot be profitably substituted for each other.

7.   Valuable social support can be provided by a variety of formal and informal helpers and helping strategies.

8.   Generally, different types of helpers and helping strategies cannot be profitably substituted for each other. In particular, formal helpers and informal helpers have quite different functional and structural advantages indicating that they generally may be used in a complementary fashion, but cannot be substituted for each other.

9.   The potential of social support provisions or helping strategies varies in important respects in relation to a range of structural dimensions, including range, level, length of commitment, reciprocity, technical expertise, openness to all in need, availability in a crisis, motivation, and skill requirements.

10.   Consistent buffering effects have been found where the focal person perceives that she or he has easy access to one or more satisfactory, confidant relationships and to appropriate emotional support and informational support.

11.   Larger, less dense networks with a more heterogeneous membership and that provide people with several intimate, reciprocal, dyadic relationships (and valued social roles) may be advantageous in supporting transitions from one social identity to another and have been associated with increased ongoing psychological well-being and a positive social identity.

12.   Smaller, dense, intimate, and homogeneous networks may have advantages in providing intense emotional support and crisis supports and in maintaining a specific social identity.

How Does Social Support Work?   3

There is consensus in the social support literature that the benefits of access to social support can be attributed to two quite different helping processes (Cohen & Syme, 1985; Cohen & Wills, 1985; Kasl & Wells, 1985; Kessler & McLeod, 1985; Rook & Dooley, 1985; Vaux, 1988):

1. by providing access to resources that help people cope with particular problems or stressful life events—the buffering effect;
2. by fostering a sense of psychological well-being and social valuation independent of particular problems or stressful life events—the main effect.

This is a basic distinction for understanding how social support works with important implications for the development of support programs. There are substantial differences between interventions designed to help with specific problems and those focusing on the long-term integration of participants. For a complete understanding of social support—and of interventions built upon these ideas—one must pay close attention to both of these social support processes.

HOW DOES SOCIAL SUPPORT WORK: THE BUFFERING EFFECT

The social support buffering hypothesis, according to Thoits (1982), is

> Individuals with a strong social support system should be better able to cope with major life changes; those with little or no social support may be more vulnerable to life changes, particularly undesirable ones. (p. 145)

Cohen and Wills (1985, p. 348), after an extensive review of the social support research, concluded that the research provided strong evidence for a buffering model of the social support process only when the studies measured the availability of interpersonal resources, as perceived by the focal person, and the functional components of social support measured included emotional and educational (informational) supports—what they described as the broadly useful coping resources. They also observed that a large

35

buffering effect of social support is regularly evident under circumstances of high stress, but that the differences between high support and low support provisions may disappear under low stress. Kessler and McLeod's (1985) review concurs with this assessment:

> After discarding unclear results, strong evidence for stress buffering was found. Evidence for a marginal effect under conditions of low stress was found in one-third of the studies where the buffering effect was significant. (p. 229)

Gottlieb (1983, p. 37) argues that the buffering effect of social support may work by:

- preserving self-esteem and confidence when confronting stressful situations;
- providing access to social resources useful in coping with various problems;
- improving ability to realistically assess problem situations and to respond appropriately.

Vaux (1988, pp. 137–141) hypothesizes that a number of intervening processes may explain how social support in general, and emotional supports and informational supports in particular, buffer against the ill effects of stress:

Inoculation:	as a result of numerous supportive exchanges around threats to a particular commitment, the well-supported person gains a strong identity with respect to that commitment, one that is less vulnerable to threats
Primary appraisal guidance:	advice/guidance may dramatically alter how a person appraises an event
Supportive direct guidance:	direct assistance may allow an environmental demand to be met or a problem to be resolved even though the person may have been unable to cope independently
Secondary appraisal guidance:	advice/guidance may lead to a more elaborate and realistic evaluation of coping resources and options than would have occurred without assistance
Reappraisal guidance:	advice/guidance may help a person think about a stressor in more realistic, perhaps less threatening fashion

Palliative emotional
support: emotional support—listening, showing empathy,
                                expressing concern, caring—plays a critical role in
                                managing emotional responses to a stressful situa-
                                tion.
Diversion: involvement in different activities (e.g., socializing)
                                disrupts persistent thinking and worrying about a
                                stressful situation.

The buffering-effect model of social support is essentially an ecological
approach that posits that access to social supports helps to achieve a better
balance between a person's personal and social resources and the problems
that have to be managed (Unger & A. Wandersman, 1985). An assumption is
that, with access to sufficient and appropriate resources, most people can be
expected to cope adequately with their problems most of the time (Rappaport, 1977). While it is striking that a positive buffering effect has been
recorded with such a diversity of populations and problems (suggesting a
global buffering effect), some argue that social support research about the
buffering effect needs to become more specific and to focus on what kinds of
assistance helps what populations with which kinds of problems—a direc-
tion similar to that proposed for other intervention outcome research such as
psychotherapy and social work counseling (Shumaker & Brownell, 1984;
Unger & L. P. Wandersman, 1985; Vaux, 1988).

RELATIONSHIP BETWEEN PERSONAL AND ENVIRONMENTAL TRAITS
AND THE BUFFERING EFFECT OF SOCIAL SUPPORT

Part of the ongoing debate about the value of access to social support
revolves around whether the benefits of social support can be attributed
more credibly to personal traits or to other characteristics of the environment. Detractors of social support research argue that these personal or
environmental variables make more important independent contributions to
well-being than does access to social support. It is a fact that access to social
support has been correlated with a plethora of personal and environmental
variables (Brown & Bifulco, 1985; Cohen & Syme, 1985; Heller & Lakey,
1985; W. H. Jones, 1985; Paybel, 1985; Pearlin, 1985; Pepleau, 1985;
Thoits, 1982; Vaux, 1988). However, unfortunately, this debate about the
relevance of social support sometimes appears to be partisan, with various
authors arguing for the primacy of factors that appear to value their particular areas of expertise.

A more reasonable conclusion would be that there is a reciprocal relationship between access to social support and many of these personal and

environmental variables. For example, individuals with a high sense of mastery and strong self-esteem may have less immediate need for social support, but under prolonged stress this self-confidence is likely to wane and their need for social support increase (Hobfoll, 1985, p. 398). Similarly, ongoing access to positive social connections may lead to increased confidence in one's ability to deal with problems and to higher self-esteem. It is also probable that personal variables and social support make independent contributions to well-being. For example, Brown and Bifulco (1985, p. 365) found that women with low support but high self-esteem had a relatively low risk of depression when confronted with a problem situation. On the other hand, this risk was also minimal for women in the sample who had high support but low self-esteem.

Research on social isolation and loneliness has shown consistent correlations with personal variables such as depression, low self-esteem, external locus of control, lack of assertiveness, shyness, negative early childhood experiences, and poor social skills (Brown & Bifulco, 1985; Cohen & Syme, 1985; D'Augelli, 1983; Hobfoll, 1985; W. H. Jones, 1985; Lefcourt, 1985; Peplau, 1985). It seems logical that many of these personal variables would not only influence access to positive social supports, but that they would themselves be negatively or positively impacted by successful and failed social involvements. This reciprocity between personal variables and social supports would suggest that there is a need for support strategies in the social services that focus both upon improving personal behaviors and abilities as well as on the creation of supportive relationships, networks, and social roles for participants.

Perhaps the most relevant finding for support programs is that there is little or no evidence for a negative effect of being more socially connected (Cohen & Wills, 1985, p. 350). While dysfunctional personal behaviors or attitudes would make the development of effective support strategies more difficult, they do not make the undertaking impossible. There are many examples of the successful creation of supportive networks for "hard-to-reach" populations such as psychiatric patients, alcoholics, victims of sexual abuse, child abusers, street kids, violent men, and juvenile delinquents (Berkeley Planning Associates, 1977; Borman & Lieber, 1984; Cameron et al., 1992; Cameron & Rothery, 1985; Edmunson et al., 1984; Family Resource Coalition, 1983; Giarretto, 1982; Levens, 1968; Lieber, 1984; Silverman & Smith, 1984). The rule of thumb for support interventions should be that positive benefits can be anticipated whenever isolated or lonely populations are consistently linked with relevant social supports during periods of high stress, or when they become more socially connected as a consequence of these efforts.

Access to social support will also be influenced by the context or environment in which the person functions. Social support will vary substantially by the social position or roles the person occupies—for example, housewife, volunteer, unemployed, employed:

> [O]ur study has found that East Yorkers with different locations in the large scale social structure (i.e., employed men, employed women, homemaking women) have networks with quite different compositions, structures, and contents. (Hall & Wellman, 1985, p. 37)

Attitudes toward and opportunities for social interactions will be affected by family and neighborhood resources, structures, and cultures. For example, social isolation and loneliness is more common among low-income populations (Cameron, et al., 1992). It is also clear that various life events such as divorce, unemployment, or serious illness can substantially modify access to social support. In addition, persistent lack of opportunities to join together with similar others or to occupy useful social roles will increasingly limit a person's ability to discover and use what supports are available in her or his surroundings. Social isolation reduces people's capacity to take initiatives to render their environment more hospitable, or even their desire to do so, as individuals increasingly tailor expectations and self-image to correspond to persisting external realities (Bronfenbrenner, 1979).

A number of researchers have suggested that there are significant patterned differences in the way men and women in North America access and use social supports (Antonucci, 1985; Cohen & Wills, 1985; House & Kahn, 1985; Kessler et al., 1985; Lefcourt, 1985; Sarason & Sarason, 1985; Vaux, 1988). The argument is that women often have more numerous confidantes and benefit more clearly from intimate confidante relationships than men, whereas men tend to emphasize more activity-focused interactions than confiding relationships (Bell, 1981, as cited in Vaux, 1988, p. 166; Cohen & Wills, 1985, p. 350). Men are more likely to have an intimate relationship only with their spouse (Antonucci, 1985). Some authors have suggested that the buffering effect of social support is clearer for women than men (Lefcourt, 1985; Sarason & Sarason, 1985)—perhaps not surprising given the observed importance of emotional support and intimate, intense relationships in the research on the buffering effect of social support (Cohen & Wills, 1985; Vaux, 1988). Kessler et al., (1985, p. 498) concluded that "men, despite their ability to empathize, structure their lives in such a way that they care about fewer people" (p. 498). Vaux (1988) hypothesizes that "relative to their male peers, women might be disadvantaged by social role but advantaged by sex role with respect to the support process" (p. 166). However, Vaux also suggests that some caution is in order in drawing firm conclusions from the research on the relationships between social support and gender:

In summary, empirical findings regarding gender differences in social support are mixed and inconsistent. Many studies suggest comparable levels of support among men and women. Differences tend to be quite specific and occur most commonly with respect to number of confidants, supportive behaviour from friends, and emotional support resources, behaviour and appraisals. (p. 169)

The data on gender and social support cautiously suggest that different support programs may be required for female and male populations. Strategies designed to foster talking and personal exchanges, confidante friendships and emotional support may be easier to develop with women. Males may respond better to task- or activity-focused strategies. The relative paucity of males participating in many social service group programs and community groups may be attributable to these differences in the social connection patterns for males and females. However, it also is worth remembering that isolated women and single mothers form a large part of the service population of many social service organizations.

It would be erroneous to conclude that social support strategies are not relevant for males, or that men do not equally need or benefit from social integration. A more reasonable interpretation may be that patterns of male and female social participation are substantially culturally determined and that the social integration benefits of North American males are more likely to be from their work involvements and from their immediate family involvements. As a result, they would be less likely to access or to benefit from informal caring responsibilities or friendships outside work than women. However, it is obvious that males deprived of employment and family involvements or of a source of intimate emotional support and guidance would be greatly at risk of psychological and physical harm (House & Kahn, 1985; Schulz & Rau, 1985). It is also not clear if these patterns will change as family structures and responsibilities evolve and as a working careers outside of the home become more the norm for both partners and as ideals of appropriate male and female behaviors and attributes change.

THE BUFFERING-EFFECT MODEL OF SOCIAL SUPPORT

The model of the relationships between social supports, personal characteristics, environmental variables, and stressful life events for this volume is summarized in Figure 3.1. This buffering-effect model is expressed in general terms. It is simply not possible to describe with precision the relationships between these different factors or to speculate about how the buffering process would vary with different problems or with different populations (Cohen

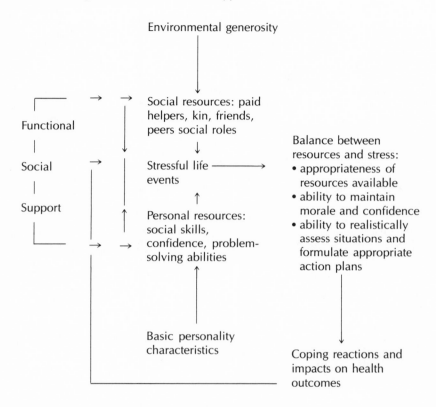

Figure 3.1 The buffering-effect model of social support (adapted from Heller & Lakey, 1985, p. 228; Gottlieb, 1983, p. 37; Kahn & Antonucci, 1980, p. 267; Vaux, 1988, pp. 70, 136).

& Syme, 1985; Cohen & Wills, 1985; Gottlieb, 1983; Thoits, 1985; Vaux, 1988).

In this buffering-effect model, social support would consist of functional contributions (emotional, educational, concrete, social integration supports) to the personal and/or social resources that a focal person can call upon in order to cope with specific stressful life events. The appropriateness of the balance between the types and levels of resources the person can mobilize and the problems that have to be managed will determine the person's ability to cope with these stressful life events. This will, in turn, influence the impact that these stressors will have upon the person's physical and mental well-being. These coping reactions and health outcomes may then augment or decrease the personal and social resources the person is likely to have available in the future.

In the proposed buffering-effect model of social support, successful and unsuccessful coping are patterns that may become increasingly self-confirming, unless there is a fortuitous or planned change in the social and/or personal resources available to the person or in the problems that they are confronting. Support strategies, within this model, would be intended to augment the availability of the personal resources (e.g., social skills, self-confidence, problem-solving abilities) and/or the social resources (e.g., access to supportive paid helpers, kin, friends, peers and colleagues, social roles) of individuals, families, and groups.

HOW DOES SOCIAL SUPPORT WORK? THE MAIN EFFECT

Benefits from positive social integration exist independently of the problems or the stressful situations confronting the person. Cohen and Wills (1985), based upon their extensive review of the research evidence, concluded that the beneficial main effect of social support is consistently evident when the research investigation measures social connectedness, that is, "structural integration into a larger social network" (p. 310). While the buffering-effect model of social support examines the usefulness of social support provisions in situations of high stress, the main-effect model of social support attempts to explain the contributions of positive social integration to well-being independent of the level of stress.

Figure 3.2 provides an overview of the main-effect model of social support for this volume. As with the buffering-effect model of social support, the main-effect model is described in general terms. It is not possible to be precise about the mechanisms that produce the benefits from positive social integration or about how the model might vary for different kinds of people and situations (Vaux, 1988). From the main-effect perspective, the benefits of positive social integration should be most evident when a person is embedded in a large and heterogeneous social network (Hirsch, 1980; Hobfoll, 1985; House & Kahn, 1985; Saulnier, 1982) that provides for his/her involvement in one or more stable, multidimensional, reciprocal relationships (Cohen & Syme, 1985; Garbarino, 1983; Hirsch, 1980; Hobfoll, 1985) and when she/he successfully occupies one or more valued social roles (Allen et al., 1983; Brown, 1986; McCall & Simmons, 1966; Pearlin, 1985; Thoits, 1982, 1983, 1985; Weigert et al., 1986). Under these conditions, the main-effect model postulates that most people will benefit from a clearer and more positive social identity, improved self-esteem and/or a stronger sense of self-worth, as well as greater life satisfaction and feelings of well-being:

> Perhaps the sheer sense of attachment is among the more important forms of support. [R]esearch dealing with events that disrupt attachments, such as resi-

• a larger and more heterogeneous social network • more stable, reciprocal intimate dyadic relationships • more enduring and valued social roles and successful role performances	→	• sense of affiliation • sense of power and mastery • positive personal valuations • attained social aspirations • appropriate norms and reference figures • more pleasant events • more development opportunities	→	• a more positive social identity • improved self-esteem • increased life satisfaction • increased ongoing feelings of psychological well-being

Figure 3.2 The main-effect model of social support (adapted from Cameron, 1990b; Vaux, 1988, p. 149).

dential changes (Stohols & Shumaker, 1982) and divorce (Pearlin & Johnson, 1977) has indicated that the loss of attachment is accompanied by psychological distress. This kind of work suggests that support systems, whatever else they provide in times of crisis and need, impact to people a general and abiding sense of security and well-being. (Pearlin, 1985, p. 51)

Shumaker and Brownell (1984, p. 23) argue that the main effect results from gratification of the person's need for affiliation, from self-identity maintenance and enhancement, as well as from self-esteem enhancement. Vaux (1988) argues that the main-effect perspective "softens the focus on social support and distinguishes it less sharply from social relationships and social integration more generally." (p. 148). He posits that the main effect benefits of social support are produced by a range of mechanisms (pp. 150–152):

Social penetration: Acquisition of more valued social roles and statuses may enhance the person's sense of power and mastery.

Belonging: Involvement in networks, mutual obligations and roles can result in a sense of belonging or affiliation.

Self-esteem: A person's self-esteem is boosted by the messages from others in their network that they are valued and needed.

Social aspirations: The existence of a set of network connections and role involvements that satisfy cultural prescriptions of what is good produces a feeling of satisfaction.

Pleasant events: An expanded set of network and role involvements may produce more varied and frequent involvements in pleasant events that enhance the person's feelings of well-being.

Norms and
reference figures: Acquisition of an appropriate set of norms and reference figures may help the person to appraise situations more effectively, to avoid harmful situations or to respond in a more useful fashion.

Social identities: Having more friends, network connections, valued social roles presents more developmental opportunities that allow the person to construct a set of social identities that enhances his/her sense of well-being and life satisfaction.

A number of social science theories have been used to explicate the relationship between positive social integration and well-being, for example, bonding and attachment theory (Pilisuk & Parks, 1986), social exchange theory (Wills, 1985), self-esteem and personal control theories (Wills, 1985), developmental theory (Boyce, 1985), symbolic interactional theory (Weigert et al., 1986). From the perspective of understanding and developing interventions based upon social support concepts, situating the main-effect model of social support within a broader theoretical context is important for several reasons. First, the theoretical rationales for the main effect highlight the essential differences of the helping processes involved in the main effect and buffering-effect models of social support. Second, these social science rationales make it clear that the main-effect model of social support incorporates processes that are basic to the construction, maintenance, and reconstruction of identities and well-being. While Vaux (1988, p. 148) worried that including the concerns of general social integration might obfuscate the focus of social support theory and research, from the point of view of understanding the importance of different kinds of social connections and how they may be used in helping strategies this broader focus seems fortuitous. Finally, these social science rationales for the main effect of social support indicate clearly that programs building on the main-effect model are very different and not substitutable for helping strategies drawing on the buffering-effect model of social support.

Three of these social science rationales for the main-effect model of social support have been selected for discussion below: ecology and human development, the social construction of identity, and the process of escape from inferiorization. These three perspectives were chosen both because of their power to explain the central importance of social integration for well-being and for their ability to indicate the types of social involvements that should be fostered if the benefits of the main effect of social support are desired.

The main-effect model of social support moves the conception of support programs in the social services well beyond short-term provisions for specific problem situations. To the extent that social service providers are concerned with the long-term well-being of those they are trying to help, as well as the prevention of individual or family breakdown, the evidence is that they are going to have to pay attention to methods of intervention that foster the core elements of social integration stipulated in the main-effect model: stable, multidimensional, intimate and reciprocal relationships, enduring and valued social roles, and accepting social networks. It is evident that these elements are missing in the lives of many users of social services (Cameron et al., 1992; Cameron & Rothery, 1985). Confronting such deficiencies represents substantially more difficult challenges than the provision of short-term supports; however, there are a number of realistic avenues to begin addressing such difficulties. Not to do so would be to leave out a central component of social support and, more importantly, to ignore circumstances of great significance in the lives of many who ask for our help.

RATIONALES FOR THE MAIN EFFECT OF SOCIAL SUPPORT: ECOLOGY AND HUMAN DEVELOPMENT

From the ecological perspective, individuals have a close and reciprocal relationship with their environment and the individual matures or develops in a positive manner as he or she acquires:

> a more extended, differentiated and valid conception of the ecological environment and becomes motivated and able to engage in activities that reveal the properties of, sustain, or restructure that environment at levels of similar or greater complexity in form and content. (Bronfenbrenner, 1979, p. 27)

Developmental opportunities increase, as do positive developmental impacts, as the person successfully participates in a broadening range of patterned activities and social roles and as the person is able to interact with others occupying a variety of social roles. People who hold few positive social identities, and who relate to few others holding such positions, represent a developmental risk (Allen et al., 1983; Bronfenbrenner, 1979; Garbarino, 1983; Thoits, 1983, 1985; Weigert et al., 1986). A positive social identity and a healthy conception of one's own worth comes not only from participation in diverse social situations, but from an ability to master or cope with this diversity.

Developmental opportunities also result from involvement in multi-faceted and intimate relationships. An individual's feeling of belonging and her/his sense of self-worth are influenced by being able to develop such relationships and by being able to consider herself/himself as an active and valued contributor to the success and continuation of these relationships:

> Developmental risk derives from a microsystem characterized by a narrowly restricted range and level of activities; impoverished experiences in playing, working, and loving; or stunted reciprocity in which genuine interaction is lacking. . . . In contrast, enduring, reciprocal, multifaceted relationships that emphasize playing, working and loving provide environmental opportunities for a person. (Garbarino, 1983, p. 12)

A sense of belonging and self-worth cannot result from repeated failures to connect with others in such mutually beneficial relationships or from a negative valuation of ourselves from significant others. Our social identities and our self-esteem depend upon our succeeding in our patterned involvements with others. Mastery over our environment is considered to be a function of the adequacy of both the personal resources and the social resources we can call upon (Garbarino, 1983). Perceiving ourselves as being competent in our environment and being able to see ourselves as a proactive participant—or as a "subject" (Freire, 1981)—in important areas of living are fundamental prerequisites of social and psychological well-being within the ecological perspective on human development.

Pilisuk and Park (1986), in their book *The Healing Web,* use attachment theory to arrive at similar conclusions about the central importance of person-environment relations to human development and well-being. Noting that the presence of a strong attachment figure in early childhood is important to the development of strong and persuasive feelings of security and provides a basis for expanding relationships with significant others beyond the initial attachment figure, they argue that the need for such attachments continues throughout the life cycle. Success at attachment and the feedback received from these involvements "contributes to a sense of mastery and security. The person then feels less vulnerable or helpless and is more likely to have the confidence to take risks, to move in new directions, and to be creative" (p. 15).

Persistent pressures from the environment will tend to mold both the behavior and the expectations of people living in that setting. Over time, the ecological perspective predicts an increased conformity between the actions and ambitions of the person and the experienced demands and opportunities in the environment. For example, Sarabin and Scheibe (1983) describe the role that social services may play in supporting a process of self-depreciation:

In our effort to be professional and humanistic, we have coined special euphemisms that for a short time conceal the strong negative valuation. Examples of
these euphemisms are "disadvantaged," "underdeveloped," "underprivi-
leged," "culturally deprived," "mentally ill," "welfare recipient," "problem
families," "patients," "inmates," and so on. These labels carry much of the
meaning of nonperson. The person so labelled is likely to be regarded as if he
or she were at the lowest grade on the status dimension and at the negative end
of the value dimension. (p. 17)

The implication of this ecological perspective is that to reverse this process people have to be provided with access to meaningful social involvements. Consideration must be given to the creation of opportunities to be
valued and loved, to be contributors as well as receivers, and, perhaps most
important, to have meaningful and successful social role performances—
challenges traditionally not emphasized in the social services where the
change process usually has been seen as an individual one.

RATIONALES FOR THE MAIN EFFECT OF SOCIAL SUPPORT: THE SOCIAL CONSTRUCTION OF IDENTITY

Individual behavior and identity are not solely determined by personal
history; they are also social constructions. From our involvement in social
roles and from our stable interpersonal relationships, we develop an idealized conception of self—an amalgam of multiple role identities—that becomes very important to us and our sense of well-being (McCall & Simmons,
1966; Weigert et al., 1986). Role identities, or the characteristics a person
takes on or is seen as having by virtue of occupying particular social positions, are basic to personal development:

Roles have a magic-like power to alter how a person is treated, how she acts,
what she does, and thereby even what she thinks and feels. This principle
applies not only to the developing person but to the others in her world.
(Bronfenbrenner, 1979, p. 6)

Classical symbolic interaction theory emphasizes the interactive process in the
"looking glass self" or mirror theory of identity. The mirror theory argues that
we are what others' reflections make us . . . identity is produced by the twin
processes of subjectivation and objectivation. We construct ourselves as we
show ourselves to be to others and self. . . . The imperative to act significantly
links the inner experience of each participant into a system of meaning real-
ized in interactions. This link is conceptualized by seeing persons as per-
formers of roles; that is, shared expectations mobilized by validated and
committed identities in the social situation. . . . Selves are committed to roles
that are relevant to their identities. (Weigert et al., 1986, pp. 50–52)

Role identities and successful role performances are important to human development and ongoing well-being in a number of ways (Thoits, 1985, p. 56):

- by providing an answer to the existential question, Who am I?
- by providing opportunities for the development and the demonstration of personal competence,
- by permitting positive social evaluations of oneself,
- by facilitating the development of enduring, multidimensional, reciprocal relationships,
- by allowing the role-holder to become a contributor to valued social exchanges,
- by linking the role-holder with socially similar others.

Our role identities are not only basic to our idealized conception of self; they are also fragile constructions. These identities require constant negotiation and legitimation. As a result, we all have a very strong need to seek out role support or ongoing confirmation of our ideal identities (McCall & Simmons, 1966). Indeed, it can be argued that a basic purpose of many formal or informal groupings of similar others is the reciprocal valuation and maintenance of the participants' conception of themselves:

> [T]his mutual over valuation may occur by default, in a sense, out of sheer delight in finding another person who shares even the vocabulary associated with a given identity . . . [T]his result is particularly likely when the opportunity structure is exceedingly limited or when the creation of the identity is more idiosyncratic. (McCall & Simmons, 1966, p. 103)

The process of developing and maintaining a social identity involves ongoing bargaining and exchanges with others with whom one has regular contact (Huston & Burgess, 1979). It has been argued that these relationships are governed by the universal norm of reciprocity; that is, for a benefit received in such a relationship a subjectively equivalent benefit ought eventually to be returned (Brown, 1986; Shumaker & Brownell, 1984). Social exchange theory would predict that these relationships, integral to the development of a positive social identity, can be maintained only if they are perceived by the parties to be mutually profitable to acceptably equivalent degrees (Brown, 1986).

It follows that the ability to engage in these intimate relationships and social roles depends upon an ability to make a positive contribution to their development and maintenance. Indeed, there is evidence from social psychology research (Brown, 1986, pp. 66–86) that unequal relationships are often terminated by the parties receiving a disproportionate share of the benefits:

Help that cannot be reciprocated poses a special problem for the recipient. Because benefits must be reciprocated in some subjectively equivalent way, accepting offered help, or worse, asking for needed help does produce a feeling of obligation in the recipient and feelings of obligation are unpleasant. (p. 86)

The language describing most social service helping relationships (for example, therapist/counselor; client/patient) indicates that these are essentially nonreciprocal, hierarchical relationships. Even in alternatives to traditional therapy such as feminist therapy (Greenspan, 1982), it remains basic to the exchange process that one party is needy (or deficient) and is helped and the other party is competent and provides. In addition, while his judgment may be harsh and ignores the evidence for the positive contributions of formal helping, this perspective supports Alinsky's (1971) critique that service takes, rather than gives dignity. For the purposes of this analysis, the relevant observation is that social involvements in which all parties contribute as well as receive, and successful social role performances, are central contributors to a positive social identity and well-being. This viewpoint challenges the restricted concept of helping that dominates most service settings.[1]

Relationships that endure and contribute to the positive social identities of the parties are more likely between similar or status-equal people. The availability of such relationships will be positively or negatively influenced by the opportunity structures in the person's environment and by the person's ability to take advantage of the opportunities that do exist. The consequences of repeated role failures, of not having multiple valued role identities, of not participating in stable, multidimensional reciprocal relationships, are likely to be feelings of unworthiness and eventually self-blame (Adam, 1978; Bronfenbrenner, 1979; Brown, 1986; McCall & Simmons, 1966; Thoits, 1985).

The social construction of identity perspective stresses the importance of social integration in the development, maintenance, and reconstruction of a positive social identity and feeling of self-worth. Support programs intending to take advantages of the insights of this perspective would concentrate upon:

- creating opportunities for people to develop enduring, multidimensional, reciprocal relationships,
- creating opportunities for people to be givers as well as receivers of assistance,
- developing new social roles and opportunities for new types of social participation for people,

- supporting successful performances in valued social roles (e.g., work, school, parenting),
- helping people to learn the new behaviors and skills and to acquire the self-confidence required for them to take advantage of above types of social opportunities.

RATIONALES FOR THE MAIN EFFECT OF SOCIAL SUPPORT: THE ESCAPE FROM INFERIORIZATION

Many of the daily experiences of users of social service cannot be comprehended uniquely in terms of individual or family problems; they need to be perceived as collective or shared experiences. To compound matters, these shared experiences are often representative of harshly oppressive realities confronting many social service populations. To share these realities means being socially stigmatized or inferiorized in relation to more powerful groups in society. Stigmas that are shared by many social service participants include being unemployed, on welfare, a poor single mother, a child welfare client, and physically or mentally handicapped (Sarabin & Scheibe, 1983).

People living in such circumstances often have a negative social identity—not of their own making—as a basis for identifying with each other. Many writers have identified the discovery that one is a devalued other as a significant psychological and social turning point in the life of an inferiorized person (Adam, 1978; Brown, 1986; Fanon, 1963; Greenspan, 1982; Lewis, 1978; Rappaport, 1977; Ryan, 1976; Sennett & Cobb, 1972; Weigert et al., 1986). Reality in the lives of inferiorized groups is more harmful and threatening. In addition, their social identities as inferiorized people—who they are and why they live as they do—is defined by powerful outside groups who control the means of cultural expression and the helping professions that define their problems. These external definitions are expressed usually in language and values alien to the experiences of the inferiorized (Adam, 1978; Illich, 1977; McKnight, 1977; Sarabin & Scheibe, 1983).

The shared inequalities of the inferiorized are typically defined by helping professions—either explicitly or indirectly by their actions—as specific inadequacies of the inferiorized group (McKnight, 1977). Given the risks involved in challenging this view of reality, it is not surprising that the natural avenue to the inferiorized is the "masochistic solution" (Adam, 1978). The inferiorized begin to internalize the negative social identity as a true description of themselves. As a result, patterns of low self-esteem, and even of self-hate, are common among the inferiorized, as are "flights from identity," where the stigmatized person tries to distance himself or herself from the inferiorized group and to emulate the more powerful and valued outsiders (Adam, 1978; Fanon, 1963; Sarabin & Scheibe, 1983; Sennett & Cobb, 1972; Weigert et al., 1986). Brown (1986) reviews a number of studies documenting this pattern of self-hatred and flight from identity among inferiorized groups. For example:

> Approximately 60 percent of the black children thought that the nice doll, the doll that was the nice color, and the one they wanted to play with, was white. The doll that looked bad to 59 percent of the black children was the black doll. . . . This is the reverse of ethnocentrism: this is in-group derogation and out-group elevation and there are many demonstrations for other subordinate groups. (Clark & Clark, 1947, quoted in Brown, 1986, pp. 558–559)

Studies of Quebec francophones found similar patterns of in-group derogation and out-group elevation in comparisons of evaluations of communications in French and English ([Lambert et al., 1960; Maurice, 1985] quoted in Brown, 1986, pp. 559–560). People who have internalized a negative social identity will have greater difficulty, not only in respecting themselves, but in valuing each other and being able to engage in collective endeavors (Adam, 1978).

What is most of interest, in terms of interventions drawing on this perspective, is the general agreement in the literature on the process of escape from inferiorization (Adam, 1978; Altman, 1971; Brown, 1986; Fanon, 1963; Freire, 1981; Greenspan, 1982; Withorn, 1984). The process of escaping involves collective or group action by the inferiorized that incorporates both disobedience and cultural affirmation.

Escaping from inferiorization requires a refusal to accept the negative definition of one's social identity and a refusal to conform to expectations of behavior for the inferiorized. The escape process demands a reevaluation and redefinition of the daily realities confronted by the inferiorized and the dissemination of counterinterpretations of these realities. Cultural affirmation on behalf of the inferiorized boosts their pride and sense of self-worth (Brown, 1986). The potential and the limitations of this process of escape from inferiorization can be gauged by the successes in redefining definitions of identity and in creating opportunities by social movements such as the women's movement, the independent living movement for the physically handicapped, the gay liberation movement, the antipsychiatric movement as well as North American First Nations' and Aboriginal People's and African-Americans' attempts at self-determination. A number of distinct components have been identified in this process of escape from inferiorization (Adam, 1978; Brown, 1986):

- the injustice of existing circumstances and the treatment of the inferiorized by the outside dominant groups has to be denounced;
- the inferiorized have to begin to see the commonalities in their circumstances and to think of themselves as an identifiable minority;
- the inferiorized have to create some social space for themselves, within which they can enjoy acceptance, intimacy, and relative security and where they can begin to exercise control and freedom of action;
- existing realities have to be evaluated by the inferiorized and counter-interpretations of these realities have to be developed and disseminated among the inferiorized and to members of the broader community.

The contribution of social service professionals to the development of legitimate collective processes of escape from inferiorization is likely to be quite limited. However, this perspective does contain a number of insights for those wishing to develop interventions exploiting the potential of the main effect of social support. Perceiving oneself and being perceived as a member of a stigmatized or socially inferiorized group of people is not an uncommon reality among social service clientele. This collective inferiorization limits opportunities of creating a positive social identity for individual members of the stigmatized group. If groups of social service participants can be identified as sharing repressive conditions, this analysis indicates that the process of escape from inferiorization cannot be exclusively individualized, but will require that the inferiorized make contact with each other and create some shared social space within which the process of reconstruction and redefinition can begin to occur. Finally, while the creation of social movements is beyond the reach of social services, this perspective does stress that exposure to the counterinterpretations of reality and identity, and to the coping strategies emanating from these movements, as well as encouraging and supporting participation in such movements, can be quite legitimate approaches to fostering the development of positive social identities and well-being with various social service populations.

SUMMARY

This discussion of the nature of the buffering-effect and the main-effect models of social support challenges the dominant helping paradigms and the allocation of energies in social service settings. The buffering-effect model of social support points to the need to combine informal and formal helping strategies to profit from their relative advantages. It also suggests that we should investigate ways of more flexibly augmenting the level and the types of personal and social resources available to children and families. Existing emphases on professional helpers in hierarchical individual, family, and group treatment roles are overly restrictive and lacking in the power and the diversity that struggling children and families often require.

The main-effect model of social support exposes important aspects of the processes of identity development, maintenance, and reconstruction as well as the roots of ongoing psychological well-being and a positive social identity. These insights are basically ignored in the helping processes dominant in professional social services today. If we are truly interested in augmenting self-esteem and empowering people, and increasing their independence, we will have to incorporate the insights of the main-effect model of social support in a central fashion into how we try to support both children and their parents.

In addition to the social support perspectives discussed in this chapter, there also are many characteristics of effective formal programs with children and families under high stress that can inform our design of useful support programs. We turn to these in the next chapter. Following this review, the task of translating these general discussions into guidelines for understanding and creating support programs will begin.

NOTE

1.   This focus on the importance of social involvements is not intended to devalue the contribution of formal helping focused on personal or family functioning, but rather to point to the need to twin these formal methods with strategies that support successful social performances (see the discussion in the next two chapters). Equally important, these deliberations need to be considered in the context of the dominant reality of poverty confronting a large percentage of users of social services. While social support strategies can be helpful even under these circumstances, they do not address the fact that many people's lives will be substantially determined by a lack of employment opportunities and economic resources.

Evidence has been accumulating over the past twenty years about the characteristics of support programs that have the potential of producing significantly greater benefits for disadvantaged children and families. However, little of this information is available to those responsible for designing and delivering services in a fashion that is useful in their decision-making. Much of the time, support programs are developed with very limited access to information about others' efforts and even less knowledge about program characteristics associated with greater efficiencies and superior outcomes.

The work presented in this chapter and the next is based on two theses: (a) general patterns of effectiveness associated with support programs with disadvantaged populations can be identified; and (b) it is possible to use available research and theory to construct a generic framework that will improve our ability to understand, develop, and assess formal and informal support programs. In the end, the most useful product of our efforts will be a systematic way of thinking when developing a support program or assessing an existing program.

In seminars about support programming, we have played a game with participants called "Have I Got a Program Model for You!" In this game, participants are presented with the rationales for several existing support program models in child welfare (e.g., intensive family preservation services, parent training programs, parent aide programs, mutual aid organizations) including their proponents' predictions of program outcomes (which are remarkably similar across these very different ways of helping families). Participants are asked to evaluate these competing claims. Of course, it soon becomes apparent that there is no credible basis for doing so. Practitioners and administrators currently have no practical means of making choices between the various approaches to helping children and families being proposed, often by very enthusiastic proponents.

This dilemma has five parts:

1. Innovative approaches to protecting children and to supporting families have the potential to produce encouraging benefits for disadvantaged children and families.

2. These promising methods differ substantially from many of the dominant ways of helping in child welfare and other service settings.
3. Not all of the actively promoted programs are effective in multiple-problem situations.
4. No single approach to helping will be effective with all populations— the real challenge is choosing an appropriate range of helping strategies.
5. There is little guidance available about how to assess these competing claims, how to combine approaches, or how to integrate these different ways of working into existing child welfare and other service organizations.

By the end of this volume, our ambition is to improve the readers' ability to generate reasonable expectations about different support programs, to understand the populations appropriate for these different approaches, to make decisions about combining approaches to helping, and to understand the organizational implications of these new ways of helping. Admittedly, we can only begin to satisfy these objectives. Nonetheless, the Support Program Impact Assessment Framework and the intervention principles highlighted in these chapters represent an advance over current ways of decision-making. Hopefully, the framework will be of both practical and scholarly importance in child welfare and in other settings.

In selecting which programs to investigate, we have emphasized methods with a potential for preventing child abuse and neglect, reducing the need for child placements, supporting families at high risk of poor outcomes, fostering successful community integration, and being cost-effective. Little attention has been paid to traditional divisions between ways of helping— protection and support, prevention and treatment, formal and informal helping. Our concern has been with the lessons that can be drawn from successful programs wherever we find them. There is a need to cross conventional boundaries in our search for effective ways of helping children and families. When we do, we find similar patterns and principles of helping emerging from many different settings—such as child welfare, juvenile delinquency, community mental health, and psychiatry.

In subsequent chapters, a selection of different types of support programs will be discussed in more detail. In this chapter, a summary of earlier reviews of support program effectiveness by the principal author and selected other reviewers is presented. The emphasis will be on highlighting the programming patterns associated with better outcomes with disadvantaged populations. In the next chapter, the Support Program Impact Assessment Framework and intervention guidelines are developed.

ROTHERY AND CAMERON (1985)

Rothery and Cameron (1985) reviewed program descriptions and/or program evaluations of eighty-six programs designed to prevent child abuse and neglect as well as reduce the use of out-of-home placements of children. Table 4.1 provides an overview of the support program alternatives that they reviewed. They pointed out that the range of supports provided and the methods of helping emphasized in these programs were quite limited. The programs essentially provided the services already familiar in child welfare but at higher levels of intensity and for the express purpose of supporting families. The authors drew several conclusions about promising formal support programs:

- Multiple services and supports have stronger impacts on families than single interventions. Many successful support programs provide a variety of supports *concurrently* to families.
- High levels of direct contact with families (e.g., five to thirty hours per week) have been characteristic of effective family support programs.
- Standard child welfare methods (e.g., counseling, skill training, homemakers) are efficacious methods of supporting families if provided in combination and at high levels.
- Skill training has demonstrated impacts on specific individual and family problems. However, this approach has not been clearly effective with isolated, "multiple-problem" families unless combined with strategies that augment the families' access to positive social networks, and/or other formal supports.
- Effective family supports have been provided in a variety of ways: crisis intervention, counseling, skill teaching, in-home services, peer groups, peer networks, mutual aid associations, recreational and social activities, etc. The more powerful program models typically build a package of these elements.
- None of the program reports indicated that greater client independence from formal services was an outcome.
- Nonprofessional staff are demonstrably effective in support programming and can be profitably incorporated into programming.
- In-home services have been associated with favorable outcomes under certain conditions.
- Groups of peers with similar problems, positive peer networks and mutual aid strategies have been associated with positive outcomes with a broad variety of participants confronting diverse situations.

Table 4.1. Overview of Common Support Program Alternatives in Child Welfare

Program Type	Services Offered	Reported Impacts
Intensive Crisis Intervention Programs (3)	• emergency help • brief intensive services (every day, 24 hrs) • time limited • high level of direct contact • broad range of supports, e.g., crisis counseling, advocacy, shelter, homemakers, foster homes, 24 hrs intake, training, and skill development	• a capacity to reduce percentage of crisis placements • an ability to return children home • cost reductions
Intensive Short/Medium-Term Programs (39)	• high level of direct contact (5–20 hrs/wk) • lower number of cases per worker (11) • dominant service package included: counseling or therapy; training and skill development; inhome practical services • clients served 6–24 months	• reduced incidence of abuse and neglect • reduction in child placement • some positive impacts on parenting and child development
Intensive Long-Term Programs (4)	• same services as short/medium term • focused on severely dysfunctional families who have been unsuccessfully served by other agencies • high risk of child maltreatment, placement	• support without high reincidence of abuse or child placement; independent functioning not expected
Skill Development/ Teaching Programs (5)	• instruction the central focus • in-home or classroom • focuses on parental skills, child management, child development • sessions 2–3 times per week • time limited • other supports may be joined, e.g., transportation, childcare, advocacy	• some positive impacts on child development and parenting • participant satisfaction • no reported impact on incidence of abuse and neglect; child placement

(continued)

Table 4.1. Continued

Program Type	Services Offered	Reported Impacts
Hospital Newborn Programs (7)	• through maternity department of a hospital • first time mothers identified as high risk • outreach services: ongoing link with pediatrician; ongoing contact with quick access; home visits by nurse or homemaker • helping new mother to understand and cope	• good research evidence on reduced incidence of serious child abuse • no reported impacts on parenting or child development

Source: Rothery and Cameron (1985, pp. 65–67).

• Family support programs emphasizing informal methods of helping are almost non-existent in child welfare. Intervention strategies that emphasize the support of families remain a very distant second to those stressing change in individual or family problems. The problems of social integration and ongoing support of families are seldom addressed.

Rothery and Cameron (1985) also assessed eight family support programs in Ontario child welfare agencies as part of a larger study (see Table 4.2). They noted the following patterns that were consistent with those gleaned from their previous literature review (p. 77):

• Programs with high support dimensions (i.e., high level of direct contact, broad variety of helpers, broad variety of help) were the only programs with an identifiable superior impact on child placement rates. However, these programs did not necessarily produce clearly superior benefits on measurements of individual and family problems.
• Some programs with moderate to high levels of direct contact with families coupled with relatively focused interventions by paid helpers had higher positive change on several measurements of individual and family problems. There were no indications of superior performance on child placements or case closure indicators for these programs.
• Programs with low levels of direct contact with families and little variety in types of help and helpers had no discernible higher positive change rates on child placement, case closure, or individual and family problem indicators.

Table 4.2. Program Parameters and Case Impacts for the Eight Family Support Programs

Program	Level of Direct Contact	Variety of Helpers	Variety of Help	Higher Positive Impacts*
Self-Help	moderate-high	very broad	very broad	less child placement less time in care more case closures personal problems parent
Afterschool II	very high	broad	very broad	less child placement more cases closed good return home rate child problems
Afterschool I	high	broad	broad	less child placement good return home rate
Family Skills	high-very high	moderate	moderate	less time in care parent/child relationship parenting
Parent Aide	moderate	low	low-moderate	parent/child relationship parenting household management
Homemaker	low-moderate	low	low-moderate	none
Child & Family Management	low	low	low	none
Child Management	low	low	low	none

Source: Rothery and Cameron (1985, p. 78).
* These ratings are in relation to several comparison groups for each of the programs reviewed.

CAMERON (1990a), CAMERON (1993)

Based upon a more current review of the literature about support programs, Cameron (1990a, pp. 281–284) presented a preliminary framework to help differentiate general support program alternatives. He argued that common structural characteristics of support programs can be used to distinguish three broad types of program strategies: personal and family change, formal support, and social integration. Besides having different administrative, staffing, and service requirements, the three program types were described as producing quite different benefits for families. Cameron also claimed that, although these basic program strategies can be profitably used to complement each other, they generally are not substitutable for each other. Finally, he postulated that the more powerful support program models incorporated characteristics from two or more of these general program types.

Cameron (1993) added crisis intervention programs to this general typology of support program models. Based upon on extensive review of the research evidence about IFPS (rapid response time, high levels of direct contact, in-home services, multiple types of assistance, one or two primary workers for a client, low caseloads, brief program involvement), he concluded that (pp. 40–41):

- The results of controlled studies of these crisis intervention programs in reducing the frequency of care and in reducing the number of days in care in "high-risk" situations were encouraging with most studies showing a marked advantage for the program group over the control group.
- There is evidence that placement aversion rates decline over time, suggesting a need for follow-up program strategies and more explicit attention to program graduation procedures in these models.

There also was convincing evidence for the cost-effectiveness of these crisis intervention programs. However, there was little information available showing any long-term changes in personal or family functioning or in daily living circumstances resulting from these interventions. Tables 4.3 and 4.4 present this general typology of family support programs and the anticipated impacts of each program type.

Commenting on the first three program types, Cameron (1990a) offered the following interpretation. Under favorable circumstances, programs with high personal and family change characteristics can be usually expected to produce positive change on the specific individual or family problems targeted. Generally, it is not reasonable to anticipate substantial spin-off effects from specific interventions, for example, to expect that improved parenting

Table 4.3. General Typology of Family Support Programs

Program Type	Common Programming Parameters	Example
Personal and family change programs	low to moderate level of direct contact (approximately 1–2 hours per week) short to moderate duration (approximately 3–18 months) emphasis upon a single formal helper or some other formal method of bringing focused technical expertise to bear upon specific problems focus upon specific individual and family problems	family therapy (Collins & Collins, 1990) behavior modification (Blythe, Hodges, & Guterman, 1990; Thomlison, 1990) parent aide programs (Bidgood & van de Sande, 1990) child management programs (Bidgood & van de Sande, 1990)
Formal support programs	moderate to high levels of direct contact (approximately 4–15 hours per week) moderate to long-term duration (approximately 6 months to several years) involves clients with a variety of formal helpers and a variety of formal program activities informal helping strategies may be incorporated but only as adjuncts to formal helping	adolescent afterschool programs (Cameron & Rothery, 1985) Comprehensive Emergency Services to Children (Cameron, Holmberg, & Rothery, 1983) Iowa Family Services (Bidgood & van de Sande, 1990)

Social integration programs	moderate to high levels of direct contact (approximately 4–15 hours per week)	Parents Anonymous (Cameron, 1990a)
	involves participants in a variety of informal helping strategies emphasizing reciprocity, multiple exchanges, social networks, mutual aid, and social role performances	Community Development Network (Cameron, 1990a)
	contacts with formal helpers may be incorporated but only as adjuncts to informal helping strategies	Cooperative Daycare (Brophy, 1990)
Crisis intervention programs	high levels of direct contact (as high as 3–5 times a week, sometimes can be 24 hours a day)	Intensive Family Preservation Services (Cameron, 1993)
	short duration (4–8 weeks)	
	rapid response to a crisis (within 24 hours of referral)	
	involves one or two well-trained formal helpers as focal point of helping	
	services focus on rational-emotive therapy, skill development, concrete supports, linking to environmental resources	

Source: Cameron (1990a, p. 282), Cameron (1993).

Table 4.4. Anticipated Impacts of Family Support Programs

Program Characteristics	Anticipated Impacts	Example
High on personal and family change characteristics	on the specific individual and family problems targeted by the intervention impacts will likely be of short to medium duration in multiproblem situations	improved parenting skills improved spousal communication more personal assertiveness personal and family gains will probably attenuate after treatment ends unless other relevant changes are made in individual's or family's environment
High on formal support characteristics	on specific individual and family problems targeted by the interventions on specific social problems targeted by the interventions on rates and duration of institutionalization and family/individual breakdown impacts will likely be of short to medium duration in multiproblem situations	improved parenting skills improved spousal communication less social isolation access to more emergency resources less use of foster care or institutional placements gains will probably attenuate after termination of program involvement unless other relevant changes are made in individual's or family's environment

64

High on social integration characteristics	on specific social problems targeted by the intervention on rates of institutionalization and family/individual breakdown on independence from formal helpers on social identity, feelings of belonging, self-worth, and confidence impacts of medium to long duration in multiproblem situations	less social isolation access to more emergency resources less use of foster care or institutional placements more case closures more confidence in ability to cope with problems better feelings about self and social identity gains can be maintained as long as social integration involvements are maintained or replaced by other positive social involvements
High on crisis intervention characteristics	on specific individual and family programs targeted by the interventions on rates of institutionalization and family/individual breakdown impacts will likely be of short to medium duration in multiproblem situations	improved parenting skills less use of foster care or institutional placements gains will probably attenuate after termination of program involvement unless other changes are made in individual's or family's environment

Source: Cameron (1990a, p. 283), Cameron (1993).

will lead to better family functioning, which will in turn translate into more parental self-confidence and improved reaching out to friends. In multiple-problem situations, few social service interventions are powerful enough to produce such repercussions. One of the basic tenets of service/support package construction is that if changes are desired in a particular social or personal factor, then it should be the focus of an appropriate intervention strategy. Finally, in such circumstances, personal and family change strategies, when used in isolation, have not consistently demonstrated a capacity to prevent child abuse and neglect or to prevent child placements—these interventions are reportedly often overwhelmed by the multiplicity of stressors in families' lives.

What we have called formal support programs in Table 4.3, because they provide high levels of service and a range of services-supports, have frequently demonstrated an ability to prevent child abuse and neglect as well as child placement. Intensive formal support initiatives have been used effectively during periods of very high family stress. These types of programs may also produce positive change in personal and family functioning in areas specifically targeted by elements of the program. However, these formal support programs are usually expensive. In addition, with disadvantaged individuals and families, formal support programs have not been consistently associated with changes that endure after contact with the program terminates or with fostering long-term independence from formal service providers.

Some social integration programs with high levels of participant involvement and multiple supports have also demonstrated their potential to lessen the incidence of child abuse and neglect as well as child placement. In addition, under favorable conditions, social integration programs are the only type of program where it is reasonable to expect benefits to be maintained over the long-term and where greater independence from formal services can be fostered. Successful social integration can also produce improved self-confidence and feelings of belonging. However, social integration programs have not been consistently associated with positive change in other personal or family factors (for example, parent-child relations) unless these are specifically addressed by elements within the social integration intervention.

ROTHERY (1990a, 1990b)

Based upon his own review of the evidence for the effectiveness of family therapy with disadvantaged families and on his interpretation of reviews of other methods of clinical service with this population, Michael Rothery

(1990a) draws several conclusions relevant to our concerns. Disadvantaged families, rich in stress but poor in resources and able to absorb high levels of service without seeming to improve, are presented as a prime example of the "hard-to-serve" family. Reviews of clinical practice with these families reveal a number of persistent principles and issues. "For many of us, these principles seem sensible and true to our clinical experience, at the same time as they imply significant deviations from what we have been trained to think and do" (p. 2):

- "The need for coordinated service packages rather than reliance on a single specialized form of help is now a widely accepted principle among people who work with 'hard-to-serve' families, and is supported by the ample evidence" (ibid.).
- "Although professional helpers have learned to value emotional support above all other kinds of help, effective service packages for maltreating families can seldom ignore the need for instrumental or concrete resources, for educational supports of various kinds, and for efforts to ameliorate social isolation" (ibid.).
- "[There is a need for] an extension of our concept of helping beyond the psychotherapist's traditional focus on the resolution of the emotional and interpersonal conflicts in which dysfunction is presumed to be rooted. [There is] an especially important focus for programs for maltreating families in recent years, emphasizing the building of . . . competence rather than the treatment of pathology. . . . Efforts to distinguish abusing from nonabusing families by identifying psychopathology or personal problems in the parents have had ambiguous results" (p. 3).
- "One of the premises . . . is obviously that a comprehensive approach to the problem of child maltreatment will draw on the talents and resources of many different [helpers]. For example . . . the traditional focus . . . has been on the parents [but] this can profitably be balanced with programs that attend to the needs of children from maltreating families. Specifically, what can preschool and daycare programs do to help very young children from such situations?" (p. 4).
- "Formal helpers have had to recognize that their impact on maltreating families is less than they would wish; at the same time, it is clear that the informal support systems to which a family is connected are very powerful in determining that family's well-being" (ibid.).
- "There is . . . strong agreement that it is best if one of the many workers involved with the family is designated as the primary worker with responsibility for the overall management of the case. . . . This clearly implies that the primary worker's role includes an overall, highly flexible coordination function. . . . There is a tendency to

downgrade case management or coordinating functions as being somehow less sophisticated than more purely psychotherapeutic kinds of social work activity. In fact, it is clear that all of the skills of a seasoned family therapist could be called into play. . . . The difference is in the definition of the client system rather than the level of technical skill employed" (1990b, p. 27).

CAMERON (1990b), CAMERON, HAYWARD, AND MAMATIS (1992)

Mutual aid organizations are relatively well-known vehicles for creating supportive relationships for a range of disadvantaged populations. Cameron (1990b) described their potential for a child welfare constituency in the following terms:

> Considering the social isolation of many child welfare clients, and their stig-matized status in the community, it seems probable that informal social sup-ports created specifically for these groups may prove to be more accessible than such supports available within the general community. The creation of mutual aid organizations specifically for various groupings of child welfare clientele may be a promising and practical way of actualizing some of the benefits of informal social supports.
>   One of the great strengths of the mutual aid model is its potential to provide a broad range of social supports. Such groups can also be flexible enough to provide benefits to participants for brief or for extended periods of time. As a model, child welfare mutual aid organizations have the theoretical potential of producing many of the main effects, as well as the buffering effects, of social support. However, the benefits of participation in a mutual aid organization— as with all family support programming—will depend on the levels and types of involvements that a particular self-help organization is able to provide. (pp. 159–160)

Cameron (1990b) also reviewed the outcome research on mutual aid organizations and described general patterns similar to those identified ear-lier for formal social support programs:

> Lieberman and Borman (1976a) concluded that "not a single adequate study of the effectiveness of self-help groups exists" (p. 459). Although research evi-dence has accumulated since the late 1970s, outcome studies of mutual aid interventions are still relatively rare. This review of the evidence on the effec-tiveness of self-help groups indicates that the mutual aid model is very flexible and that many different interventions are incorporated by mutual aid organiza-tions. To predict the possible impacts of a self-help group on its members, it is necessary to consider explicitly the types and levels of involvement of group

members, as well as their personal characteristics. This investigation of the research evidence suggests that the impacts of mutual aid groups parallel roughly the pattern identified by Rothery and Cameron (1985) for formal family support programs in child welfare:

1. Mutual aid groups that demonstrate a clear reduction in the rate of institutional placement and in the use of formal services emphasize strong network connections among members, and enmesh their members in a variety of activities;
2. Mutual aid groups that stress particular methods of skill development and personal change techniques borrowed from professionals have a clear impact on some individual and family problems; [and,]
3. Mutual aid groups with minimal levels of contact with their members do not produce very encouraging results.

Although no individual study of a mutual aid group is conclusive, there is a consistency in these findings that is convincing. A conservative conclusion would be that they indicate the value of continued investigation of the potential of the self-help or mutual aid model in child welfare. (p. 162)

ONTARIO MINISTRY OF COMMUNITY AND SOCIAL SERVICES (1990), BETTER BEGINNINGS, BETTER FUTURES

Prior to implementing the multiple-site Better Beginnings, Better Futures (BBBF) Prevention Demonstration Project in Ontario, teams of experts were engaged in reviewing the outcome evidence available on prevention interventions with poor children and families (Ministry of Community and Social Services, 1990). They assessed program models from health, child care, primary schools, and social services. In general, they agreed that the proposed demonstration project should build on the following themes identified from the literature:

- "Children's functioning must be understood within an environmental context . . . children in the context of family (however it is structured) and the family in the context of community."
- "To be most effective, prevention programs must address the needs of children and their families throughout the developmental cycle, with special attention to the critical transition periods."
- "Primary prevention programs must be comprehensive. [T]o produce positive outcomes for significant number of children and for these outcomes to last, programs must address a number of risk factors."
- "Components identified in the literature . . . associated with successful prevention programs, should be included as priority components before designing untested components. Examples of such well-

documented components include parent training, child development
education, parent support groups, diet supplements, drop-in centres
and parent-child resource centres, as well as components which address food and shelter."
- "Programs need to be flexible and tailored to community conditions."
- "Parental involvement helps to stabilize the family and consolidate
  gains made through the program" (pp. 107–110).

The Better Beginnings, Better Futures review summarized the outcome
research for several promising approaches to working with disadvantaged
children and families. Their conclusions about these different approaches
are highlighted below.

Prenatal/Infant Development Programs

- "Programs with the greatest impact had:
  —multiple components (e.g., home visits, parent-support groups,
    plus daycare or nursery school); and,
  —long-duration (e.g., two to five years)" (p. 18).
- "Outreach (home visits) [was] a major program component. This component was important for disadvantaged families in all programs with
  broad impact, at least for the child's first year" (ibid.).

Preschool Programs

Hundreds of studies, both publicly and privately sponsored, evaluated the
effectiveness of these prevention programs. In addition, two major meta-
analyses report aggregate data: the Head Start Evaluation Synthesis and Utilization Project (McKey, Condelli, Ganson, Barrett, McConkey, & Plantz, 1985),
which synthesized data from 210 Head Start studies; and the Consortium for
Longitudinal Studies (1983), which pooled data, including long-term follow-
up, from 12 of the most carefully designed, implemented and evaluated studies. Nine of the Consortium studies were not part of the Head Start program,
but were privately sponsored initiatives that were well-funded and profession-
ally staffed.

The effectiveness of [these] primary prevention programs to produce positive changes in the lives of socially disadvantaged children is well-
documented (see Zigler and Valentine, 1979, Consortium for Longitudinal
Studies, 1983; Woodhead, 1988 for reviews of this literature). High quality
preschools are associated with positive outcomes in cognitive functioning
(e.g., lower rates of retention in grade, referrals to special education and early
school leaving), and social and emotional development (e.g., higher rates of
social competence, self-concept, positive attitudes and motivation about
school and better relationships with family). Long-term positive outcomes of
note are lower rates of juvenile crime and arrest, fewer teen pregnancies,

higher rates of employment, earnings and success at becoming self-supporting.

Although some measures are not direct indicators of mental health, the relationship of these factors and the general well-being of their child is apparent. In discussing the long-term effectiveness of preschool programs, Woodhead (1988) suggests the effects are probably not simply attributable to an increase in intellectual functioning " . . . but in the impact on a complex, interrelated set of events (attitudes, expectations, behaviours) taking place over an extended period of time with the child, school, family and community." These programs have had a broad impact across many areas of functioning of the child and the environment in which s/he operates. (pp. 25–26)

Preschool programming can be effective as a mechanism for early detection and intervention of children with developmental problems. (p. 37)

In order to stabilize the positive child outcomes, the two year programs were more successful than one-year programs. However, it is likely that even longer programs would produce more stable short-term effects and larger long term effects. (p. 37)

Child-Centered/Skill Development Approaches

Such programs as stress coping, assertiveness training and arts/sports in schools . . . have yet to demonstrate lasting impact on psychosocial competence or long-term prevention of mental health programs. (p. 57)

The authors of the Better Beginnings, Better Futures report offered the following general observation:

There exists, in the field of primary prevention, a myth that single, simple, relatively inexpensive, one-shot programs can produce long-term positive outcomes for economically disadvantaged children. Such myths are illusory. In order for prevention programs to produce positive outcomes for a significant number of children, and for those outcomes to last, programs must address a number of important risk factors. (p. 107)

SCHORR (1988)

Schorr (1988), reviewing program models for disadvantaged, poor families that focused on unwanted pregnancies, prenatal care, children's health services, family support in child welfare, and primary schools, corroborates these conclusions from Better Beginnings, Better Futures (Ministry of Community and Social Services, 1990):

We can significantly change the odds for youngsters growing up in environments that threaten healthy development by building on programs that have already proven successful. . . . Where I looked, in health, social services, family support, or education, the programs that worked for families and children living in concentrated poverty differed in fundamental ways from traditional programs that seemed to work for those in less devastating circumstances.

The programs that work best for children and families in "high-risk" environments typically offer comprehensive and intensive services. Whether they are part of the health, mental health, social service, or educational systems, they are able to respond flexibly to a wide variety of needs. In their wakes they often pull in other kinds of services, unrelated in narrowly bureaucratic terms but inseparable in the broad framework of human misery. These programs approach children not with bureaucratic or professional blinders, but open-eyed to their needs in a family and community context. Interventions that are successful with "high-risk" populations all seem to have staff with the time and skill to establish relationships based on mutual respect and trust.

These findings about the attributes of successful programs are not novel, but their convergence is striking. Their empirical support is now sturdy because similar patterns emerge from so many different arenas (pp. xxi–xxii)

The most striking fact about the programs that have accomplished the seeming miracle of helping "high-risk" families to change the conditions in which their children grow up is how much these successful programs have in common. All of them offer services that are comprehensive and intensive. All have highly professional staffs (some of whom work closely with paraprofessionals). All use insights and skills from psychiatry and child development in working with families to establish an atmosphere of trust and confidence. (pp. 175–176)

Services for families at greatest risk work if they are comprehensive and intensive enough to respond to the full range of their needs, and if they are prepared to provide help as concrete as a ride to the hospital or a box of diapers and as subtle as trust and understanding. (p. 177)

Schorr (1988, pp. 257–259) lists a number of attributes of interventions that work, particularly those which have been successful, in comparison with prevailing services, with high-risk children:

- Offer a broad spectrum of services.
- Cross traditional professional and bureaucratic boundaries.
- Be flexible.
- See the child in the context of family and the family in the context of its surroundings.
- Staff are people who are perceived by those they serve as people who care about them and respect them, people they can trust.
- Services are coherent and easy to use.
- Find ways to adapt or circumvent traditional professional and bureaucratic limitations when necessary to meet the needs of those they serve.

- Remove barriers—money, time, fragmentation, geography, and psychological remoteness—that make heavy demands on those with limited energy and organizational skills. "Rather than wait passively to serve only those who make it through the daunting maze, these programs persevere to reach the perplexed, discouraged, and ambivalent, the hardest to reach, who are often the ones who would benefit most" (p. 259).
- Professionals are able to redefine their roles to respond to severe, but often unarticulated, needs. "These professionals have found a way to escape the constraints of a professional value system that confers highest status on those who deal with issues from which all human complexity has been removed" (p. 259).

GENERIC LESSONS FOR SUPPORT PROGRAMMING

In the next chapter, a Support Program Impact Assessment Framework is developed. The information from this chapter can be used to spell out a number of generic lessons for support programming. The following lessons were relevant in creating the Support Program Impact Assessment Framework and can be helpful in working with this tool:

- There does not appear to be any single, focused program that will prevent child abuse and neglect or reduce the need for child placements in families coping with multiple problems. Rather, support programs capable of sustaining families and protecting children through situations of high stress are characterized by their provisions of multiple kinds of support and by a high level of contact with program participants.
- Traditional formal methods of helping (e.g., counseling, skill training) in child welfare can prevent child abuse and neglect and reduce child placements if they are provided in combination and in an intensive fashion. The power of these interventions seems to be increased if joined to other ways of helping.
- Focused professional helping tends to produce specific personal and family functioning benefits. The power of these interventions seems to be increased if joined to other ways of helping.
- Constructing packages of simultaneous and sequential supports for families seems to be a sound intervention guideline in multiple-problem situations. Case management/service-support coordination is a valuable function.
- Informal helping can be a powerful complement to formal helping or the basis for effective program models by itself. Informal helping has

been demonstrably useful with a variety of individual and family difficulties and, if provided at an adequate level, in preventing child abuse
and neglect and in reducing child placements. Informal helping and
social integration are greatly undeveloped considerations in support
programming.

- Gains from formal program involvement frequently attenuate after
  program involvement terminates. Informal supports and social connections can significantly lessen reliance on formal service providers
  and help to maintain gains and foster successful living in the community.
- Rapid response and intensive supports can help maintain families and
  protect children in their homes through periods of crisis.
- Effective programs often assertively cross traditional bureaucratic and
  professional boundaries to get families the support that they need
  when they can use it. They often have an expanded concept of what
  are relevant concerns and appropriate ways for them to help.
- Effective programs consciously work at reducing concrete, psychological, and social barriers to consistent participation in the program.
  They often actively reach out to involve people.
- Helpers need to strive to develop warm and trusting relationships with
  the people participating in the program.
- Programs need to focus upon participant strengths and competence
  and not only upon dysfunctional areas of their lives. This involves both
  fostering competence and creating opportunities for participants to
  demonstrate and be recognized for their competence.
- Mutual aid and participant involvement in program decision-making
  can be empowering components of programs.
- Good programs are often flexible and adaptable to the challenges and
  experiences participants bring to them.
- There are a number of proven program components that can be profitably incorporated into many program models (e.g., crisis supports,
  in-home visits, child care, mutual aid, education or training, emotional supports).
- Long-term involvements often produce superior outcomes with disadvantaged children and families. Graduation procedures—or what
  happens after program involvement ends—need explicit attention.

This volume has investigated the relevance of social support to interventions with children and families as well as the characteristics of formal support programs with more satisfying benefits in multiple-problem situations. While this has provided insights into promising helping approaches, more is required to guide decision-making in a practical fashion. It will be useful to have a way of thinking that will permit various approaches to helping to be compared. Such a framework would help decision-makers to make informed choices about support programs and provide them with guidance in combining these helping approaches on behalf of children and families. This chapter begins the process of articulating this framework.

This practical problem in deciding about support programs has several components. How do you decide between support programs as different as in-home intensive family preservation services, parent training, and parent mutual aid organizations? What are reasonable outcome expectations from each approach? What populations or circumstances are more appropriate for each method of helping? Can these different methods of helping be used to complement each other? What range of helping methods should be available in most child welfare agencies? It is not possible to provide a conclusive answer to all of these questions. However, we can abstract intervention principles and guidelines from the reviews in previous chapters to construct a more systematic approach to considering such questions. We can apply what we have learned about working with disadvantaged families and become more rigorous in assessing how we are trying to help and in building more effective ways to work in the future.

The Support Program Impact Assessment Framework developed here has three elements: intervention principles, method guides and impact questions. The intervention principles represent general concepts that can guide our thinking about support programs. These are ideas that clarify important elements that should be considered in program assessment or development and, *along with the patterns highlighted in the social support and support programs reviews,* provide a reasonable basis for our expectations from various approaches to helping. The method guides are presented as conceptual tools that can be used in gathering information about helping approaches. They also can help us to clarify and justify our expectations about various support programs. The impact questions are intended to be used in evaluating an existing program or to be answered in developing a rationale for creating a new program. Together, these three elements—while admittedly only a beginning—represent a more systematic and informed way of thinking about support programming than is common in child welfare and other settings.

INTERVENTION PRINCIPLES

A Concern with Effectiveness

This principle should be self-evident; unfortunately, in practice, it is not. Program outcomes—whether our interventions are truly helpful—are among the most neglected considerations in delivering service. This may be a harsh judgment. However, a strong argument can be made that social service personnel do not learn in their education or in their practice that outcomes matter and deserve our priority consideration. Professional and agency cultures do not support the need for evidence of program effectiveness nor do they encourage the development of convincing rationales for our approaches to helping. Too often, there seem to be strong personal and organizational attachments to particular ways of working that are dissociated from a consideration of their usefulness and a willingness to look for better ways.

In social work, students spend a great deal of time learning the values and techniques of particular ways of helping (e.g., individual, family or group counseling) but often, do not spend much time looking at the available evidence about the effectiveness of these ways of helping. In particular, in our experience, they are not encouraged to think about the limits of these ways of helping or to search for better ways of working when these traditional ways are found wanting. Child welfare agencies have evolved around a narrow range of interventions, and new ways of working have to overcome substantial obstacles to gain a foothold—even if they are demonstrably effective (Cameron et al., 1992; Rothery & Cameron, 1985). There are very limited time and resources committed to considering whether interventions work or whether more promising alternatives are available. These assertions are not meant to deny the principled efforts of child welfare and other service personnel nor the many excellent innovations that have taken place despite daunting constraints. Nonetheless, considerations of whether what we are doing works do not occupy a central position in either our helping paradigms or our organizational cultures.

What would a concern for effectiveness resemble? First, questions such as What do those coming here for help need? and Does what we do produce good results? How can we do better? would be acceptable and expected topics of discussion. A basic principle behind practice and administration would be, outcomes matter. Attachments to predetermined ways of helping would be downplayed. To the extent possible, available theory and outcome research would be considered in decision-making. At the very least, existing or proposed support programs and helping approaches would be expected to give a rigorous rationale for their efforts, including a discussion of reasonable outcome expectations and the reasons for these expectations, and a consideration of the limits of the approach. These would be discussed in decision-making. Whenever possible, programs would incorporate program components with proven effectiveness (Ministry of Community and Social Services, 1990a). When they do not, good rationales for doing things differently would be required and defended. When feasible, support programs and other key helping approaches would be formally assessed and modified as required. If formal evaluations are not possible, support programs and more traditional approaches would be periodically reviewed in a systematic fashion, for example, using the impact questions described later in this chapter. There would be experiments in better ways of helping. It would be a requirement that such experiments be assessed. They would be expanded if successful and discontinued or changed if not.

Obviously, social service organizations cannot run exclusively on these "effectiveness guidelines." Organizational realities are much too complex to be molded completely by intervention outcomes (Cameron, 1983). However, there is substantial scope for augmenting our concern with program/intervention effectiveness. Our purpose is not just to do what we have done before or what our professional training predisposes us to do. We want to be helpful. We want to learn and to improve what we do.

Theory-Driven Interventions

It is axiomatic that sound support programs should be "theory-driven" (Ontario Ministry of Community and Social Services, 1990a); that is, they need to be built upon credible explanations of why the desired and unwelcome phenomena occur and what factors are most likely to prevent the unwelcome occurrences and foster the desired ones. It is common in child welfare and other agencies to find support programs with very general rationales for their existence and without any explicit elaboration of the explanatory paradigm on which they are based (Rothery & Cameron, 1985). Programs are seldom reviewed in light of the credibility of the explanatory paradigms that they incorporate. While this avoidance may increase organizational harmony, it makes the creation of effective support programs a hit-or-miss phenomenon. It sometimes happens, but we generally do not know when it does and why or why not (Cameron & Rothery, 1985).

This volume focuses on programs/interventions designed to prevent child abuse and neglect and to reduce the need for out-of-home placements of children. In order to decide how to help, it is necessary to have a perception of what is happening in families' lives and an explanation about how these characteristics result in child abuse and neglect and/or family breakdown. It is important to be explicit about how our program/intervention might counteract these ill effects.

There are many possible competing explanations. Numerous programs presume powerful single factors leading to child maltreatment, for example, inadequate parenting knowledge and skills, parental or family pathology, or periodically occurring periods of very high stress. Still others view child maltreatment and family breakdown as resulting from a multiplicity of immediate and long-term stressors and dysfunctions in family life. How we perceive families' lives heavily influences how we try to help.

It is important to be clear and public about our program rationales. Our theories or explanations also should be subject to the rules of evidence and logic. They should be assessed and debated.

The reviews earlier in this volume suggest the value of explanatory perspectives that acknowledge the contribution of multiple factors to child abuse and neglect and to family breakdown. Table 5.1 presents a descriptive profile of the problems and concerns of 547 families from a study in Ontario child welfare agencies. Several conclusions can be drawn from these data. First, it is evident that many of these families are confronting multiple individual/family and social challenges at the same time. In addition, there is no conceptual or empirical way that one, or even a few problems can be credibly isolated as the core reasons for child maltreatment in most cases. For example, interventions should not be focused exclusively on parenting abilities and parent-child relations, if families' resources are being deflated by financial difficulties, lack of access to relief/vacation opportunities, children's school difficulties, caregiver loneliness, family violence, and so on. Finally, service worker, program, and organizational responses to these family realities require both a range of helping responses that can be called upon for families coming for help and flexible ways to marshall resources for particular families.

Bagley and Thurston (1989) recommend the use of an "additive model of stress" and the idea of early interventions to guide the design of programs with disadvantaged populations:

> The best we can do is propose an additive model of various stressors which may or may not interact in imposing unbearable strain on a particular individual. The most rational intervention strategy is to try and remove as many of the stressors as possible. (p. 132)

Table 5.1. Presenting Problems of Child Welfare Families

Individual or Family Problems
- parents unable to provide necessary/realistic limits for child (60%)[a]
- inability to relate to child as a person with own needs (60%)
- few occasions for positive parent-child interaction (55%)
- overreliance on negative reinforcement (54%)
- parents have unrealistic expectations of child (46%)
- poor homemaking skills (38%)
- chronic marital discord (51%)
- violent behavior (parent) (36%)
- substance/alcohol abuse (parent) (39%)
- emotional disorder (parent) (44%)
- inability to cope with normal everyday tasks (parent) (42%)
- chronic discord with parents (child) (51%)
- violent behavior (child) (22%)
- criminal/delinquent behavior (child) (25%)
- school problems (40%)
- emotional disorder (child) (31%)
- developmental delay (25%)
- poor male-female relationships (parent)[b]
- low self-esteem, confidence (parent)[b]
- etc.

Social Problems
- inadequate money for food/clothes/utilities (49%)
- unable to regularly meet financial obligations (40%)
- inadequate housing facilities (25%)
- low-income neighborhood (65%)
- families in neighborhood move often (38%)
- inadequate access to temporary relief from child care responsibilities (36%)
- lack of activities for children/youth (39%)
- opportunities to participate in illegal or antisocial behavior (49%)
- social isolation, loneliness, no positive friendships[b]
- restricted access to emotional support[b]
- no meaningful social role[b]
- unemployment, welfare (70%)
- coping as a single parent (52%); managing a single adult household (36%)
- coping as a young mother[b]
- lack of relief/vacation opportunities[b]
- no access to emergency resources[b]
- etc.

Source: Rothery and Cameron (1985, p. 5).
[a]The percentages indicate what proportion of reviewed cases showed these problems.
[b]While these were common problems in this sample, it was not possible to calculate percentages.

Logically we would suppose that the earlier that supportive intervention takes place the more likely it is that a positive outcome will occur in the long-term. American studies in early intervention with at risk groups provide support for the idea that such interventions can be successful in the medium term at least. (p. 147)

It would be difficult for an individual child welfare or other service agency to have elements in place to respond to all of the challenges identified in Table 5.1. However, it may be possible to identify a group of generically helpful resources that could be profitably incorporated into standard helping responses, for example, rapid response and intensive crisis supports; in-home and outreach services; parent training; home management supports; parental relief and child care opportunities; created networks and mutual aid groups for various populations; individual, family, or group counseling; a resource/drop-in center and specialized treatment services. It also seems that case management or linkage efforts—to *both* formal and informal sources of support—would need a priority emphasis.

Finally, a perspective that considers parenting and parent-child relations to be valid child welfare foci but views topics such as health and nutrition, school difficulties, loneliness, and isolation as the concern of other systems greatly reduces our capacity to help. We need an expanded concept of helping and a willingness to cross professional and bureaucratic boundaries to support families and to truly protect children. We should investigate helping formats that efficiently allow various formal and informal resources to focus on protecting children and supporting families (see the discussion in Part III of this volume).

Competence and Empowerment

It is essential in support programming to focus on people's abilities and their positive resources, and not only on their difficulties. Programs should emphasize supporting program participants in recognizing and in developing their own positive attributes and potential. In particular, by creating opportunities for participants to demonstrate their competence, to be recognized for their achievements, and to be helpers, we can open powerful avenues for growth that are often closed in their lives. It is hurtful to always be a client, the one who perpetually needs help.

There is a much greater potential for parents and for children coming to child welfare agencies to create, to do for themselves, to learn and to do for others than our traditional methods of helping permit. However, the process of empowering child welfare service users is complex. It requires supporting people in personal change as well as fostering the benefits of positive social integration and community involvement. Cameron et al. illustrate this concept of empowerment in reference to the Parent Mutual Aid Organizations in Child Welfare Demonstration Project:

> Empowering members in the mutual aid organizations required a merging of empowerment ideas drawn from both community development and clinical service perspectives. Finding a viable balance between these divergent approaches was sometimes a controversial undertaking in the Demonstration Project.
>
> The clinical perspective focused upon empowerment as personal or individual growth. In practice, this meant a style of working with members that provided a lot of encouragement and acknowledgement of members' efforts and, to a substantial extent, an attempt to insulate members' from tasks at which they might fail. Frequent opportunities were provided for receiving emotional support and help with problem-solving around a myriad of personal and family concerns and members were also encouraged to try new things in their lives. Teaching focused upon developing understanding and learning skills relevant to personal and family functioning. This focus on personal concerns, providing emotional support within a caring group environment and supporting people in their efforts to make changes in their own lives, all became essential helping processes within the PMAO. However, they represented [an] incomplete concept of empowerment for a mutual aid organization.
>
> The community development perspective on empowering members stressed the shared realities of members and members' abilities to control their own mutual aid organization. This translated into creating new (non-social service) experiences for members, opening up new areas of responsibility and roles for members, allowing for leadership opportunities, encouraging members to become helpers, and reflecting upon shared realities. Teaching emphasized the skills and knowledge members would need to be responsible for the mutual aid organization. These elements also became pivotal for the empowerment processes within the PMAO. [Table 5.2] provides an overview of the clinical and community development perspectives on empowerment articulated for the Demonstration Project.
>
> An exciting characteristic of the PMAO model was that it required the program developer to cross traditional boundaries in ways of thinking and helping. The nature of the mutual aid organizations meant that members needed to be empowered both as individuals and as members of a participatory organization. Crossing these boundaries was not always easy but, in the end, was one of the strongest reasons for the power of the PMAO model of helping. (1992, pp. 131–133)

Semi-Independence of Program Impacts

Many programs/interventions in child welfare predict substantial spin-off benefits from changes in one or a few areas of family functioning. However, meaningful ripple effects (for example, improved parenting skills → greater self-esteem → more confidence in solving diverse problems → access

Table 5.2. Clinical and Community Development Perspectives on Empowerment for the Demonstration Project

	Clinical Empowerment	Community Development Empowerment
Major Focus	• on individual behaviors • on personal and family issues • empowerment conceptualized in terms of personal change and growth	• on shared realities • on competencies and behaviors as members • on resource acquisition and environmental change • on collective destigmatization and redefinitions of identities • empowerment conceptualized as a shared and collective process
Common Methods in PMAO	• encouragement about potential for change; emphasize strengths • identify manageable coping tasks • insulate from insolvable tasks and failures (negative feedback) • teach interpersonal skills • encourage members to support and connect with each other • provide opportunities for emotional support, information, and problem-solving around personal and family problems • use group facilitation to provide caring and safe environment • role-model appropriate behaviors • emphasize proper behaviors at group meetings	• creating new community (non-social service) experiences • creating new roles and responsibilities for members • creating opportunities to successfully experience their new collective influence; build group power and capabilities • create leadership roles and governance structures (recognize different motivations, ambitions, talents) • teach organizational skills; what the program worker knows • teach how to cope in non-social service settings • encouraging people to connect with each other • encourage reciprocity and opportunities to contribute

Observations for PMAO	• when done well, this process is very good at creating a safe and caring environment for members; norms of caring • enables members to confront important personal and family issues • these methods leave the worker in the central helping and power position in the organization, since focus is on members' individual behaviors and problems, issues of transfer of power and collective empowerment of members do not arise as important concerns • the process does not emphasize creating real life opportunities for people to learn (i.e., non-social service experiences and successes) • the process does not emphasize the importance of new roles and new responsibilities in empowerment of individuals	• emphasize competencies but temper with real-world task requirements • encourage norms of responsibility and accountability • methods do recognize the pivotal importance of non-social service performances for empowerment • methods recognize the power of roles and responsibilities for personal empowerment • (at least in theory) methods recognize the need to move the worker off centre stage if empowerment of members is to be maximized • methods recognize that social involvements and joining with others can be empowering • leaders and governance structures are necessary for collective empowerment of members and real participation in running of PMAO • methods seriously underestimate the central importance of dealing with personal and family issues to empowerment • methods underestimate the importance of stressing norms of caring • methods underestimate the need to help with personal crises and problem-solving

Source: Cameron et al. (1992, p. 132).

to more social resources → less reliance on professionals → less child maltreatment) are often far less than anticipated by ambitious program rationales.

Focused interventions frequently produce benefits in the specific areas addressed without producing noticeable benefits in other important areas or without impacting on successful community living. For example, it is quite possible to increase understanding of parenting yet not to have a discernible impact on the frequency of child placements. Or, families can be supported through a crisis without substantial or enduring changes in parent-child relations or family dynamics. In addition, parents can become more socially connected and feel better without a major change in parenting competence or vice versa.

A useful general rule of thumb for support program development is that if improvements in particular aspects of individual, family, or community functioning are desired, they need to be addressed *directly* by specific initiatives.[1] Generally, our interventions are not powerful enough to reasonably anticipate benefits in important aspects of living peripheral to the foci of our helping efforts. This clearly suggests the need for packages of services and supports when helping populations confronting multiple challenges in their lives.

Change-Support-Integration

When considering support programs, it is useful to be clear about the difference between changing, supporting, and integrating children or parents. All three purposes are basic to a complete concept of protecting children and supporting families, yet they differ in very important ways:

Change: to make different in some particular . . .
            to give a different position, course, or direction (*Webster's Ninth New Collegiate Dictionary*, 1984, p. 225)
Support: to hold up or serve as a foundation for . . .
            to keep from fainting, yielding, or losing courage . . .
            to keep (something) going. (p. 1186)
Integrate: to combine in such a way that it becomes fully a part of something else
            to become fully a member of a community, rather than remaining in a separate group. (*Oxford Advanced Learner's Dictionary*, 1989, p. 651)

In the social services, change goals have typically been considered the most legitimate rationales for our helping efforts; however, support and integration goals also are fundamental to assisting disadvantaged families. There are several reasons why these distinctions are important to support programming. First, the daily living realities of families using child welfare and many other social services indicated that attention should be paid to all three goals. Second, the challenge of changing a person's or family's functioning is quite different from supporting them through times of crisis or from integrating them into a supportive network or community. A family can change in a positive fashion yet still collapse from too much stress. Or a family can be supported through a crisis without substantial change in their functioning and without linking them with ongoing community supports. Third, the practical programming requirements of changing, supporting and integrating families are often very different from each other (see Table 4.3). Finally, change, support, and integration program/intervention strategies can be expected to bring very different benefits to families (see Table 4.4). While a particular program or service package often focuses on two or three of these purposes, it is useful to distinguish when and how programs are intended to change, to support and to integrate participants.

Survival and Development Needs

Rothery (1990a) makes a simple, but useful distinction between survival and developmental needs. As a general rule, both survival and developmental concerns need to be addressed if stable and substantial progress is to be made in helping disadvantaged children and families. For example, in multiple- problem situations, there is a good deal of evidence that personal or family developmental issues can seldom be confronted successfully, or gains in these areas maintained, unless the pressures of survival needs are reduced (for example, see Edmunson et al., 1982; Edmunson et al., 1984; Fairweather, Sanders, Maynard, & Cressler, 1969; Gottlieb, 1983; Hawkins & Fraser, 1983; Wahler, 1980b; Whittaker, 1986). In addition, not only are survival concerns—such as coping as a single parent, being socially isolated, lacking money, lacking child care or parent relief—very common difficulties for many families using child welfare and other services, but a strong case can be made that addressing such survival needs is at least as important as addressing developmental concerns in preventing child abuse and neglect. Intellectually, most child welfare professionals would be likely to agree with this position; however, in practice, interventions targeted on survival concerns are much less common. Nonetheless, there is a range of small-scale initiatives, accessible to social service personnel, that can be helpful in eliminating or in managing important survival issues.

Finally, it is overly simplistic to suggest that development concerns call for

Table 5.3.   Selected Survival and Developmental Needs and Relevant Helping Strategies

	Survival	*Development*
Needs	• coping as a single mother • social isolation of mother • lack of money • separating from an abusive partner	• poor self-esteem • negative social identity • limited confidence in ability to cope with everyday problems • poor child management skills • deciding to separate from an abusive partner
Helping Strategies	• arranging access to daycare • creating opportunities for parent relief, family vacations • information on community resources • parent training • supportive and educational counseling • creating or arranging access to support group, mutual aid organization • job retraining, return to school • women's shelter, second stage housing	• individual and family therapy • facilitating or creating opportunities for successful social involvements • parenting and life skills training • group therapy • support group • mutual aid organizations • job retraining, return to school

professional therapy while survival needs require case management and community work skills. A range of formal and informal helping strategies should be considered in relation to both survival and development needs. This point is illustrated in Table 5.3.

METHOD GUIDES

Social Support Typology

The social support typology outlined in Table 5.4 can be used to focus attention on the nature and range of assistance available in a support pro-

Table 5.4. Typology of the Functional Components of Social Support

Concrete Support	Providing some form of material aid such as money, clothing, accommodation, and/or assistance with carrying out everyday tasks such as parent relief, homemaking services, transportation
Educational Support	Providing the information and knowledge or developing the skills required so that the person will be more able to cope effectively with specific problems and/ or so that the person will be more capable of access-ing and benefiting from available supportive relationships
Emotional Support	Providing access to intimate relationships that serve to meet the person's need for acceptance or encourage-ment and understanding when coping with particular stressful events and the challenges of everyday living
Social Integration	Providing access to positive contacts with members of an enduring social network and/or providing access to valued and stable social roles to foster the person's sense of affiliation and personal validation

gram. While the typology includes only general categories, it is important, when using it as a guide, to be specific about the assistance provided in a particular program, intervention, or relationship. (See the discussion later in this chapter about the support program impact questions.) In addition, Table 5.5 illustrates how this typology also can be a helpful guide when compar-

Table 5.5. Potential Social Support Contributions by Helpers

	Concrete	Educational	Social Integration	Emotional
Family	+++	++	++	+++
Friends	++	+	+++	+++
Neighbors	+	0	+	+
Mutual Aid Group: Peers with Similar Problems	++	+++	++	+++
Co-Workers	+	+	+++	+
Professional Counselors	+??	+++	?	++
Intensive Family Preservation Intake Worker	++	+++	?	++

Legend: 0, no anticipated contribution; +, minor anticipated contribution; ++, significant anticipated contribution; +++, highest anticipated contribution; ?, the anticipated contribution is dependent upon how these helpers define their role.

ing the helping potential of various kinds of programs, interventions and relationships.

Structural Dimensions

Besides the functional content of programs, their potential impact is determined by a number of structural dimensions. These dimensions, as listed below, can help us to be more specific about what is happening, or potentially can happen, in a particular helping relationship and to develop more realistic expectations about the benefits that may accrue from these involvements (see the discussion later in this chapter about the support program impact questions). In partnership with the typology of the functional components of social support, these structural dimensions can be used to compare the potential benefits of different types of helping programs and relationships and to consider how various approaches might complement each other. Tables 5.6 and 5.7 illustrate these comparisons.

(a) *Range of Supports:* How many and which types of stressors are being directly relieved by the program elements? What protective factors are being enhanced by the program? Benefits should only be anticipated in areas that receive explicit attention in the helping processes. In multiple-problem situations, the helping strategy has to be able to reduce a range of *important* stressors and/or provide relevant protective elements if substantial progress is to be made.

(b) *Level of Support:* How many total hours of support will be available to participants? How intensive will their involvement be in a specified time period? In a period of crisis? In crisis situations and in multiple-problem situations, there has been a shift toward program models that provide high levels of direct contact with families to counteract the levels of stress that they are facing.

(c) *Length of Involvement:* How long will people be able to have access to the support? What provisions are made for continued access to support after formal program involvement ends? Social service users often present difficulties in terms of their long-term social integration and continuing access to resources for daily living. Gains made in formal programs often attenuate markedly without suitable changes to the person's external living environment. Substantial changes to personal, family or social functioning are often more pronounced for longer-term interventions. Graduation concerns (what happens after the formal intervention ends) are a frequently neglected aspect of many programs/interventions.

(d) *Availability in a Crisis:* Many users of social services experience periodic crises in their lives. These periods of high stress are associated with higher risks of child maltreatment and child placement. Rapid and intensive

Table 5.6. Potential Performance on Structural Properties of Supportive Relationships by Helpers

	Range of Support	Reciprocity	Technical Expertise	Length of Commitment	Level of Contact	Openness to All in Need	Availability in a Crisis	Motivation/ Skill Requirements
Family	+++	++	+	+++	+++	+	+++	++
Friends	++	+++	+	++	+++	+	++	+++
Neighbors	+	+++	+	++	+	+	+	++
Mutual Aid Groups: Peers with Similar Problems	+++	+++	++	++	+++	++	++	++
Co-Workers	+	+++	+	++	++	+	+	+++
Professional Counsellors	+??	+	+++	+	+	+++	++	+
Intensive Family Preservation Intake Worker	++	+	+++	+	+++	++	+++	++

Legend: +, low; ++, medium; +++, high; ?, the anticipated contribution or requirement is dependent upon how these helpers define their role.

Table 5.7.   Comparing Formal Helpers and Informal Helpers

On both tables 5.5 and 5.6, formal helpers and informal helpers approximate mirror opposites in terms of their strengths and weaknesses in providing support. The implication is that, while formal and informal support strategies can be complementary, they cannot be easily substituted for each other.

Some types of informal helpers are characterized as potentially providing broader ranges of functional social support than formal helpers.

Only informal helpers such as family, friends, peers, and co-workers can directly foster a feeling of positive social integration. The contributions of formal helpers to social integration can only be indirect.

The role of the formal service provider can be pivotal in that what the worker does often determines what supports a child or parent will or will not receive. If the worker includes an emphasis upon linking the participants with other types of helpers, then the potential range of her/his direct and indirect support contributions can be quite broad.

Formal, individualized methods of helping rate relatively low on structural properties such as range of support provided, reciprocity and length of commitment. Once again, the implication is that the direct contribution of these helping strategies to the construction of a positive social identity for clients may be quite limited.

Formal helpers may have advantages on structural properties such as technical expertise, openness to all in need, availability in a crisis and minimal motivation and skill requirements. Such helpers are likely to be more accessible to many people and useful in short-term periods of crisis. They may also have the ability to facilitate participants' access to more enduring and reciprocal informal relationships.

Some mutual aid/peer groups can acquire high levels of specialized technical expertise and be able to provide good crisis support. They can provide either short-term or long-term supports. Groups often have higher motivation and skill requirements than individualized helping methods.

responses in crisis situations are often a prerequisite for avoiding bad outcomes.

(e)   *Openness to All in Need:*   Some difficulties have considerable social stigma attached to them (e.g., child abuse, substance addiction, AIDS) and some helping options (e.g., friends, family) may be unavailable under these circumstances. Professional helping and specialized groups (e.g., Parents Anonymous, Alcoholic Anonymous, AIDS committee) may be more available to people with socially stigmatized challenges.

(f)   *Motivation and Skill Requirements:*   Some helping options are highly proactive in going to potential users and in reducing obstacles to participation. Others, by their nature, require certain basic levels of participant motivation and some need basic social skills. Group approaches often have higher motivation requirements than many individualized helping methods. Some groups may also require some basic interpersonal skills. However, professionals need to guard against a common tendency to underestimate family members' willingness and ability to participate in groups and to learn to do for themselves (Cameron et al., 1992; Rothery & Cameron, 1985).

(g)   *Focused Technical Expertise:*   Some difficulties benefit from access to expert knowledge and specific intervention techniques. Helping strategies vary in their ability to bring this expertise to families. Professional helpers and specialized self-help groups often are able to bring focused expertise to participants.

(h)   *Social Integration and Reciprocity:*   There is ample evidence of the usefulness of various kinds of informal supports and social relationships for coping with a variety of problems. There are good theoretical and empirical rationales for the importance of involvements in intimate, reciprocal relationships and positive social roles for an ongoing sense of well-being and for the construction, maintenance, and reconstruction of a positive sense of identity. Being appreciated, doing for oneself, and helping others are fundamental to psychological well-being. In addition, informal involvements often can be legitimately long term and they can reduce reliance on formal service providers.

Continuum of Social Support Interventions

Based upon an analysis of the buffering-effect model and the main-effect model of social support, a continuum of types of social support interventions can be identified as in Figure 5.1: This social support intervention continuum can be seen as progressing from support strategies that are relatively accessible to child welfare service providers to those that will be more difficult to mobilize. Obviously, it will be easier to develop a formal support program that provides specific short-term supports to parents and children in periods of crisis than it will be to create enduring social support networks or social roles for parents or children. However, it must be emphasized that the various strategies in this continuum of social support interventions are not substitutable for each other. In addition, the more difficult main-effect interventions are often those that are the most needed and desired by social service users. Clearly, social integration strategies are greatly underdeveloped in child welfare and other social service programming. This continuum also can help us to be clear about what kinds of support benefits we are trying to provide and what results we can anticipate from these involvements.

most accessible and most common

least accessible and least common

- short-term access to concrete, educational, and emotional supports to cope with specific problems and/or to increase personal competence, for example, counseling, homemakers, parent effectiveness training
- short-term access to peer supports, for example, adolescent day program, parent support group
- access to and successful performances in varied social and recreational activities (preferably of an enduring nature), for example, amateur theatre group, ethnic meal club
- access to and successful performances in opportunities to be a helper, to contribute to a larger purpose, to reciprocate help received, for example, peer tutoring, volunteering, teaching skills
- access to and successful performances in a few enduring, intimate friendships
- access to and successful performances in valued and stable social roles, for example, student, employee, officer in a volunteer association
- involvement in redefining in a collective fashion the social identities of participants and explanations of their life circumstances, for example, women's movement, independent living movement for the physically disabled, native and aboriginal people's organizations

IMPACT QUESTIONS

Based upon the intervention principles and method guides in this chapter, and the earlier reviews of the social support and formal support program literature, a list of questions that constitute the Support Program Impact Assessment Framework has been constructed. By answering these questions in designing a support program, or using the questions to guide a program assessment, a coherent approach to decision-making can be developed. In answering the impact questions, it is essential to be specific and to focus on the realities of participants' daily living circumstances and the actual func-

Table 5.8. Support Program Impact Assessment Framework Questions

1. What are the predominant problems confronting the children and parents: economic, social, family, personal?
2. What competencies and resources can the participants bring to the program? Existing? Potential?
3. In operational terms, what helping components are incorporated into the program model: concrete, educational, emotional supports, social integration assistance?
4. How does the program model make its services accessible and acceptable to participants?
5. What kind of helper(s) will be used to provide the assistance?
6. What level of direct contact with participants is provided?
7. How long is service/support to be provided?
8. Are personal and family issues to be addressed? If so, how? If not, why not?
9. Are issues of lack of access to concrete resources to be addressed? If so, how? If not, why not?
10. Are social integration issues to be addressed? If so, how? If not, why not?
11. Are participants to be encouraged to demonstrate their own competencies and power? If so, how? If not, why not?
12. What provisions are made to support successful coping and maintenance of gains after formal involvement is terminated? If none, why?
13. Are crisis supports provided? If so, how? If none, why?
14. In light of the above factors, what outcomes can be reasonably expected from the program model with the target population?
15. Are there economic advantages for the program sponsors expected from this approach? Why?
16. On what basis are these outcomes predicted: explanatory paradigms and confirming evidence for participating population's circumstances, theoretical and research evidence supporting these predictions, logical arguments?

tional content and structural parameters of the support program. In predicting program outcomes, rationales for these expectations should draw on explicit explanatory paradigms and, whenever possible, be based on available outcome research. At the very least, a sound argument should be developed and defended for these expectations. While the questions could be adapted for considering services/supports for a specific individual or family, they were constructed with support programs and the populations using various support programs in mind. However, in the final analysis, the thought process is generic: What are families' daily living realities? What services/supports are they likely, *in fact,* to receive? What outcomes can we reasonably anticipate given families' realities and service/support content and structural dimensions? Why should we expect these outcomes? Does the method offer economic advantages? Table 5.8 outlines the Support Program Impact Assessment Framework Questions. Tables 5.9 and 5.10 present

Table 5.9. Support Program Impact Assessment: Hypothetical Intensive Family
      Preservation Services Program

---

1. Types of Support Provided

Concrete
- help with homemaking
- help with child care
- help to find emergency resources

Emotional
- empathy
- opportunities to ventilate
- opportunities to discuss personal
  concerns

Other
- availability during crisis times
- short-term counseling/therapy
  around specific issues

Educational
- hands-on modeling of parenting
- hands-on modeling of homemaking
- problem-specific advice
- one-to-one teaching about life skills if
  necessary

Social Integration
- encourage/assist to use low-cost community resources but only a modest
  amount of time for this

---

2. Level of Direct Contact

- rapid response (within 24 hours)
- 24-hour availability if necessary
  (limited in practice)
- inhome service provision

- 2–3 times a week
- 6–10 hours a week
- 40–80 hours total contact

---

3. Duration of Provision

- 6 to 10 weeks

---

4. Problem Profiles of Participants

*Common Individual and Family
    Problems/Characteristics*
- families often in high-stress periods
  or crises
- moderate risk of child maltreatment
- no immediate safety concerns for the
  child
- children at risk of placement in the
  near future
- some parental delinquency
- parents willing to try inhome support
  services
- parents able to learn basic skills
- high levels of difficulty in coping
  with everyday tasks common
- parent-child relationship difficulties
  common

*Common Social Problems/
    Characteristics*
- 50% moms under 25
- 50% single parents
- almost all poor
- 70% unemployed
- most lonely and socially isolated
- most coping with unsafe, unstable
  neighborhoods
- some with negative peer/family networks
- high dependence on formal service
  providers
- limited vacation/parent relief opportunities
- etc.

(continued)

Table 5.9.   Continued

4. Problem Profiles of Participants

- parenting/child management concerns common
- home management difficulties common
- low parental self-esteem common
- some low functioning parents
- social skills/relationship skills difficulties common
- problems in male-female intimate relationships common

5. Program Impacts	

Individual/Family Problems
- some measurable gains on parenting/ child management skills, parent-child relations but likely to attenuate after program involvement ends

Social Problems
- none anticipated unless specific program elements added in these areas

Family Breakdown/Placement
- good ability to avert short-term to medium-term crisis placements
- less child maltreatment over short- to medium-term
- gains in maltreatment/placement likely to attenuate after program involvement ends in many cases

Self-Reliance/Independence
- generally heavy reliance on formal service providers will continue unless specific program elements added

Economic
- good cost-saving benefits from averted crisis placements if program in fact reaches mostly families at risk of having a child placed

Source: Hayward and Cameron (1993), based on selected questions from the framework in Table 5.8.

a brief review of two support program models based on selected questions from this Framework.

SUMMARY

Over the past ten years of support program research in child welfare settings (Cameron et al., 1992; Cameron, Holmberg, & Rothery, 1983; Cameron & Rothery, 1985; Hayward & Cameron, 1993; Rothery & Cameron, 1985; Rothery & Cameron, 1990), we have learned that support programs

Table 5.10.   Support Program Impact Assessment: Hypothetical Parent Mutual Aid Organization Program

---

1. Types of Supports Provided

Concrete
- babysitting and other concrete exchanges between members
- parent relief while at meetings
- small amounts of emergency resources

Educational
- life skills and parenting courses
- variety of guest speakers
- practical advice on specific problems
- new roles and responsibilities in organization
- new role models

Emotional
- understanding of problems
- sharing of experiences
- empathy
- opportunities to ventilate
- acceptance
- valued as a person

Social Integration
- recreational and social activities
- new friends
- peer group at meetings
- new roles and responsibilities
- new experiences
- new social contacts
- people to call when in difficulty or lonely
- daycare for children 2–3 times a week

---

2. Level of Direct Contact

- 2–3 times per week in formal program activities (4–8 hours)
- 1–3 contacts per week with peers outside of program activities

- 16–32 hours per month in formal program activities
- 150–300 total hours in formal program activities (high variance)

---

3. Duration of Provisions

- 4 months to several years in formal program activities

---

4. Problem Profiles of Participants

Selected Individual/Family Problems/Characteristics
- mostly preschool to preadolescent children
- moderate risk of child maltreatment
- no immediate safety concerns for children
- low to moderate risk of child placement in the future
- some parental delinquency
- parent motivated to come to a group

Selected Social Problems/ Characteristics
- 80% single moms
- 50% moms under 25
- almost all poor
- almost all unemployed
- almost all lonely and socially isolated
- many coping with unsafe, unstable neighborhoods
- some with negative peer/family networks

(continued)

Table 5.10. Continued

4. Problem Profiles of Participants	
• some parent-child relationship difficulties • parenting/child management concerns common • moderate to high levels of difficulty in coping with every day tasks common • problems in intimate male-female relationships common • social skills/relationship skills difficulties common • partner/ex-partner conflict common • low parental self-esteem common • etc.	• moderate to heavy users of formal services • limited vacation/parent relief opportunities • etc.

5. Program Impacts	
Individual/Family Problems • better problem-solving of parents • more parent self-confidence • better coping with stress • some improvement in parent-child relationships/parenting • gains may attenuate after program involvement if other connections not available *Family Breakdown/Placement* • fewer children to care • less child maltreatment	*Social Problems* • more access to concrete and problem-solving resources • new friends • new network of peers • more social activities • for some new roles and responsibilities • for some more role successes and recognition • some return to school, employment • for some new community involvements • for many these gains may attenuate after program involvement ends • for some program involvement and/or social connections will be long term
Other • good cost-savings to child welfare agency in averted placement costs and in less use of professional services	*Self-Reliance/Independence* • a high percentage of protection cases closed to child welfare agency • substantially less reliance on child welfare and perhaps other professional services

Source: Cameron, Hayward, and Mamatis (1992), based on selected questions from the framework in Table 5.8.

typically are developed in an ad hoc fashion. Program rationales often are quite general and are not built on a well-articulated theoretical or empirical foundation. Helping methods usually are variations on approaches already well-established in child welfare. Efforts to exploit the power of informal helping or positive social integration as well as helping methods that allow participants to demonstrate their own competence and power are particularly underdeveloped. The range of child and family concerns considered appropriate for child welfare remains quite limited. Finally, service/support coordination, program graduation, and community linkage responsibilities seldom receive a priority investment of time and resources.

Hopefully, these intervention principles, method guides, and impact questions can help to improve support programming in child welfare and other service settings. Following these guidelines can focus our attention on an appropriate range of child and family daily living realities, help us to design useful interventions, and assist in developing reasonable expectations for our efforts. We can be more optimistic and better informed in our work with disadvantaged families. We can try a broader repertoire of ways of protecting children and supporting families and, in particular, consider using these various helping approaches in more flexible and complementary fashions. We need to respect hard-won lessons about helping populations dealing with multiple challenges and we need a basic commitment to the effectiveness of our helping efforts. We can be more helpful in allowing people coming to us for help to connect with each other and to build their own abilities and their own dignity.

These are profound challenges to how we "do business" in child welfare. The focus would be less on investigation and more on being supportive and empowering. In the end, the suggestion is to stand child welfare services on their head. Ways of helping that have been marginal to child welfare would move into the center. Individualized, professional ways of helping would become just one choice among other approaches. Organizational philosophy, structures, resource allocations, and staffing profiles would change in order to be more flexible and more helpful (see the discussion in Part III of this volume). Our ability to respond in a practical fashion to these challenges remains largely unexplored. The obstacles are daunting; the potential benefits are intriguing.

NOTE

1.   While in fact some interventions do produce benefits in unanticipated areas and outcome expectations should be a matter for empirical investigation, the emphasis here is on principles to guide program/intervention design and, from this perspective, it is wise to have conservative expectations about spin-off benefits not directly related to the helping methods used.

The Nature and Effectiveness of Support Programs II

1The following chapters summarize the available literature and outcome research on five groupings of support programs relevant to child maltreatment: intensive family preservation services, home health visitor and parent aide programs, parent training programs, lay home visitors and mutual aid/community living networks, and comprehensive support programs. These types of programs were selected either because they are common program approaches when children are considered to be at risk of maltreatment or they are promising, yet underutilized methods of helping.

No type of support program is always effective or produces the same outcome in every setting. Drawing conclusions from the research about support program effectiveness is plagued by intractable variability in program dimensions (for example: family characteristics, worker characteristics, service content, service delivery format, administration) as well as by differences in research designs and methods. It is not reasonable to expect that all outcome research about the same support program model would find identical or even similar outcomes. There will always be exceptions. However, if the thesis developed in the first part of this volume is accurate, then information about the functional content and the structural dimensions of support programs should be useful as general predictors of their effectiveness. This means that, while some studies will be discordant, there should be patterns across multiple studies indicating similar outcomes for support programs of a particular type, if they have reasonably comparable program content and structural dimensions. It also means that we should be able to use individual program characteristics to understand at least some of the outcome differences between support programs of the same type. Finally, if program content and structural dimensions are very different across various types of support programs, there should be patterned differences in the outcomes for these types of programs. These expectations largely are sustained by the reviews in Part II's five chapters.

The support program reviews in the following chapters serve several purposes. Each review provides information on support program rationales, service content, and structural parameters. Knowing these program characteristics is helpful in interpreting the outcome patterns described for each type of support program. Second, these reviews summarize what is known about the effectiveness of each support program model based upon the available outcome research. For some support program models, the evidence for their effectiveness is convincing; for others, the research suggests a limited relevance with disadvantaged children and families. Yet other support programs seem promising but the quality of the research on their effectiveness is poor. All of the types of support programs reviewed have their respective strengths and weaknesses. These reviews facilitate a better understanding of the potential of these various program models and how they might complement each other in protecting children and supporting families. Finally, these reviews of support programs provide additional evidence for the relevance of the Support Program Impact Assessment Framework's principles, method guides, and impact questions detailed in the previous chapter. In order to make these linkages more accessible to the reader, a summary for each grouping of support programs is provided that is consistent with the Support Program Impact Assessment Framework. These summaries also allow for an easier comparison of the strengths and limitations of the support program models reviewed. The conclusion to Part II includes an overall summary of all of the support program types examined.

HOW TO READ PART II

Each of the chapters contains a detailed description of particular support programs and a review of the studies assessing the effectiveness of these programs. These chapters will be of most interest to readers wanting to know, in some depth, about these programs and their effectiveness. These people may choose to read all five chapters or just the chapters on the support programs that are of interest to them. Readers preferring a summary of the research can examine the summaries provided for each program model. Reading all of the summaries for the five chapters and the conclusion to Part II provides a good overview.

Intensive Family Preservation Services*   6

INTRODUCTION

There is growing concern about the high cost of family breakdown and the placement of children in foster care or residential settings—in terms of the financial consequences of these options as well as their prohibitive toll on children, parents, and community. At the same time, there is a growing recognition that program models have been created that reduce the need for out-of-home child placements and seemingly produce better outcomes for disadvantaged families than traditional child protection services (Frankel, 1988; Pelton, 1981). One of the most popular of these program models is Intensive Family Preservation Services (IFPS), a home-based, crisis-intervention model that is prevalent in the United States and more recently has become popular in Canada. This chapter examines the literature specifically on the Homebuilders IFPS model, as well as IFPS programs fashioned after the Homebuilders model, and identifies some of the principles and lessons from the IFPS model that are relevant to child welfare practice.

Part of the original rationale for the Homebuilders approach was the argument that clients experiencing the pain of crises would be more highly motivated to learn and to try new ways of coping, and this would permit significant and enduring personal and family change to be made during and immediately following the crisis period. This rationale is somewhat at odds with the ecological perspective behind many current approaches to family support and prevention, which holds that in multiple-problem situations a variety of personal, family, and environmental stressors have to be addressed in a simultaneous and sequential fashion over time for enduring progress to be made (Ministry of Community and Social Services, 1990a; Cameron, 1990a; Weiss & Jacobs, 1988; Whittaker & Garbarino, 1983). Also, in some of the literature on family therapy with poor, distressed families, the exact opposite case is made that "survival" concerns need to be addressed before meaningful progress can be made on "developmental" issues (Geismar & Ayres, 1958; Rothery, 1990b). In a book devoted exclusively to the

---

*This chapter is adapted from Hayward and Cameron (1993). Homebuilders™ is the trademark of Behavioral Science Institute. Subsequent references to Homebuilders throughout the book should be regarded as implicitly carrying the registered trademark.

Homebuilders approach, Barth (1990) also questioned this component of the Homebuilders rationale:

> Early crisis theory cited evidence that stress and learning are related along an inverted U-shaped curve so that too much or too little crisis-related arousal worked against learning more adaptive strategies. . . . This evidence is consistent with recent evidence that the higher the prestress arousal the less the poststress arousal adjustment and the less the prestress arousal the better the poststress adjustment. . . . Both early and late versions of crisis theory suggest that intervention will work best with families not in full crisis state. (p. 91)

The diversity and intensity of service described by the Homebuilders model, however, is consistent with a large body of research on social support (for review, see Cameron 1990b; or see Chapter 3 of this volume) and on formal support programming (for reviews, see Cameron 1990a, 1990b; Cameron et al., 1983; Cameron & Rothery, 1985; Rothery & Cameron, 1985; Chapter 4 of this volume). These studies demonstrate that providing families who are experiencing dysfunctional levels of stress with access to high levels of appropriate personal and social resources enables them to cope with a range of problems and helps to prevent family breakdown. This support orientation would help to explain the positive impacts of Homebuilders and other intensive family support programs on rates of child placement that sometimes appear without clear evidence of major enduring changes in variables such as child development or family functioning (Wald, Carlsmith, & Leiderman, 1988). It would also explain the decline in placement aversion rates over time as formal program involvement terminates, a finding that has been noted in several projects (Fraser, Pecora, & Haapala, 1991; Hayward & Cameron, 1993).

In addition, the support perspective also suggests that the positive placement aversion rates associated with the Homebuilders program may be less due to the integrity of this particular configuration of program elements and more attributable to the levels and range of supports provided to families. This would help to explain comparable aversion rates that have been associated with support program models that are quite different from Homebuilders (Cameron & Rothery, 1985; Rothery & Cameron, 1985).

In theory, the program model draws from Rogerian, cognitive-behavioral, crisis, and ecological perspectives:

> The family and its social support system are viewed as the focus of service, with an emphasis upon promoting client independence and psycho-social skill-building. In addition to teaching skills, Homebuilders therapists provide or arrange for a variety of concrete services to assist families to obtain food, clothing, housing, and transportation. Other community resources that provide families with food stamps, medical care, day care, and employment

training may be recommended by the worker as well. Therapists also use a variety of clinical methods, including parenting training, active listening, contracting, values clarification, cognitive-behavioural strategies, and problem-management techniques. (Pecora, Fraser, & Haapala, 1990, p. 2)

Homebuilders proponents suggest that this model allows more "difficult-to-serve" families to be served by seeing them in their own homes. While this claim seems credible, Frankel (1988) suggested that Homebuilders, and other intensive in-home programs, are in fact screening out the more serious cases of child abuse and neglect even though such families potentially should be able to benefit from these programs. He stated that physically abusive families make up only about 10% of Homebuilders clientele and wondered whether certain selection criteria (at least one parent agreeing to participate, and no family member objecting to the reunification goal) may not unnecessarily rule out many "underorganized, abusive and neglectful families."

Notwithstanding these observations, there is evidence presented in the following review of outcome studies that intensive, in-home programming can be used to good effect with very precarious child welfare populations. The practical problem may be making sure that the desired clientele are reached by these programs.

The Homebuilders model (in addition to individualized treatment goals) projects a standard set of positive outcomes from the programs:

- allows more hard-to-serve families to be served;
- enables families who would otherwise not do so, to use more traditional services and resources;
- reduces the frequency and length of child placement;
- reduces the risk of future child maltreatment;
- saves money through averted placement costs and other formal service costs;
- increases parenting skills;
- maintains and strengthens family bonds;
- increases the level of use of formal and informal resources;
- promotes client empowerment and independence from formal service providers.

PARAMETERS OF THE HOMEBUILDERS MODEL

At this time, Homebuilders is probably the most recognized model of Intensive Family Preservation Services. Developed in Tacoma, Washington, by Jill Kinney and David Haapala in 1974, the Homebuilders model has several characteristics that make it an IFPS model according to criteria set by the Child Welfare League of America:

- families receive a variety of clinical and concrete services,
- service is of short duration (ninety days or less), and
- service is intensive (eight to ten hours of face-to-face contact per week).

In addition to these characteristics, Homebuilders is also considered a crisis intervention program designed to respond rapidly (within twenty-four hours of referral) to families with one or more children at risk of placement in alternative care. The model stresses making help available at the times when families naturally experience difficulties and in their home environments. Services are intended to be available twenty-four hours a day, seven days a week, and are usually limited to four to six weeks.[1]

The Homebuilders program is designed to focus on two to four immediate goals contracted with family members. Progress on these goals should be reviewed regularly with the assistance of a formal goal-attainment scaling procedure. The model is described as placing a high priority on case management efforts to link families with other resources during and subsequent to formal involvement with Homebuilders. Homebuilders delivers services through one "highly qualified" worker per family, which according to Homebuilders proponents (Fraser et al., 1991; Kinney, Haapala, Booth, & Leavitt, 1990) permits easier development of relationships with family members, and better service planning and integration, and utilizes naturally occurring therapeutic opportunities during service delivery. Finally, although not unequivocally supported by the available family support theory and research, Homebuilders is presented as an integrated family support intervention model that works best when all of its prescribed elements are present.

Homebuilders workers carry small caseloads of two to four families at a time. Direct service involvement reportedly averages about ten hours per week in the initial stages of contact and five to eight hours per week thereafter. Available program data suggest that in some instances providing access to concrete services and teaching families how to access such resources can be the most time-consuming portion of the intervention.

Fraser, Pecora, and Haapala (1989) stated that research and program data provide considerable evidence of the wide-ranging and eclectic nature of home-based treatment. The model stresses the development of individually tailored service packages and relies on the skills of single workers to respond to a broad range of needs and circumstances. This can result in patterned differences in services provided by various workers based on their different strengths and weaknesses. Fraser et al., 1989), however, suggest that there are some commonalities in the service provided despite individual differences in workers. For example, concrete supports were provided to about 75% of Homebuilders families. The most common service goals included increasing parenting skills (79%), increasing anger management skills (62%), increasing communication skills (56%), increasing compliance with house rules (52%), establishing trust (45%), and improving school performance (35%).

Fraser and Haapala (1987–1988) carried out a process assessment of a Homebuilders program looking for service aspects or "critical incidents" related to placement aversion from initiation of treatment through termination and a three-month follow-up period. Forty-one single parent and two-parent families were purposively selected. A one-page interview guide was developed to gather client and therapist descriptions of treatment sessions and these data were gathered within twenty-four hours of each session. Fraser and Haapala found that global reports of program helpfulness had no predictive validity regarding placement aversion. In addition, therapist reports were not related to placement aversion. However a significantly higher proportion of mothers whose children remained in the home reported the provision of concrete services by the therapist compared to mothers whose children were placed outside the home.

Lewis (1990) investigated the service-related correlates of placement aversion for 453 families in two IFPS programs, including one Homebuilders program. When he examined the impact of providing concrete services, he discovered that although the overall time spent providing concrete services significantly reduced the risk of placement, only one specific service activity—help in obtaining household goods—significantly reduced the risk of out-of-home placement. Three other activities approached statistical significance in reducing the risk of placement: providing food, financial assistance, and help in arranging housecleaning.

Lewis also investigated the impact on placement outcomes of clinical services offered to clients. The results indicated that the combination of teaching parents both time and money management significantly reduced the chance of out-of-home child placement. There were also specific clinical activities associated with reducing the risk of out-of-home placement, which included how to use a journal, track/chart behaviors, attend/testify in court, time out, negotiation skills, and rational-emotive therapy techniques.

OUTCOME STUDIES OF THE HOMEBUILDERS MODEL

The primary outcome of the IFPS intervention documented in the literature is reduction of placement rates. A predominant characteristic of early studies is the large reduction in reported placement rates. However, subsequent studies with more rigorous evaluation designs have called some of these earlier findings into question (Frankel, 1988; Rossi, 1991). More recent studies have also begun to focus on a broader range of outcomes such as family functioning and child behavior. The evidence of impacts of the Homebuilders model on these additional variables is mixed.

Kinney, Madsen, Fleming, and Haapala (1977) described a study conducted during the first sixteen months of the original Homebuilders program. It involved a sample of eighty families (134 people) judged by child protection workers to be at high risk of having one or more children placed in alternative living situations. Three months after service termination, 97% of the children avoided placement in an institutional setting. Assuming that all the children would be placed, and using worker judgment to predict the most likely kind of placement setting, the researchers estimated that the program cost $2,331 less per family served than it would to have placed the children in alternative care.

This type of study design is typical of much of the earlier research done on intensive in-home programming and must be interpreted with a great degree of caution. Without a control/comparison group, it is not possible to estimate credibly the percentage of placements averted in relation to normal child welfare caseloads and other service alternatives. As the studies below with control/comparison groups and the information on control/comparison group child placement rates show, the assumption that all of these children would have been placed is not credible, even as an approximation.

Haapala and Kinney (1988) reported on a study of 678 status-offending youth served by Homebuilders between September 1, 1982, and December 31, 1985. Sixty-eight percent of this sample of youth had never lived in a foster or group home or other residential placement before their Homebuilders involvement. Drug abuse was suspected in 22% and substantiated in 9% of the cases, and alcohol abuse was suspected in 17% and substantiated in 11% of the cases. Twelve months after the initial Homebuilders intake, 87% (592) of youth had avoided out-of-home placements. However, without a comparison group, there is no way to estimate how many of these youth would have been placed without Homebuilders intervention.

Pecora et al. (1990) provided details of an investigation of 453 families in two programs—one in Washington State and one in Utah—that were judged to have at least one child at risk of placement. In Utah, about 40% of the cases came directly from a juvenile court judge or a screening committee, which had determined that the child would be placed immediately if family preservation services were not offered. Virtually all eligible families in the Utah program chose to participate in the study, but in Washington 46% refused. Cases were tracked over a twelve-month period using computerized information and interviews with primary caregivers. Ninety-three percent of the children remained with their parents or their relations at the end of the program (which lasted four to six weeks). A subset was tracked for twelve months after intake and overall 70% of children remained with their parents or with relatives. A child was considered to have been out of the home if he or she ran away or was placed for two weeks or more. These results show that some attrition of placement aversion rates over a twelve-month period is not an unreasonable expectation. Of course, if Homebuilders support was available during subsequent crises, then continued high placement aversion rates might be anticipated—but at a higher program cost.

Pecora et al. (1990) also included a substudy in their investigation with a "small case overflow control group" (p. 7) of thirty-eight Utah families that were referred to the Utah Homebuilders program but were not served because no spaces were available. These cases then received regular child welfare services and were also tracked for twelve months. Twenty-six of the thirty-eight families were able to be tracked, and some differences were found between this comparison group and the sample of Utah Homebuilders cases. The child placement aversion rate for the Utah comparison group was 14.8% in contrast to 58.8% for the Utah Homebuilders group. When the comparison group was matched on a case-by-case basis with a subset of Homebuilders cases, the placement rate for the Homebuilders cases was 44.4%, which was substantially lower than the control group's placement rate of 85.2%. The results of this study suggest that the Homebuilders program can effectively reduce placements compared to traditional child welfare services. However, the small size of the comparison group ($n = 26$) and the nonrandom assignment to group conditions indicate that caution should be used in extrapolating from these findings.

Spaid, Fraser, and Lewis (1991) provided further information on family functioning outcomes from the study reported above. The instruments that were used included a risk assessment measure (Family Risk Scales; Magura, Moses, & Jones, 1987), a family functioning scale (FACES III; Olson, Portner, & Lavee, 1985), a measure of social support (Milardo Social Support Inventory; Milardo, 1983), and a self-report measure of problem ratings completed by parents, which was developed by the investigators of the study. The results revealed that according to therapists' ratings, children, parents, and the family environment appeared to have improved significantly, as indicated by the Family Risk Scales. According to the results of the social support measure, there were also reductions in aversive social interactions between spouses, and increases in empathic friendships with extended kin and network members. Furthermore, parents rated family problems as much reduced at the close of treatment. However, there were no significant improvements noted on the family functioning scale. The authors speculated that given the short-term nature of the program, it may be unrealistic to expect changes in enduring family characteristics.

A report from the Behavioral Sciences Institute (undated) described a small study of the use of the Homebuilders program as "an alternative to psychiatric hospitalization for mentally ill and severely behaviorally disturbed children and youth" (p. 1). Nineteen of the twenty-five (76%) children and youth served by Homebuilders remained with their families. All five of the cases included in the comparison group of clients who were referred but not served because the program was full were placed—four in psychiatric hospitals and one in a correctional institute. The researchers estimated the average cost of serving one family through Homebuilders for their cases was $5,130 and the projected cost of institutionalization for the comparison group was $17,623 per case. This study suggests the promise for the effectiveness of the Homebuilders program for a specific population, but more research is necessary before general conclusions can be drawn with confidence.

An evaluation was also conducted on a Homebuilders program in the Bronx, New York. Mitchell, Tovar, and Knitzer (1989) reported on an evaluation of the first forty-five families served by the Bronx Homebuilders program during the first year (May 1987 through April 1988). The evaluation included a small comparison group ($n = 15$), comprised of clients who were referred to the program but could not be served because the program was full. The clients of the Bronx Homebuilders program were referred by two main agencies: the Child Welfare Administration (CWA) and Pius XII, an agency serving children and youth who were brought to court because of their "incorrigibility." The comparison sample was composed solely of clients referred by Pius XII. Cases were tracked for a twelve-month period. Outcomes examined included placement aversion rates, as well as scores on the Child Well-Being Scales (CWBS), developed by Magura and Moses (1986). Placement in this study was defined as an officially mandated removal of the child from the home for greater than two weeks.

The findings revealed that at the three-month follow-up there were no CWA placements in 81% of the CWA-referred Homebuilders families, and no placements in 77% of the Pius-XII families. At the twelve-month follow-up, these rates had dropped slightly: 76% of CWA-referred families and 73% of the Pius XII-referred families had averted placement. Twelve of the fifteen comparison families were tracked during the follow-up period. At four months following referral to the program (or the equivalent time period to service plus the three-month follow-up for the Homebuilders families), there had been no placement in 83% of the Pius XII-referred families. As well, at thirteen months following referral (or the equivalent time period to service plus the twelve-month follow-up for the Homebuilders families) there had been no placement in 75% of the Pius XII-referred families. Thus, the aversion rates were similar for the Pius XII-referred Homebuilders families and the comparison group, also composed of Pius XII-referred families. In this study the Homebuilders program appeared to have no significant effect on rates of placement. However, because of the small sample size of the comparison group, caution should be used in interpreting these results. In addition, no details were provided about the services and supports received by comparison group families.

In addition to placement rates, this study also examined the impact on child well being and family functioning using the CWBS. No differences were found on the CWBS between the Pius XII program and comparison families. For the CWA families who experienced subsequent placement, the CWBS scores indicated a greater number of areas of concern at termination compared to those CWA families who did not experience placement.

Mitchell et al. (1989) also reported on the results of qualitative interviews conducted with Homebuilders families. The families who consented to be interviewed (twenty-six at termination; twenty-one at three months; eighteen at twelve-month follow-up) had higher placement aversion rates than the families who did not consent to be interviewed. The results indicated that many of the mothers (or mother-figures) reported school-related concerns. For example, 81% reported concerns about whether the child who was of concern in the intervention was attending school. Also, seventeen of the twenty-six mothers or mother-figures reported serious health or mental health problems. All of the women reported feeling positive about the Homebuilders intervention. Mitchell et al. (1989) also noted that "families did not always have a clear understanding of the limits of the Homebuilders intervention" (p. 17). That is, the caregivers had wanted to call their worker or receive more help after the intervention was terminated. The respondents suggested that Homebuilders' workers be "on call" when new crises occurred.

It is worth noting that, in all of these studies of Homebuilders programs, placements of less than two weeks are not reported. Such information could be useful in gaining a greater understanding of the Homebuilders model. Because it is a crisis intervention model, it could be argued that short-term use of care would not be expected. Thus, even though short-term use of care can be an effective way of bridging a family crisis, it might not be a welcome outcome from this type of program model.

Overall, there has been very little outcome research published specifically on the Homebuilders program. This review identified only three small studies that included a comparison group permitting an estimate of the percentage of placements averted by the program. For two of these studies, the results were very encouraging, showing an advantage in placement aversion for the Homebuilders clients of between 40 and 76%. However, the samples for these two studies were very small and in one instance represented a distinct subgrouping of child welfare clientele. In contrast, the Bronx Homebuilders program showed very little difference in placement aversion rates between the Homebuilders clients and the comparison group clients. Nonetheless, as with the above two studies, the Bronx Homebuilders program also had a very small sample size. Thus, we should be cautious in accepting the results of these studies as predictive of the results of a broad use of the Homebuilders model in diverse settings.

There is also evidence that the Homebuilders program can produce quite different placement aversion rates with different populations and in different settings. These data also show that placement aversion rates may decline as time lengthens from program involvement. This may indicate the need for placing greater emphasis on graduation and community linkage procedures as well as the need for follow-up with clients served by the Homebuilders program.

These studies also focused almost exclusively on placement aversion as the primary outcome variable and provided little information on the impact of Homebuilders participation on personal or family variables. Only two studies were identified that reported any data on outcomes other than placement aversion. There was some evidence to indicate improvements in child well-being, social support, and reduced risk to the child. However, more enduring patterns of family functioning showed no improvements. All of these results have to be seen as very preliminary. In addition, there are substantial cost savings reported from the Homebuilders program in some of these studies; however, no detailed cost analyses were available to support this finding. Nonetheless, cost savings would be a reasonable expectation if out-of-home child placements are used as infrequently as reported in these studies.

Fraser, Pecora and Haapala (1989), clearly advocates of the program model, provide the following summary:

> [T]he research studies conducted thus far provide a foundation to support cautious optimism that intensive home-based services are able to improve child, parent, and family functioning to the extent that child placement is prevented for at least a short (six month) period of time. Which specific client, service, or worker factors are most responsible for treatment success is not clear. (p. 36)

OUTCOME STUDIES OF OTHER INTENSIVE FAMILY PRESERVATION SERVICE PROGRAMS

As indicated previously, in-home support program models have proliferated in child welfare over the past ten years, particularly in the United States, where they have become a frequent response to the desire to reduce the level of child placements. Many of these programs are modeled directly after the Homebuilders program, while others have a variety of programming parameters in common with the Homebuilders program.

In recent years, there have been several controlled studies of home-based programs. Feldman (1991) evaluated a family preservation program in New Jersey's Division of Youth and Family Services, modeled after the Homebuilders program. Feldman explained that the "study was designed to address one of the gaps in the research literature to date—the minimal use of control groups to determine the net effect of the Homebuilders' intervention" (p. 48). Families referred to Family Preservation Services (FPS) were randomly assigned to either the program or to a traditional community service. The intervention delivered to clients in the control group was the responsibility of the referring agency; this intervention typically involved less intensive counseling and referral to other community resources. However, detailed information allowing a useful comparison of the services received by FPS and comparison group families was not available.

Results revealed that the experimental group (FPS) had lower placement rates at the termination of service than the comparison group: placements occurred in 7.3% of the FPS cases compared to 14.9% of the control group. However, this difference was not statistically significant. As well, the placement rates increased throughout the follow-up period for both the FPS and control groups. At the three-month follow-up, placements had occurred in 21.9% of the FPS group and 36.8% of the control group; at six-month follow-up these rates had increased to 29.2% for the FPS group and 49.4% for the control group. Both of these differences were found to be statistically significant. By the twelve-month follow-up, placements had occurred in 45.8% of the FPS cases and 57.7% of the control group cases—still a statistically significant difference. However, while the differences noted during the follow-up periods were all statistically significant, the gap between the groups was less than reported in many of the Homebuilders studies previously discussed. The largest variation was found at the six-month follow-up—a difference of 20.2%. At the twelve-month follow-up the gap between the two groups narrowed, with the placement rates increasing more quickly for the FPS group than for the control group.

The importance of a control group in studying placement aversion rates is clearly illustrated by this study. That is, although all of the referring clients were considered to be "at imminent risk" of out-of-home placement, only 57.7% of control group clients had experienced a placement after twelve months. This study also suggests that the success in averting out-of-home placements demonstrated by IFPS models attenuates over time, indicating the importance of graduation procedures to the model. As well, these results demonstrate that follow-up interventions may be useful.

In addition to placement aversion rates, Feldman (1991) also examined the intervention's effect on several other variables, including family environment, child well-being, and social support. Results demonstrated that, to some extent, FPS families were functioning at a higher level at case closure relative to their own baseline. On ten of eighteen scales assessing support and family functioning, the FPS families scored higher at the three-month follow-up than at the initiation of service. Child well-being scores also improved for the FPS families between initiation and termination of service: improvements were noted for the composite scale, as well as for the Parental Disposition and the Child Performance subscales. No improvements were made on Child Well-Being scales measuring household adequacy. Nevertheless, the families receiving the intensive service *did not* generally improve to a greater extent than did the control group families. The most significant difference between the FPS and control groups was noted for the Parental Disposition subscale of the Child Well-Being Scales and the Intellectual-Cultural subscale of the Family Environment Scale, with the FPS group showing greater improvement than the control group.

McDonald and Associates (1990) conducted an evaluation of in-home care projects, modeled after the Homebuilders program, that also included a comparison group in the research design. The consultants evaluated the effectiveness of intensive, short-term, in-home therapeutic services in averting placement for eight projects in California. In addition, the cost-effectiveness of these projects was investigated. During the last year of this three-year demonstration project, referrals were randomly assigned to the project group to receive the intensive service or to the comparison group to receive "traditional" services as determined by the referring agency. Once again, little information about the nature and the extent of services received by comparison families was available. To ensure that referrals were at "imminent risk" of an out-of-home placement, the referring source had to agree that action would be taken within the next two weeks to place the child, unless intensive services were provided. All placements were considered in the analysis. Cases were followed for eight months past the termination of the intensive service, which was approximately four to six weeks in duration.

The results revealed that the project group and the comparison group had comparable rates of placement. Specifically, placements occurred in 25% of the project families during the follow-up period, compared to 20% of the comparison group families during that same time period. The project group, however, did use nearly 1,500 fewer days of placement than the control group, although this difference was not statistically significant. As well, the children in the comparison group were placed earlier than the children in the project group. That is, within sixty days of referral, 13% of the comparison children had experienced a placement compared with 7% of the project children, a statistically significant difference. For both groups, placements in relatives' homes accounted for the highest percentage of placement days:

41.5% for the project group and 55.1% for the comparison group. Little difference was found in overall placement costs for children placed from either the comparison group or the project group (McDonald & Associates, 1990). Based on their findings, McDonald and Associates argued:

> Expectations will need to be tempered based on the findings to date. There is evidence to indicate that while intensive in-home services have high success rates in terms of placement outcomes, the rate may not differ significantly from the baseline rate of a comparable group of families who do not receive intensive in-home services. Communities will need to consider the referral process, and the availability of other family service resources as well as their placement resources, when defining expectations. (p. 7.3)

Prior to the completion of these two studies, the literature on the IFPS models was quite enthusiastic about the outcomes associated with these interventions. These two controlled studies were somewhat of a departure from this previous research, prompting some researchers (K. Nelson, 1990; Pecora, 1991) to challenge the findings from these studies.

In reviewing the results from the California study, Pecora (1991) identified several factors that need to be considered when interpreting the results. First, he argued that there was some evidence that the services received by the experimental and comparison groups were similar. Second, there was considerable variation in direct client hours across the eight program locations. He also contended that there was some evidence to suggest that service provision may have varied among some of the locations. Pecora argued, therefore, that aggregating data may be problematic. Third, the children were younger than those served by other IFPS programs, and therefore the results may not be generalizable to all IFPS programs. Lastly, because of the data gathering techniques used (payment records and case reviews), private placements and runaway episodes were not included in the analysis.

Pecora also reviewed the findings from the New Jersey study and observed that it was unclear what levels of service were received by the comparison group. Therefore, there is the possibility that the services received by the experimental and comparison groups were similar. He also argued that only 8.8% of the program group families received concrete services—a proportion that is much lower than other IFPS programs.[2] This may help to explain why program clients did not show improvements on the Household Adequacy subscales of the CWBS, as reported previously.

K. Nelson (1990) argued that the results from the California and New Jersey studies, as well as from the Bronx study described earlier, do not mean that IFPS programs are ineffective. She contended that "imminent risk is proving to be a very elusive standard for referral" (p. 2). Therefore, she argued that the children in these studies may not have been at "imminent risk" of placement. As well, she pointed out the possibility of "contamination" of the comparison groups. That is, referring agencies may likely have known about the research and may have made special efforts with the families who were included in the comparison group. Furthermore, she maintained that different results may emerge if different sites and subpopulations (e.g., neglect cases, physical abuse cases, status offenders) are analyzed individually. Lastly, she discussed the possibility that the placements for families receiving the IFPS program may be more appropriate, shorter-term, and more stable, because of the intense assessment that these families received.

Schwartz, Auclaire, and Harris (1990) described a study of a unit of eight specially trained social workers created in August 1985 within the Hennepin County Child Welfare Division of the Minnesota County Services Division. The program worked exclusively with seriously emotionally disturbed adolescents who had been approved for placement. Services were typically limited to four weeks and were provided in the client's home. Workers carried an average caseload of two families and provided intensive services (no details provided) available at irregular hours, and made use of case teams and structural family therapy—parameters generally similar to the Homebuilders model.

This demonstration project involved adolescents assigned to enter care and thus allows an estimation of placement aversion rates with a difficult-to-serve child welfare population. An adolescent was eligible for participation in the study if he or she was approved for out-of-home placement, was twelve to seventeen years of age, was not a ward of the state, and was not under court order into placement. An experimental and a comparison group were created by selecting cases from the adolescent pool and randomly assigning them to the two conditions (fifty-eight in home-based program; fifty-eight in comparison group). The cases assigned to the comparison group were placed in foster homes, hospitals, group homes, or residential treatment centers. The program group and the comparison group differed significantly on only two of sixteen background variables: more program families resided in the city of Minneapolis than did control group members, and control group members had experienced more past placement episodes than did program families. While not statistically significant, the experimental group was composed of more single parents (53 and 36%, respectively), and the control group parents and adolescents were more favorably disposed toward care placements.

Results revealed that of the fifty-eight cases referred to the home-based program, twenty-five remained in their own homes throughout the entire study period (twelve months to sixteen months). Seventeen (68%) of the program group clients who were placed experienced multiple placements compared to thirty-four (58%) members of the comparison group. The total number of postassignment days in placement for the home-based program group was 4,777 days compared to 12,037 days for the comparison group receiving regular services—a 60% reduction in days spent in care. Both groups used about the same number of days in short-term shelter care. There was some indication that families receiving more treatment days (forty-six to 114 days) and more treatment hours (twenty-one to fifty hours) made less use of placement alternatives. Schwartz et al. (1990) concluded optimistically that:

> the results indicate that the model of intensive home-based care services can be an effective model for preventing placements and keeping families together. This is the case even for youth approved for placement in such costly and restrictive settings such as residential treatment centres, group homes and hospitals. (pp. 16–17)

While no cost analysis is provided, it would not be unreasonable to anticipate good cost savings by reducing placements through such use of in-home services in child welfare.

Frankel (1988) described a study in which seventy-four families were randomly assigned to one of three traditional child welfare units or to the Ramsey County, Minnesota, Family-Centered Home-Based Demonstration Project. This project had some program parameters in common with the Homebuilders model. Home-based services were described as primarily consisting of counseling and concrete services provided by the caseworkers. Cases in either the child welfare units or the demonstration project remained open ten to twelve months. No information was provided on the levels of direct contact in this program. Three months after service termination, 67% of the families in the experimental group had no children placed compared to 45% of control group families. Moreover, the experimental group children spent considerably less time in care.

Frankel made two salient points about this study. First, children who were considered extremely likely to be placed in long-term care within three months were excluded from the program and, despite this, the prevention placement rate was lower than in similar uncontrolled studies. This pattern is hard to interpret without more information on program intensity, context, and client characteristics. Second, the "high-risk" group excluded from the program received the same child welfare services as the control group and experienced a similar rate of placement (44%). Frankel interpreted this as evidence that only a portion of children considered very high-risk end up in care in the absence of intensive programming. Unfortunately, no information was provided on the cost savings derived from the 20% advantage the experimental group had on placement aversions and the shorter time periods in care.

Thus, the results from the controlled studies of IFPS programs other than

Homebuilders are inconsistent. Most of these studies demonstrated better outcomes for the groups receiving the intervention, as compared to the comparison groups. However, these studies indicate that not all of the comparison group children will experience child abuse or neglect incidents, or subsequent placement despite being identified as at risk of "imminent" placement. In addition, there was considerable difference in outcomes across settings and populations.

In addition to the studies described above which included random assignment control groups, many nonexperimental (nonrandom assignment) studies of IFPS or home-based program models have also been conducted within the last decade. Pearson and King (undated) evaluated an intensive family preservation program in Baltimore. This IFPS program was somewhat different from the Homebuilders model. Although the service was intense and a variety of clinical and concrete services were offered, the service lasted ninety days and utilized a team approach (a family service worker and a parent aide), carrying a case load of no more than six families. A quasi-experimental research design was exercised. That is, all referrals made to the program were assigned to either the intensive experimental group, or to the traditional services offered by the Department of Social Services, based on the level of risk of placement. Those families referred to the experimental group were considered to be most at risk.

For the comparison group, sixty of 180 families (33%) experienced a foster care placement during the six-month period between intake and reassessment. Thirty-two of these placements occurred at intake, and therefore were not considered in the comparisons with the group receiving Intensive Family Services (IFS). At termination of service, eight of eighty IFS families (7.5%) had experienced a placement. This placement rate was significantly lower than the comparison group, where the placement rate was twenty-eight of 148 families (18%). At the twelve-month follow-up, the IFS group had two (3%) cases open in foster care compared to twelve (8%) cases open in foster care for the comparison group. The purposive sampling used in this evaluation suggests some caution in interpreting these findings. However, if indeed the experimental group represented a higher risk of placement than comparison cases, then these results are promising for IFPS programs.

Pearson and King (undated) also examined the cost effectiveness of the IFS program. They sought to determine if the IFS program was too costly to be offered by public services. To determine the cost effectiveness, Pearson and King compared the cost of delivering traditional services with IFS. They then compared the placement costs incurred per one hundred families for the two types of services, based on the placement rates found in their study. The IFS program was considered much more costly to run: $282,000 versus $102,000 per year for the traditional services. However, foster care placement prevention savings were projected to be $216,750 if IFS was utilized.

Thus, the overall cost savings predicted for one year was approximately $37,000. The actual savings would be more substantial considering that the average length of time for foster placement was 2.2 years.

Fixsen, Olivier, and Blase (undated) reported on a home-based family centered treatment program initiated in Alberta. Alberta Family Support Services program was based on the treatment methods of the Teaching-Family model and the service delivery system of the Homebuilders model. Treatment was intensive (ten to thirty hours a week), short-term (six to ten weeks), and flexible as dictated by the Homebuilders model, but treatment focused more on teaching as the method to help family members improve family functioning. In addition, the program offered "booster visits" after formal treatment ended to help with subsequent crises and provide occasional support. Clients were referred to the program after placement had been approved by the Planning, Assessment, and Review Committee (PARC) of the Department of Social Services. Eighty-seven children from fifty-two families were included in this evaluation of the program. Data were collected on placement rates, as well as on variables reflected in measures such as the Child Behaviour Checklist (CBCL) and the Parent Conflict Behaviour Questionnaire (PCBQ). A cost analysis was also conducted.

Of the eighty-seven children included in the evaluation, seven were placed during the intervention. Children were followed for a twelve-month period following the intervention. Results revealed that placement rates were quite low throughout the twelve-month period. The highest rate of placement occurred at the six-month follow-up with a placement rate of 16%; the lowest rate occurred at the twelve-month follow-up with a placement rate of 5%. Without a comparison group, however, it is impossible to know whether these rates would be better than those for children not receiving this program.

As mentioned above, information was also collected using the CBCL and the PCBQ. At intake, the children included in the evaluation scored in the low functioning range on both measures. However, in another report on this same program (Oostenbrink et al., 1990), follow-up outcomes on both these measures were reported. Results revealed that improvements were made on several of the scales of the CBCL for the children tracked from pretest to termination ($n = 17$). As well, improvements were noted on the PCBQ at pretest, posttest, and the three-month follow-up period. Indeed, at the three-month follow-up, the PCBQ scores at termination were not only sustained, but a further improvement had been made.

In their cost analysis, Fixsen et al. (undated), calculated the cost savings based upon cost of placements if all of the children recommended by PARC to be placed were actually placed. If all of the children had been placed in care for an eight-month period (indicated by the authors to be a conservative estimate of the typical time in care), the cost savings was calculated to be over $600,000. Nonetheless, without a comparison group the credibility of these estimates is extremely questionable.

A number of other studies of in-home programs have been conducted over the last ten to fifteen years (Dunu, 1979; Frankel, 1988; Heying, 1985; Hinckley & Ellis, 1985; Magura, 1981). These in-home programs shared service parameters similar to Homebuilders, and were designed to help prevent out-of-home placement for children. These programs all demonstrated good placement aversion rates, with varying populations and in different settings. Nevertheless, with little detail provided on service content, and without the benefit of comparison groups, the findings reported from these studies are suggestive *at best*.

Several studies reviewed by Frankel (1988) revealed some evidence of lower placement aversion rates for cases with a physically abusive history or where reunification of a child in care with his or her family was the goal of treatment. As well, there was some indication that families who were new clients of the child welfare system may experience greater success. Other studies have demonstrated that placement is more common in cases in which substance abuse or mental health difficulties are involved, the child at risk has a placement history, the primary caretaker is uncooperative, or the child is at risk due to chronic neglect (Nelson, 1991; Yuan & Struckman-Johnson, 1991). However, without comparison groups, knowing conclusively whether the home-based programs described in these studies fared better or worse with such subpopulations than other interventions is not possible.

Rivera and Kutash (1994) completed a review of the research evidence for the effectiveness of IFPS. Their review included several experimental or quasi-experimental studies in addition to those previously discussed:

> Henggeler, Melton, and Smith (1992) conducted a study to examine the efficacy of a family preservation program using multisystemic family therapy (MST) in decreasing the rates of institutionalization of youthful offenders and in reducing antisocial behavior. Eighty-four juvenile offenders, judged to be at risk for out-of-home placement, participated in the study. Results revealed that at 59 weeks post-referral, youth who had received family preservation services using multisystemic treatment had approximately half as many arrests as youth who received traditional services. Recidivism rates (rates of re-arrest) were 42% for the treatment group and 62% for the comparison group. Further, results revealed that a composite measure of family cohesion indicated that families participating in the family preservation program experienced greater cohesion, while families receiving traditional services experienced decreased cohesion. A composite measure of aggression toward peers revealed that those youth in the treatment condition had a decreased level of aggression, while those in the control condition experienced no change in aggression as a result of treatment. These findings support the efficacy of a family preservation pro-

gram using multisystemic therapy in reducing out-of-home placements and in decreasing criminal activity as compared to traditional service delivery methods.

Through a search of archival data, long-term, follow-up data on re-arrest for the above sample (n - 84) were gathered for an average of 2.4 years post-referral (Henggeler, Melton, Smith, Schoenwald, & Hanley, 1993). Results revealed that multisystemic family preservation was more effective than traditional services in prolonging the time to re-arrest for this sample. The mean time to re-arrest for those receiving multisystemic family preservation services was about 56 weeks, while the mean time to re-arrest for those receiving traditional services was about 32 weeks. At 2.4 years (120 weeks) post-referral, 39% of those in the multisystemic family preservation group had not been re-arrested, while 20% of those receiving traditional services had not been re-arrested.

Other controlled clinical studies examining the effectiveness of family preservation using multisystemic treatment with adolescents having substance abuse and serious criminal behavior have been conducted (see Henggeler et al., 1994, for a brief review of these studies). Findings from the Missouri Delinquency Project represent the most comprehensive and extensive evaluation of family preservation using MST. Chronic juvenile offenders ($n = 200$) were randomly assigned to either a group who received MST or a group who received individual therapy. In addition to recidivism data for 4 years following treatment, pretest-posttest self-report and observational measures were collected to assess individual, peer, and family functioning. Observational measures revealed that families who received MST exhibited more supportiveness and less conflict/hostility in mother-adolescent, father-adolescent, and mother-father relations as compared to those families in the individual therapy condition. Those in the MST condition also reported more family cohesion and adaptability. Adolescents in the MST group displayed significantly fewer behavior problems following treatment and parents reported less symptomatology. Four-year follow-up data indicated that recidivism rates were 22% (MST group) and 71% (individual therapy) for those who completed therapy. Of these recidivists, those in the MST condition were arrested less often and for less serious crimes than those in the comparison group.

Another randomized, controlled study examining the effectiveness of family preservation using MST was conducted in Charleston, South Carolina. Adolescents ($n = 112$) exhibiting both substance abuse and delinquency problems were randomly assigned to either the MST condition or the usual services condition. A battery of assessment devices were administered at pretreatment, posttreatment, and at 6- and 12-month follow-up periods. Preliminary results from 20 cases revealed that the MST group experienced more gains in abstinence from substance abuse and delinquency resulting in decreased institutionalization as compared to the usual services group (Henggler et al., 1994). . . .

An evaluation (Michigan Department of Social Services, 1993) was conducted to determine the program's effectiveness in comparison to foster care services in averting children from out-of-home placements. The evaluation involved a group of children ($n = 225$) who received family preservation services through the Families First Program and a matched group of children (n = 225) who received traditional foster care services. The study covered a 3-year period and utilized multiple data sources. In an examination of out-of-home placement rates for the two groups, results revealed that children in the Families First program evidenced a consistently lower out-of-home placement rate at 3, 6, and 12 months following the intervention. At 3-month follow-up, out-of-home placement rates were 7% for the Families First group and 15% for the foster care group. Six-month follow-up data revealed out-of-home placement rates of 12% for the Families First group and 26% for the foster care group. Out-of-home placement rates at 12-month follow-up were 24% for children in the Families First group and 35% for those in foster care. Even more striking differences were noted in out-of-home placement rates for the two groups when 39 pairs of children referred due to delinquency and reunification were removed from the analysis. For the matched pairs of children (n = 186 pairs) referred due to abuse and/or neglect, respective out-of-home placement rates at 3, 6, and 12 months were 5%, 13% and 19% for the children in the Families First group and 12%, 26% and 36% for children who received foster care services. . . .

A quasi-experimental design was employed to measure outcome differences between youth in the Family Ties program and a group of juveniles not served by the program. Primary outcome measures included rates of re-arrest, re-conviction, and re-incarceration for the year following release from the Family Ties program or, for those in the comparison group, from the state youth facility. Positive behavior changes exhibited by program youths also were used to assess outcome. Former program youth (n = 93) were randomly selected for inclusion in the study. Of that number, 57% (n = 40 families) consented to an interview. The comparison group was comprised of randomly selected juvenile delinquents (n = 40) who were adjudicated in Family Court and placed in a state youth facility. Groups were found to be comparable in background and at-risk variables and had been in the community about the same length of time (1 year) before follow-up. . . .

Rates of re-involvement were significantly lower for those in the Family Ties program than for the comparison group. For those in the program, the rate of re-arrest was 20%, while re-conviction and re-incarceration were rates were 18%. For the comparison group, the rate of re-arrest was 42% and the rates of re-conviction and re-incarceration were 40% each. As another measure of outcome, the evaluation focused on the amount of placement time saved as a result of the Family Ties program. On average, in 1992, the program averted almost 6 weeks of placement time during the program and nearly 10 months following participation in the program. . . .

Rather than focusing on the use of family preservation as a way of preventing out-of-home placements, Walton, Fraser, Lewis, Pecora, and Walton (1993) examined the effectiveness of family preservation services in reunifying children with their families. This study, conducted in Utah, utilized a posttest-only experimental design. Families were randomly selected from a computer-generated list of children in out-of-home care. The sample was randomly assigned to either the treatment or control group. The treatment condition was comprised of a group of families (n = 57) who received family preservation services, while those in the control condition consisted of families (n = 53) who received traditional family foster care reunification services. Data were collected at the beginning and end of the 3-month treatment period. Findings revealed that at the end of the 90-day treatment period, 93% of the families in the treatment condition were reunited as compared to only 28% of the families in the control condition. Six-month data revealed that some of the children in the treatment group who had been reunited with their families had returned to an out-of-home placement, while more of the children in the control group had returned to their homes. Of the 53 children in the treatment group who were living at home at the end of the treatment period, 40 (70% of the total treatment group) remained in the home 6 months later. During this time, an additional 7 children in the control group returned home, resulting in a total of 22 (41.5%). Data collected at 12 months after the termination of services revealed that 43 (75.4%) of the children in the treatment group were in their homes as compared to 26 (49%) of the children in the control group. Further, those receiving family preservation services spent significantly more days living at home during the 90-day treatment period and follow-up periods than those receiving traditional services. (pp. 62–69)

Rivera and Kutash draw several conclusions from their review of the effectiveness of IFPS programs:

> It appears that family preservation services have been effective in averting the placement of a high percentage of children. . . . [T]he percentage of children averted from placement tended to decrease at follow-up. However, percentages were greater for those receiving family preservation services at follow-up than for those in comparison or control groups. . . .
> While the percentage of children [already in care] reunified [with their families] was greater in the treatment as compared to the control groups, those percentages decreased as the amount of time from discharge increased. . . .
> While it appears that many family preservation programs have proven effective at keeping families intact and preventing or delaying the placement of children deemed at-risk for substitute care, the effects do not appear to be long-lasting and families continue to be at-risk following service termination. . . .
> Moreover, research has shown that the majority of children admitted to intensive family preservation programs would not have been placed without the program. (1994, pp. 71–74)

The results from the controlled and comparison group studies reviewed in this chapter were not consistent. The five controlled studies reviewed described differing program impacts on placement aversion rates. The Feldman (1991) study indicated moderate placement aversion rate advantages for the IFPS program, but these declined over the twelve-month follow-up period, and became more similar to the placement prevention rates demonstrated by the comparison group. As well, improvements on indices such as family functioning and child well-being were not substantially greater for the intervention group than for the comparison group. The McDonald and Associates (1990) study showed comparable rates of placement between the IFPS and comparison groups. The results from the other three controlled studies were more encouraging, showing better outcomes for the intervention groups than for the comparison groups. The superiority of the program groupings in frequency of use of care and fewer days in care was marked, particularly in the study focusing on "high-risk" adolescents approved for placement. The Pearson and King (undated) quasi-experimental study also showed better placement aversion rates for the IFPS group. The research summarized by Rivera and Kutash (1994) generally showed comparably superior benefits for the program groups, particularly for programs working with young offenders and for the reunification of families with children in care.

The inconsistent findings from the controlled and comparison group studies may be the result of differential program content, structural dimensions, and service user characteristics. That is, the actual services received, the methods by which they were delivered, and the children and families served may have been very different across settings, resulting in different outcomes. These investigations reported generalities about these service characteristics, making it difficult to interpret these different outcome patterns.

The findings of Feldman (1991) and Rivera and Kutash (1994) corroborate findings reported earlier that aversion rates decline over time. These findings may indicate the necessity of follow-up procedures or, at the very least, greater emphasis being placed on the graduation procedures from the program.

The results from the McDonald and Associates (1990) study, as well as from the other controlled studies reviewed, may indicate the need for accurately defining the target population. The disappointing results demonstrated by the McDonald and Associates investigation may have been the result of the target population not being at "imminent risk." Recently, Rossi (1992) examined this issue and argued that because the assessment for imminent risk of placement is so difficult to judge, "it would seem to be more sensible to intervene at a point *after the decision to place has been made,* perhaps after court decisions to place have been made" (p. 173; italics added).

The controlled studies reviewed show that, even in very precarious situations, a substantial number of families identified as at risk of immediate child placement will not have a child enter care while receiving mainline child welfare services. This again indicates the difficulty in focusing IFPS on a population who are considered to be at "imminent risk" of out-of-home placement.

Generally, the studies of in-home programs that did not include comparison or control groups reported similar placement aversion rates to the Homebuilders studies without such control/comparison groups: generally between 75 and 90% of clients served. This was true despite substantial variations in the service parameters of these programs. However, without comparison/control groups, such studies are not helpful in assessing if their programs had any comparative advantages over other intervention options.

In the uncontrolled studies, there was some evidence of higher placement aversion rates if the in-home program was used as an early intervention strategy, and lower placement aversion rates for cases involving substance abuse or mental health problems, documented incidents of abuse, past placement histories, or when family reunification was an objective. However, without comparison/control groups, it was not possible to determine if these are superior outcomes with such populations.

SUMMARY: INTENSIVE FAMILY PRESERVATION SERVICES

According to the Child Welfare League of America, Intensive Family Preservation Services must have certain characteristics: families receive a variety of clinical and concrete services, service is of short duration (ninety days or less), and is intensive (eight to ten hours of face-to-face contact per week). Homebuilders and many other IFPS models are considered crisis intervention programs designed to respond rapidly (within twenty-four hours of referral) to families with one or more children considered to be at risk of placement in out-of-home care. The model stresses making help available at the times when families naturally experience difficulties and in their home environments. In theory, services are available twenty-four hours a day, seven days a week, and are usually limited to four to eight weeks. Services typically are delivered by one worker, or a small team of workers, who carry lower caseloads (two to six families) than regular child protection workers. IFPS is not a stand-alone program model but, in principle, places a priority on concurrent and ongoing connections with other formal and informal resources. Also, as an intention, provision of concrete services is an important component of IFPS programs.

Generally, the outcome research on the IFPS model is more extensive and more conclusive than the research available on the other support program models reviewed for this volume. However, the IFPS research has concentrated on avoidance of out-of-home child placements as an outcome indicator and includes little information on other child, parent, or family changes.

There also is considerable evidence that IFPS programs have had great difficulty focusing their services on children who were indeed at imminent risk of out-of-home placement. Studies that have included control or comparison groups consistently demonstrated that most of the families not receiving IFPS services did not have a child placed during the study period.

A number of structural program dimensions drawn from social support as well as support program theory and research (see Chapter 5 of this volume) can be used to summarize our understanding of IFPS programs and the other support programs models that will be reviewed in this volume. In this section, a selection of these programming parameters and anticipated program impacts are used to situate IFPS programs within a broader support program context:

The Range of Supports Available. Because of the amount of time spent in face-to-face contact with family members, IFPS programs should be able to provide a variety of help. Research evidence suggests that education and skill development around parenting, child management and home management concerns, counseling and emotional support, and concrete assistance are among the most common supports provided to families. However, the reliance upon a single helper in many IFPS programs may constrain what supports can be provided directly by the program. There also may be substantial variation in supports provided from worker to worker. The focus on case management, when it is adequately implemented, can increase the types of support available to families.

The Level of Support Available. IFPS programs provide high levels of direct contact (e.g., several times a week for a few hours a day) with family members as well as, potentially, increased access to external supports. This is a major strength of the program model, which is consistent with the prescriptions in the support program literature, for supporting disadvantaged families.

Availability in a Crisis. Additional strengths of IFPS programs are their potential for rapid responses to crisis referrals and the amount of time that can be spent with family members during periods of high stress whenever they might occur.

Motivation and Skill Requirements. The in-home services and the flexible service hours should advantage IFPS programs in reaching out to and in involving less motivated and less skilled parents, particularly in the early stages of service involvement. These features, coupled with the supposed emphasis on linking clients with other services and supports, suggest that IFPS programs potentially might be effective as a transition service for "hard-to-reach" clientele. However, the selection criteria of at least one parent agreeing to program involvement and no one objecting to the idea of the child(ren) remaining at home may eliminate some more resistant families who might profit from a IFPS program.

Focused Technical Expertise. IFPS programs were designed to focus professional expertise on selected personal and family concerns in naturally occurring circumstances. However, reliance on a single helper may limit the range of expertise that can be brought to bear in comparison to some multiple-helper support program models. Program evidence about the large amount of time case management responsibilities might require as well as the time that may be spent providing concrete supports to families provide some evidence of this limitation.

The Length of Time Supports Available. The IFPS program model is a short-term crisis intervention model (four to ten weeks). The original Home-builders rationale assumed that because of the crisis, motivation in families would allow quick, substantial, and enduring personal and family changes to be made by the program; however, this assumption is not well supported by support program theory or research nor by the outcome research on IFPS programs. There is no clear indication that the requirements of successful program graduation and families' ongoing need for supports have been well articulated in the IFPS model. This is a major limitation of IFPS programs.

Reciprocity and Social Integration. Taking advantage of the benefits of informal supports and fostering positive social integration are under-developed considerations in IFPS programs. IFPS programs do not empha-size family members doing for themselves or being helpers of others in similar circumstances or developing connections with peers. These are ad-ditional important limitations of IFPS programs.

Anticipated Program Impacts and Rationales. There is convincing evi-dence that, when they are focused *in fact* on "high-risk" populations, IFPS programs often reduce both the frequency that children need to be placed outside their homes and the amount of time children spend in care. Because of these averted placements, IFPS programs can result in substantial cost savings for the host agencies. In all likelihood, these results can be attributed to the broad range of supports, the intensity of services, and the crisis availability features of the IFPS program model. While research evidence is scarce, because of their ability to bring professional expertise to bear on selected personal and family functioning concerns, it seems reasonable to expect limited positive changes in these areas would result from IFPS in-volvements. Because of the short-term nature of IFPS programs and the complex, ongoing challenges faced by many involved families, it also is anticipated that some of the gains in personal and family functioning as well as in placement aversion would lessen or disappear over time. There is some research evidence that IFPS benefits to families attenuate with the passage of time after program involvement ends. Finally, there are no reasons to expect

IFPS involvement to lessen families' reliance on professional services, after IFPS participation ends.

NOTES

1.   Process studies of IFPS programs in child welfare and children's mental health in Ontario show clearly that in practice IFPS programs can deviate in significant and substantial ways from the program parameters (Hayward, Cameron, & Peirson, 1995).

2.   For example, as cited in an earlier section, Fraser et al. (1989) report that concrete supports were provided to about 75% of Homebuilders families.

In-Home Programs in Child Welfare: Home Health Visitors and Parent Aides 7

With a focus in recent years on prevention and on providing services from an ecological perspective, home-based programs have become increasingly popular (Frankel, 1988; Mamatis & Morrison, 1991). This chapter reviews the literature about programs that are offered in the home specifically for families involved in the child welfare system. These programs have been described as "all those supportive or supplemental services to a family in or near the family home" (Maybanks & Bryce, 1979, p. 20, cited in Bidgood & van de Sande, 1990). Bidgood and van de Sande (1990) added that "the primary goal of these services is typically the prevention of child abuse and neglect and the avoidance of family breakdown" (p. 107).

This review primarily includes evaluations of programs that were specifically intended for families using child welfare services. However, many home-based programs are intended for socioeconomically disadvantaged families. Many of these families have come to the attention of a variety of health, education, and social services providers. For this reason, some program evaluations have been included that were not designed for child welfare populations, but nonetheless have relevance for such families.

There is a great deal of variety among the many different home-based program models that have been tried. While there may be some common principles and values—such as an ecological approach, prevention, social support, and empowerment (Mamatis & Morrison, 1991)—there are few common guiding formulas for these services and it is difficult to neatly categorize them. A previous review (Bidgood & van de Sande, 1990) identified four major models in the literature on home-based programming for child welfare clientele: health visitors, parent aides, home training in child management, and multifaceted programs. Chapter 6 focused exclusively on in-home Intensive Family Preservation Services. This chapter concentrates on home health visitor and parent aide programs. Chapter 8 reviews child management programs, many of which are offered in the home. Chapter 10 examines multifaceted or comprehensive programs, which typically involve a combination of services to families and which often include some kind of home-based service.

HOME HEALTH VISITORS

The programs included in this section send a visitor to the home who focuses on health concerns of the family. Home health visitor programs have been developed primarily in the public health sector. A focus on prevention has seen health services include the home as an appropriate setting in which to deliver services to families. The majority of these programs have focused on families with infants, since prevention theory and research suggest early interventions in disadvantaged children's lives produce more promising results than efforts at later stages of development (Ministry of Community and Social Services, 1990a). Many of these programs have among their objectives the reduction of the frequence of incidences of child abuse and neglect.

Program Parameters

Few home health visitor programs specifically attempted to decrease rates of child maltreatment. Instead, most programs were designed to foster changes that were considered to be related to the reduction of child abuse and neglect. For example, Siegel, Bauman, Schaefer, Saunders, and Ingram (1980) stated that "our concept of abuse and neglect is one extreme on a continuum of maternal attachment" (p. 183).

Many of the programs emphasized supporting the relationship between a mother and her baby (Ashem & Kurz, 1988; Barnard et al., 1988; Barrera, Rosenbaum, & Cunningham, 1986; Breakey & Pratt, 1991; Halpern & Larner, 1987; Larson, 1980; Madden, O'Hara, & Levenstein, 1984; Metzl, 1980; Olds, Henderson, Tatelbaum, & Chamberlin, 1986b; Siegel et al., 1980). A variety of methods were used to increase the quality or quantity of interactions between mother and baby, and to strengthen the bond or attachment between mother and baby. Typically, the home visitor provided information and ideas to mothers about the kinds of activities that they could engage in with their babies. For instance, they taught the mothers songs, rhymes, and games they could do with their babies, or demonstrated different kinds of interactions during regular caretaking routines such as bathing, dressing, and feeding. This also often included information about infants' developmental needs, for example, beneficial kinds of physical contact, interpreting babies' cries and other clues, and understanding babies' needs.

Several programs focused on the mother and/or the family in addition to the child. In some of these programs, volunteers or paid paraprofessionals, who were similar to the parent in terms of ethnicity or socioeconomic status, played an informal, supportive role (Ashem & Kurz, 1988; Barth, 1991; Breakey & Pratt, 1991; Halpern & Covey, 1983). Other programs provided assistance to mothers around concrete needs, such as completing household chores, grocery shopping, transportation, child care, or food (Barth, 1991; Heins, Nance, & Ferguson, 1987; Olds, Henderson, Chamberlin, & Tatelbaum, 1986a; Olds, Henderson, Tatelbaum, & Chamberlin, 1986, 1988; Wieder, Poisson, Lourie, & Greenspan, 1988). A few of the programs offered training to increase the mothers' skills in accomplishing specific tasks (Barth, 1991; Breakey & Pratt, 1991; Halpern & Larner, 1987). Other programs focused on mothers' socialization, emotional development, and mental health (Barnard et al., 1988; Wieder et al., 1988), usually with the assistance of a professional home visitor.

Several of the programs reviewed were designed based upon research about supporting the development of children, particularly cognitive development in early infancy (Barrera et al., 1986; Larson, 1980; Metzl, 1980; Scarr-Salapatek & Williams, 1973). These programs usually involved visits by a trained professional, and typically followed a structured curriculum that was designed to provide opportunities for the infant to be exposed to stimuli intended to promote cognitive development.

Differences were also evident in the way the programs were structured. Elements such as the length and duration of the visits, the type of home visitor, and the training received by home visitors varied across programs.

Seven of the programs reviewed began their visits during the mothers' pregnancy (Gutelis, Kirsch, MacDonald, Brooks, & McErlean, 1977; Halpern & Larner, 1987; Heins et al., 1987; Lally, Mangione, & Honig, 1988; Larson, 1980; Olds et al., 1986a; Wieder et al., 1988). Of the other programs, the majority began visits within the first month after birth; one program (Metzl, 1980) began visits between six and eighteen weeks after birth, while another program offered some visits prenatally, and others beginning at six weeks (Larson, 1980).

The length and frequency of visits varied as well. The length of home visiting ranged from three months (Barnard et al., 1988) to five years (Breakey & Pratt, 1991; Lally et al., 1988; Wieder et al., 1988), with the majority of programs offering home visits for one to three years. Frequency ranged from twice weekly to four times per year. A unique feature of several programs was an arrangement in which visits began with greater frequency and then decreased in frequency over time (Ashem & Kurz, 1988; Barrera et al., 1986; Breakey & Pratt, 1991; Gutelis et al., 1977). The rationale for a greater number of visits in the beginning was to develop trusting relationships between home visitor and family members. The frequency of visiting was reduced to promote greater independence in the mothers and to bring the relationship to a close.

While diversity was evident in the qualifications and the characteristics of the person who visited the home, nearly all the programs included some kind of training for the home visitors prior to beginning visits with families. Many of the programs' home visitors were professionals (Barnard et al.,

1988; Barrera et al., 1986; Gutelis et al., 1977; Larson, 1980; Madden et al., 1984; Nurcombe et al., 1984; Olds et al., 1986a; Scarr-Salapatek & Williams, 1973). Of these programs, half of the visitors were nurses (Barnard et al., 1988; Gutelis et al., 1977; Nurcombe et al., 1984; Olds et al., 1986a), while the other half were visitors trained specifically for their role: social workers (Scarr-Salapatek & Williams, 1973), infant-parent therapists (Barrera et al., 1986), university undergraduates in psychology (Larson, 1980), and toy demonstrators (Madden et al., 1984).

Research Evidence

Evaluations of the impacts of health visiting programs typically assessed outcomes in three areas: (a) the relationship between parent and child, and the behaviors and attitudes of the mother; (b) the physical health of the child and child development; and (c) the incidence of child abuse and neglect.

Several studies have investigated the effect of health visiting on the relationship between the mother and the child. Barrera et al. (1983) investigated the effects of a one-year home visiting program on preterm infants. Preterm infants were randomly assigned to one of three groups: home visiting focusing on improving the child's developmental level of functioning ($n = 16$), home visiting focusing on improving the quality of interaction between parent and child ($n = 22$), and no intervention ($n = 21$). An additional group of full-term babies ($n = 24$) was also included as a second control group.

The social environment subscale of the Home Observation for the Measurement of the Environment (HOME) was used, as well as videotaped observations of parent-child interactions using a standardized recording and coding format, to measure parent-child relations. The results for the HOME showed "significantly higher maternal responsivity and variety of stimulation in the parent-infant group than in the preterm control group" (Barrera et al., 1983, p. 26). The videotaped observations of parent-infant interactions also showed that both intervention groups and the full-term group engaged in more verbal independent play than the preterm control infants, even four months after the intervention. As well, mothers of preterm control babies were less responsive to their infants than mothers in both program groups and the full-term control group.

Breakey and Pratt (1991) conducted a study involving 241 families, but with no comparison or control groups. Families who were designated as "high risk" according to a fifteen-item checklist received home visits from paraprofessionals. Weekly visits began at birth and gradually moved to once every three months by the end of five years. Home visitors used a set curriculum focusing on parent-child interaction, setting goals with families, and linking families to other resources. The study showed improvements over time in parent-child interaction. However, in the absence of comparison groups, it is impossible to know whether the improvement in these families would be different than for families not receiving these services.

Barnard et al. (1988) conducted a study that did not show any effects on parent-child relationships. One hundred eighty-five families were randomly assigned to one of three groups receiving either eight, six, or four home visits from birth to three months. Participating families were identified as having multiple risks including poverty, difficult birth history, low income, and low education. The study found no significant differences between any of the three groups at the end of the visits, or at the seven- and twenty-month follow-ups, on measures of the parent-baby relationships. However, this program provided substantially lower levels of contact and shorter duration of involvement with families than the programs reporting positive impacts.

In addition to parent-child interactions, some studies have focused on the parents' behaviors and attitudes about parenting. Barth (1991) conducted a study involving ninety-seven program families and ninety-four control families. All mothers were pregnant and were identified as having two or more risk factors of abuse according to ratings made by referring professionals. Trained paraprofessionals, who were matched with families in terms of ethnicity and social background, provided home visits twice a month from the third trimester of pregnancy to six months after birth. This study found no significant differences between control and program mothers on four different scales addressing mothers' well-being, attitudes, and parenting behavior: the Child Abuse Potential Inventory, the Center for Epidemiologic Studies Depression Scale, the State-Trait Anxiety Inventory, and the Pearlin Mastery Scale. However, once again, this program also had substantially lower levels of contact and shorter duration of involvement with families than the more successful programs.

Olds and his associates (Olds et al., 1986a, 1986b, 1988) developed and evaluated an intensive and comprehensive program of nurse home visitation for first-time mothers, most of whom were poor, low-educated, and unmarried teenagers. Women who were older than teens, better educated, and middle income were also included to reduce the stigma of participating in the program. Being poor, teenage, and a single parent were identified as being risk factors for maternal and child health problems. Four hundred women initially participated, yielding a control group of 165 and a program group of 189.

Trained nurses visited families from pregnancy until the child was two years old. The program consisted of three activities: (a) parent education about pregnancy and child development, (b) enhancing families' informal support networks by encouraging the involvement of other family members and friends, and (c) linking families to community resources. This study focused on three different types of outcomes: prenatal outcomes, postnatal outcomes, and maternal educational and life course development outcomes.

The prenatal outcomes (Olds et al., 1986a) showed that program mothers were aware of more of the community services available to them, attended childbirth education classes more frequently, received more welfare vouchers, and reported that they talked more frequently with service providers and members of their informal networks about the stresses of their pregnancy. The women who had received home visiting services also had made greater improvements in the quality of their diets, particularly for women who were smokers. As well, program women who were smokers reduced their smoking more than control group women. Olds et al. (1986b) also found that among women identified at greatest risk (poor, unmarried teenagers), observations of the mothers when their babies were ten and twenty-two months old showed that women participating in the program punished and restricted their children less frequently than their counterparts in the control group.

Finally, Olds et al. (1988) reported that, among women who did not have high school education at the beginning of the study, 59% of all program women (and 69% of teen mothers) had either graduated or enrolled in an educational program by the time their babies were six months old, compared to 27% of all control women (and 35% of teen mothers). However, at follow-ups at ten, twenty-two, and forty-six months, these differences in educational achievement had disappeared.

From the time of their babies' birth to age twenty-two months, the poor, non-teen program mothers had also worked an average of 9.17 months compared to 3.61 months for their control group counterparts. At forty-six months after birth, the poor, non-teen mothers still had worked more (16.41 versus 7.14 months) than control women. By this time, the teen mothers had also begun to work more than their control group counterparts, working an average of 14.9 months compared to 10.03 months.

Home-visited mothers also had fewer subsequent pregnancies and more time between pregnancies than control group women. Seventeen percent of program women had had a second pregnancy by the time their first child was twenty-two months compared to 51% of control group women. Among women who had subsequent children, program women had an average of 49.33 months between first and second children, compared to 37.28 months for control group women.

In summary, Olds and his associates (Olds et al., 1986a, 1986b, 1988) demonstrated a number of positive changes in mothers' attitudes and behaviors from prenatal through to their child's forty-sixth month. These positive changes were seen as suggesting a reduced risk for abuse and neglect of children. Amount of support during pregnancy and delivery, maternal diet, methods for managing children's behavior, employment, education and additional children are all factors seen as potentially influencing the likelihood of parents abusing or neglecting their children.

Supporting the findings of Olds, Henderson, Chamberlin, and Tatelbaum (.986), and Olds, Henderson, Tatelbaum, and Chamberlin (1986, 1988), Halpern and Covey (1983) conducted a qualitative evaluation of a home visiting program for adolescent mothers. The mothers were described as "socially and geographically isolated" and received weekly visits from birth to at least one year. Based on ongoing observations by home visitors, and by mothers' responses to questionnaires before and after the program, the researchers found the biggest impact was on the mothers' personal development in the areas of education and employment. They also reported experiencing improvement in mothers' knowledge of their children and mothers were observed to be more responsive to their children.

Other studies have demonstrated an impact on the child's physical health. Some studies have reported increased birth weights, and decreases in other health problems. Olds et al. (1986a), in the study described above, reported no differences between control and program women in their babies' birth weights. However, among teenage women, nearly 12% of the control group delivered their babies early (before the thirty-seventh week gestation), compared to no preterm births among program women. Heins et al. (1987) conducted a study in which 565 teenage mothers were randomly assigned to either home visiting services or to no program. Visits began during pregnancy and continued to the babies' first birthday. Visits included highly structured learning objectives, as well as meeting concrete needs such as transportation. This study found that significantly fewer program babies were low birth weight, and that there was a lower percentage of small-for-gestational-age babies among program babies compared to control babies. Scarr-Salapatek and Williams (1973) provided home visiting services to unmarried, poor, black teenage mothers with premature infants. Home visits were provided about once a week from birth to one year. The home visitor was a social worker who demonstrated a variety of methods for interacting with the infant and encouraged mothers to do the same. Fifteen women received visits and were compared to fifteen control group women. After four weeks, the researchers found that the program babies had significantly better weight gains than the control group babies. However, the authors pointed out that since there were also some in-hospital services, it was not clear whether the weight gains were due to the in-hospital or home visiting services.

Studies have examined the effect of home visiting on the child's development. Barrera et al. (1983) found, in the study described above, that preterm infants who received home visiting focusing on development of the parent-child relationship did significantly better on the Bayley Mental and Motor Scales than did preterm infants who received no home visits. As well, the

difference between the full term control and the home-visited preterm infants on the Bayley scales decreased over time, which was not true for the
preterm control infants. Metzl (1980) also found that infants who received
home visits did better on the Bayley scales. Forty middle-class families
received visits: twenty mother-only families and twenty two-parent families.
Home visitors visited three times from six to 18 weeks after birth and used
language stimulation to enhance parent-infant interaction as well as the
cognitive development of the baby. Metzl found, however, that the improvement on Bayley scores was greatest for families with both parents present.
Nurcombe et al. (1984) conducted a study in which married couples with
preterm infants participated in home visits and hospital visits from a pediatric nurse. Families received eleven visits from birth to age three months,
with a focus on increasing sensitivity of parents to infants' cues, and promot-
ing enjoyment of play. At six, twelve, and twenty-four months, there were no
significant differences in measures of infant cognition; however, significant
differences appeared at thirty-six and forty-eight months. Finally, the study
described above by Scarr-Salapatek and Williams (1973) also showed that
the babies of families who had received the home visiting services did
significantly better on a measure of infant cognition than the babies in the
control group.

The evidence that home health visiting programs for "at-risk" families
with infants have an impact on incidence of child abuse or prevention of
out-of-home placements is contradictory. Four of the best designed studies
showed opposite effects.

Gray, Cutler, Dean, and Kempe (1977) reported on a study of a home
health visiting program for families considered to be at high risk of having a
child placed outside the home. High-risk was defined in this study as the
potential for "abnormal parenting practices." Collecting and analyzing information through interviews and observations during the prenatal period,
during labor and delivery, and after the baby was born, one hundred women
were identified as having characteristics that might result in abnormal parenting practices. Half of these women were assigned to a group that received a combination of hospital services and home visits including contact
with a pediatrician, plus home visits by public health nurses or lay home
visitors. The other fifty families received no additional services following
discharge from the hospital other than those services normally available in
the community. In addition to these 100 families, another 50 families were
identified as "low-risk" and served as a second comparison group.

The study found that there was no statistically significant difference between the group receiving home visiting services and the high-risk group
receiving no services in the number of reports of abuse from the local child
abuse registry. However, five children in the "high-risk" group receiving
normal services sustained severe injuries thought to be related to abnormal

parenting practices, compared to no such injuries for either the "low-risk" group, or the "high-risk" group receiving the home visiting services. The authors concluded that:

> Immediate, effective intervention by physicians, public health nurses and/or lay health visitors can significantly decrease many "abnormal parenting practices." In this study, such intervention prevented serious injury in a 'high-risk' population. (p. 53)

The study described above by Olds et al. (1986b) also showed that home visitation by public health nurses can be effective in reducing the incidence of child abuse and neglect. Information about occurrences of child abuse and neglect was collected from child abuse registries and from other sources (agencies, neighbors, family members). Among women who were poor, unmarried, and teenage, significantly more children in the comparison group (19%) had been abused compared to children receiving home visits (4%). For women who were at lower risk (i.e., nonpoor, older than teen, and married), the differences in occurrences of child abuse did not reach statistical significance, but followed the same pattern. As well, for the comparison group, as the number of risk factors accumulated the incidence of child abuse and neglect increased. With families receiving home visits, however, the incidence of abuse and neglect remained relatively low, even in those groups at greatest risk. Olds et al. concluded that "nurse home visitors are capable of preventing . . . child abuse and neglect. The positive effects of the program were concentrated on those women at greatest risk" (p. 76).

There is a need for some caution in interpreting these results. First, the population sample was largely poor, rural, and white, and the findings may not generalize to other populations, especially in large urban and inner-city areas. Another limitation is that the nurses received very specific and intensive training, and had small, manageable caseloads, which may be difficult to replicate. The fact that much of the data was collected by the nurse home visitors suggests that there may have been a bias toward overreporting positive outcomes.

In contrast, Siegel et al. (1980) found that paraprofessional home visiting had no statistically significant impact on incidence of reported child abuse and neglect. Women who were poor, with low education, and mostly nonwhite were eligible to participate in the study if they had "uncomplicated" pregnancies, labor, and delivery, and if they delivered "normal" infants. There were 202 women who met these criteria and they were randomly assigned to one of four groups: early and extended contact plus home visiting ($n = 47$), early and extended contact ($n = 50$), home visiting ($n = 53$), and no intervention ($n = 52$). Early and extended contact consisted of mother-baby contact during the first three hours after birth and in the first several days in the hospital. Home visiting consisted of paraprofessionals visiting once in the hospital and nine more times during the first three months of the infants' lives. Home visitors were given over two hundred hours of training before the program, and ongoing weekly supervision and training during the program.

Reports of child abuse and neglect were collected from a variety of agencies and the local abuse registry and covered the time from birth until the child's first birthday. For groups receiving either the home visits or the extra mother-infant contacts or both services, there were no significant differences from the nonintervention group in occurrences of abuse or neglect. The authors noted that the brief duration of home visiting services (three months) may have been one reason why there was no impact on abuse and neglect. Another reason may have been that the visits did not begin until after the babies were born, perhaps creating difficulties for the home visitors in establishing relationships with the mothers.

Barth (1991), in a study mentioned above, also showed limited impact of a home visiting intervention on child abuse and neglect. In this study, 313 women were initially referred to the project by public health, education, and social service professionals, yielding a control group of ninety-four and a program group of ninety-seven. Using a ten-item risk checklist, plus situational risk factors such as age, income, education, relationship with child's father, number of children, and ethnicity, families were accepted to the program if they had two or more risk factors; the typical family had more than four.

Paraprofessionals, called parent consultants, visited families for approximately six months, usually from the third trimester of pregnancy to about four months postpartum. The average number of home visits was eleven with a range from six to twenty. The focus of the intervention was a task-centered approach in which parent consultants worked with families to identify areas that needed work and developed strategies to address these needs. Examples of tasks included eating two good meals per day, preparing one clean room for the baby to come home to, acquiring appropriate baby clothes and supplies, enrolling in specific programs, and arranging for repairing of essential appliances such as a refrigerator.

Only two differences were found between the program and control groups. First, the control group had a significantly greater increase in the number of unsubstantiated reports of abuse than the program group (forty-one unsubstantiated reports in the control group versus twenty for the program group). Second, the program families who had no previous abuse reports prior to program participation had lower total abuse reports after the program than their control counterparts. Other than these two findings, there were no significant differences between groups on rates of abuse or increases in rates of abuse. In fact, the program group showed a slightly higher, but not statistically significant rate of substantiated abuse reports than the control group.

The author concluded that there may be a slight primary prevention effect, but not an intervention effect; that is, the program demonstrated a decreased rate of abuse reports for families that had no prior history of abuse, but did not show differences for families that already had reported incidences of abuse.

These four home visiting programs had quite different lengths and frequencies of home visits. The program studied by Olds and his colleagues (1986a, 1986b, 1988) had weekly visits from pregnancy to the child's second birthday, for a total of about twenty-six months of visiting, and up to 120 total contacts. By contrast, the program studied by Barth (1991) only had six months of contact, with a maximum of twenty contacts, and the program examined by Siegel et al. (1980) had only ten contacts over three months. Second, the content of the interventions and the roles of the home visitors were different. For example, the program studied by Olds and his associates 1986b, 1988) focused on a set curriculum and approach that looked at parent education, improving informal supports, and links to community resources, while the program examined by Barth (1991) focused on task identification and accomplishment. Another major difference between these programs, which is related to the differences in the duration and frequency of contacts, may well be the development of a positive relationship with the home visitor. A third important distinction may be the type of person doing the intervention. The program studied by Olds et al. (1986b, 1988) employed professional nurse home visitors, while the programs investigated by Barth (1991) and Siegel et al. (1980) used paraprofessional visitors. Barth (1991) concluded from his results that the lack of effect may be due to the fact that "paraprofessionals may be overmatched by the multiple problems of families" (p. 372). Well-trained and highly skilled workers may be important contributors to the success of home health visiting programs.

It may be that a minimum number of contacts needs to be part of a home health visiting program in order to provide adequate levels of support and to allow meaningful relationships to develop between home visitors and families. For the more intensive and long-term programs, there is evidence that such home visiting programs can reduce the incidence of child abuse, at least in the short term. There is some evidence that in order to make a difference, these interventions should also include a variety of supports. For instance, the program studied by Olds et al. (1986, 1988) focused on building informal support and linking to other community resources.

The importance of establishing relationships was also highlighted by Heinicke, Beckwith, and Thompson (1988), who reviewed twenty studies investigating early interventions with families. Their review found that eight of the twenty programs used a home visiting approach. They commented that:

> [this] does reflect a certain duration of contact in permitting the development of a relationship. In the studies reviewed, the development of an ongoing relationship occurred most frequently with a home visitor. (Heinicke et al., 1988, p. 136)

They also found that the relationship formed between the intervenor and the family was the only variable to have a statistically significant effect on achieving positive outcomes:

> [A] significantly greater number of effects in different areas of family function-ing was reported when the contact with the family began early in the infant's life (before 3 months and typically right after birth), lasted for at least 3 months, and involved at least 11 contacts. (p. 135)

Overall, our review shows that home health visiting sometimes produces significant improvements in prenatal care, in postnatal outcomes such as mother-child interactions, parenting attitudes, childbirth weight, child men-tal and motor development, and the social and economic lives of the moth-ers. Perhaps most directly relevant to child welfare, the review showed that home visiting, if the program is intensive and of long duration, may reduce rates of child abuse and neglect among program participants.

Summary: Home Health Visitors

Home health visitor programs visit parents (generally first-time mothers) who are expecting or recently have had a baby. The primary focus of most programs is on improving the quality of mother-child relationships and the physical care and cognitive stimulation of the infants. Trained visitors pro-vide information to mothers, model new behaviors, and assist the mothers in learning to implement these practices with their babies. Many programs also emphasize providing emotional support and encouragement to mothers about their parenting responsibilities and other areas of their lives. Some programs encourage the mothers to link with available community re-sources and support their connections with friends and families. Home health visitor programs have been used with a variety of disadvantaged populations, including many parents considered to be at "high-risk" of mal-treating their infant.

There has been great variation in the programming parameters of home health visitor programs. Many programs began home visiting during preg-nancy, but some began visiting within a month of the birth of the child.

Programs ranged in duration from a few months to five years. Parents received visits once a week in some programs and four times a year in others. Many, but not all programs followed a structured curriculum in instructing and informing parents. Some programs used highly trained professionals (usually nurses), while others employed paraprofessionals. Most programs provided specialized training in home visiting for their visitors.

Home health visitors programs have been the subject of more extensive and convincing evaluation research than most other types of support programs. Home health visitor programs that have produced clearer benefits for children and for mothers have tended to be more intensive (three to four times a month) and of longer duration (one to three years). Initial contact with mothers was established during pregnancy. There is some suggestion that professional and highly trained home visitors produced better results than paraprofessional visitors. There also is some evidence that programs that included more types of support (e.g., emotional support to mother for her own career and educational goals, linkages to community services, encouraging informal support) produced more positive changes for families.

The Range of Supports Available: Home health visitor programs with weekly face-to-face contact with mothers and children should be able to provide a moderate range of supports to families. Research evidence suggests that the main supports will be information and education about child development and caring for an infant, as well as emotional support to the mother in her parenting role. A few programs also emphasize linking the mother and child with available informal and formal supports in the community. As with the IFPS programs, reliance upon a single helper may limit the range of supports home health visitor programs can provide directly to families. There may be variation in the supports provided from home visitor to home visitor; however, this variability may be less in programs following predetermined educational and child stimulation curricula with families.

The Level of Support Available: The more intensive home health visitor programs would visit families from two to four times a month. This moderate level of support may be supplemented in some programs by linking families with additional community services and supports.

Availability in a Crisis: Home health visitor programs were not described as rapid response or as crisis intervention programs. Rather, they have been used as early intervention or prevention programs reaching out to disadvantaged families prior to a serious crisis developing. None of the programs reviewed served families in which child abuse and neglect had already been substantiated. This early contact with families is a unique feature of this support program model.

Motivation and Skill Requirements: Actively reaching out to disadvantaged families and providing services to families in their own homes is an advantage for home health visitor programs in serving "hard-to-reach" families. In addition, providing assistance to families in less threatening and less stigmatizing ways should make home health visitor services more acceptable to many disadvantaged families. The program does seem to be best suited for parents willing to participate and who have some ability to learn the program concepts and skills. However, focusing on new parents during pregnancy or immediately after the child is born should maximize parents' motivation to have a home health visitor. Early intervention and acceptable service formats to disadvantaged families seem to be major strengths of the program model.

Focused Expertise: Home health visitor programs seem very well suited to bringing expertise on parenting, child development, nutrition and health, child development, and infant care to families. This may be particularly true for programs using specially trained professional home visitors (generally nurses). This is a strength of the program model.

The Length of Time Support Available: Many of the home health visitor programs reviewed provided supports to families for one to three years. This ability to provide relatively long-term support to families during critical early years of child development and parent-child attachment is a substantial strength of the home health visitor program model.

Reciprocity and Social Integration: The home health visitor programs were not designed to increase positive informal social support or meaningful social integration for family members. These programs did not emphasize family members doing for themselves or being helpers for others in similar circumstances or developing connections with peers. These are important limitations of home health visitor programs.

Anticipated Program Impacts and Rationales: Home health visitor programs that connect with disadvantaged mothers during their pregnancies and provide intensive services for one or more years through well-trained home visitors have been associated with impressive benefits to families. These programs through their instruction and emotional support to mothers have consistently produced improvement in mother-child interactions and in parenting attitudes and behaviors. Through early connections with mothers, by providing child development and health information and instruction, and by modeling and encouraging infant stimulation activities, these programs have often resulted in less premature and low-birth-weight and -size babies and in increased mental and motor skill development in infants. There is also some evidence that the more intensive programs may reduce the frequency of child abuse and neglect in participating families. One of the more intensive programs that also focused on the mothers' personal development reported greater awareness and use of community resources, better maternal diets, and greater maternal employment or attendance in school. Several programs reported fewer subsequent pregnancies for participating mothers. Finally, because of early intervention, it may be that intensive and ongoing home health visitor programs reduce subsequent use of professional services by lowering the incidence of future family problems. There were no cost-benefit studies available on these home health visitor programs. However, on face value, they seem to be promising economic investments.

PARENT AIDE PROGRAMS[1]

Parent aide programs characteristically have been developed under the auspices of a child welfare agency as a supplement to traditional protection services (Alexander & Kempe, 1982; Cameron & Rothery, 1985; Hornick & Clarke, 1986; Miller, Fein, Howe, Gaudieo, & Bishop, 1984; Rosenstein, 1978; Zimrim, 1984). The parent aide model uses nonprofessionals as home visitors. Zimrim (1984) has suggested that this is a less costly intervention, which may prove as effective as standard child welfare services. In support of Zimrim's statement, there are studies that suggest that paraprofessionals may be as effective as professionals in helping clients. For example, Hattie, Sharpley, and Rogers (1984) performed a meta-analysis of the comparative effectiveness of professional and paraprofessional helpers in thirty-nine studies and concluded that "paraprofessionals are at least as effective, and in many instances more effective, than professional counsellors" (p. 540). Furthermore, there is also evidence that natural helpers (friends and peers) may be effective in helping child welfare clientele solve their problems (Ballew, 1985; see also Chapters 3 and 4 in this volume).

Numerous authors have suggested that the help received from parent aides may be substantially different than that received from professionals. The diminished social distance between helper and family may result in reduced stigmatization and increased trust (Zimrim, 1984). Parent aides often are more readily available to clients in times of crisis and sometimes are on call twenty-four hours each day (Alexander & Kempe, 1982; Epstein & Shainline, 1974). Unhindered by professional obligations and professional definitions of helping, the parent aide may be free to provide a wide range of supports including concrete support with household chores and child care. Finally, and perhaps most significantly, the parent aide has been described as being primarily concerned with helping the parent (Lines, 1987).

Program Parameters

Parent aide programs tend to vary with respect to the criteria for selecting a home visitor. A number of programs have asserted that personal qualities such as warmth, empathy, emotional stability, and experience as a parent are the most important qualities in selecting a parent aide (Alexander & Kempe, 1982; Cameron & Rothery 1985; Carol & Reich, 1978; Miller et al., 1984). Other programs, while acknowledging the importance of personal qualities, have suggested that parent aides should be selected on the basis of specific socioeconomic or demographic characteristics. For example, Zimrim (1984) suggested that parent aides should be of similar socio-economic status as the primary caregivers. Others (Arch, 1978; Harnett, 1989) have asserted that older adults, over fifty-five, are well-suited to the parent aide role due to their important life experiences. In addition, Epstein and Shainline (1974) have reported that former social service recipients are uniquely qualified to fulfill the parent aide role due to their intimate knowledge of the social service system.

Another question is whether parent aides should be paid or unpaid. Some programs used volunteer parent aides and have suggested that these programs hold the best potential in cost savings (Harnett, 1989; Zimrim, 1984; Lines, 1987). Programs using unpaid helpers are reviewed in Chapter 9. The parent aide programs discussed in this chapter have relied upon paid parent aides (Cameron & Rothery, 1985; Carol & Reich, 1978; Hornick & Clarke, 1986; Miller et al., 1984).

Overall, there was agreement that the most important quality of a parent aide is an ability to develop supportive relationships with family members. None of the programs reviewed stressed formal education or training as a prerequisite for choosing a parent aide. However, virtually every program provided some form of initial orientation and ongoing training. The content, duration, and intensity of this training varied greatly across programs.

The goals of parent aide programs were most commonly described in global terms, and often sounded more like helping strategies than outcomes. A number of studies have described the goal of parent aide programs as parenting or nurturing the parent (Alexander & Kempe, 1982; Cameron & Rothery 1985; Hornick & Clarke, 1986; Rosenstein, 1978). It has been suggested that child abuse is rooted in the unhappy childhood of the parents; therefore, these individuals will require long-term nurturing to relinquish their distrust of others and to overcome their emotional problems (Alexander & Kempe, 1982; Hornick & Clarke, 1986). Others described the primary goal of parent aide programs as developing a friendship with the parent (Carol & Reich, 1978; Zimrim, 1984). While the practical differences between parenting and befriending a parent were not clear, the latter seemed to prescribe a more reciprocal relationship between the parent and the parent aide. There did appear to be a general consensus that a primary purpose of the parent aide was to provide emotional support to the parent.

The work of the parent aide has been described as providing various types of assistance:

1. modeling parenting behavior (Arch, 1978; Cameron & Rothery, 1985; Hornick & Clarke, 1986; Miller et al., 1984);
2. providing knowledge of community resources (Carol & Reich, 1978; Rosenstein, 1978);
3. offering counsel and guidance (Alexander & Kempe, 1982; Epstein & Shainline, 1974; Miller et al., 1984);
4. supplying concrete supports such as housekeeping and child care (Alexander & Kempe, 1982; Cameron & Rothery, 1985; Epstein & Shainline, 1974; Zimrim, 1984);
5. teaching parenting and homemaking skills (Cameron & Rothery, 1985; Hornick & Clarke, 1986; Rosenstein, 1978);
6. identifying goals with parents (Rosenstein, 1978);
7. mobilizing parent strengths (Miller et al., 1984);
8. providing crisis support (Alexander & Kempe, 1982; Cameron & Rothery, 1985).

The role of the parent aide has been delineated in the literature from that of a child protection worker: the parent aide has not been responsible for making independent service decisions and has not been expected to provide legal protection services for the child (Alexander & Kempe, 1982; Carol & Reich, 1978). However, child protection workers have played a role in parent aide programs. In most programs, parent aides were supervised by child protection workers (and sometimes by additional staff hired to coordinate or supervise the parent aide program), and child protection workers generally worked together with the parent aide and the family to establish goals and to monitor progress.

Few descriptions of parent aide programs included detailed information about the frequency and duration of contact with families. When this information was available, the actual amount of face-to-face contact between the parent aide and the family members varied widely across program reviews supplying this data—estimates ranged from approximately thirteen hours per month (Cameron & Rothery, 1985) to thirty-six hours per month (Zimrim, 1984). The average duration of parent aide involvement was six to eight months in Cameron and Rothery's studies (1985), but ranged from three months (Miller et al., 1984; Zimrim, 1984) to three years (Alexander & Kempe, 1982) in other programs. Another characteristic of parent aide programs was the fairly low caseloads for parent aides compared to the number of cases for most child welfare caseworkers. Cameron and Rothery (1985) reported that parent aides in their studies were typically involved with a small number of cases—two or three families at a time. Most of the remaining programs reported average caseloads of two to three families, but some reported average caseloads as high as six (Hornick & Clarke, 1986). Factors such as the duration and level of involvement are likely to play an important role in determining the impacts that can reasonably be expected of different parent aide programs.

Research Evidence

A review of the literature revealed few rigorous research studies on the effectiveness of parent aide programs. Many program descriptions included case examples as evidence of the positive impact of the programs (Arch, 1978; Epstein & Shainline, 1974; Harnett, 1989; Lines, 1987). Still other programs cited increased referrals and case closures as indications of effectiveness (Miller et al., 1984; Rosenstein, 1978). While these sources suggest encouraging results for the parent aide model, it is difficult to come to any strong conclusions on the basis of these predominantly descriptive reports.

However, a number of studies have attempted to demonstrate the impacts of the parent aide model for child-abusing and disadvantaged families. Carol and Reich (1978) reported on the Parent Aide Project, which began in Phoenix in 1974. Five parent aides were hired, each for twenty hours of service per week. The parent aides were given training, focusing on developing skills in relationship building, listening, and problem solving. Families were referred by the state child protective service and an effort was made to select families who would offer "realistic" challenges for the parent aides: not too difficult so as to frustrate and overwhelm the parent aide, but hard enough to challenge them. Carol and Reich (1978) concluded that their program was effective since it resulted in 85% of the participants discontinuing their abusive behavior; 20% of the families who did not receive parent aide services had to be re-referred to protective services.

Miller et al. (1984) described a parent aide program that emphasized short-term service focusing on setting goals with the participating families. Thirty-seven families completed the program in its first eighteen months of operation. Families were referred by a variety of service agencies and the majority of families were poor and headed by single mothers. Professionals worked closely with the parent aides to assist them in setting clear and realistic goals with families. A major part of the program was a contract between the family and the parent aide, which limited the program to three months. However, there was flexibility based on families' needs, as indicated by the fact that in 24% of the cases, service was extended beyond three months.

The study examined the goal attainment ratings made by parent aides and child welfare workers on indices of parenting, personal functioning, daily living, social resources, and community resources. Miller et al. found that on a scale of −10 (much worse) to +10 (goal completely achieved) the average rating for all thirty-seven families in all goals was +5.6. The area that had the largest number of goals was parenting. The data also showed that the greatest success was in the area of social resources (average rating of +6.0) and the least success was in the area of community resources (+4.6). Miller et al. concluded that two features of their program were important: the use of the professional in teamwork with the parent aide to supervise the service, and the focus on short-term service.

In a study designed to investigate the cost effectiveness of the parent aide model, Hornick and Clarke (1986) examined data collected from social workers, parent aides, and disadvantaged mothers on 17 indices related to parental nurturance, attitudes and beliefs, and parent behavior ratings. Parent aides in this program were called Supportive Home Helpers and had an average caseload of six families. The main goals of the home helpers were to provide nurturance to the mothers, to act as a parenting model, and to teach homemaking skills.

Parents who had abused their children or were considered at risk of abusing their children were randomly assigned to receive the home helper services ($n = 27$) or standard child welfare services ($n = 28$) for a period of twelve months. Data were collected before program involvement, at six months and at twelve months. The results showed that the two groups of families improved at both six- and twelve-month intervals. However, families receiving home helper services showed a slightly greater improvement, and fewer had dropped out of the program (24%) at twelve months than families receiving standard services (50%).

A cost analysis of the program showed that home helpers spent an average of 17.46 hours per month per family. In comparison, social workers spent an average of 5.54 hours per month with standard services families, and only 3.16 hours per month with home helper clients. Despite the time saved by social workers with home helper families, the lay therapy approach was more expensive ($255 per family per month compared to $93 for standard service families) due to the greater amount of time spent on each case. Unfortunately, no information about program impacts on child placements or cost-savings from averted placements was provided in this study.

Cameron and Rothery's (1985) evaluation of the Parent Aide Program in Hamilton, Ontario, revealed a high level of client satisfaction as well as very optimistic appraisals by key informants involved with the program. Parent aides were hired by a child welfare agency to provide more service time to families than child protection workers were able to provide. Parent aides were paid and were supervised by a parent aide coordinator, in conjunction with the child protection worker assigned to the family. Parent aides received twenty-six hours of training over thirteen weeks before beginning work with families, as well as ongoing monthly training and supervision. The parent aide, child protection worker, and parent(s) met to draw up a written contract outlining specific goals. Each parent aide had two to three cases at a time, and the average case was open for seven months. The parent aide program was made available only to families with young children, and did not include families with adolescents.

The evaluation of this program was based on a sample of sixteen families who received parent aide services, and comparisons were made with a similar group of families from the same agency receiving normal services (n = 28), and with a sample of cases from the same region (n = 107). Compared to the same agency group, the parent aide cases showed significantly more improvement on workers' ratings of indices of parent-child relationships, antisocial/delinquent child behavior, and child behavioral/emotional problem. However, compared to the larger, same region group, the only significant difference was on the index of inadequate parent-child relationships. This evaluation also showed that the number of placements was significantly lower for the parent aide families compared to the same agency group, but showed no significant difference compared to the same region group. The authors conclude that, "considering the relatively small size of the Parent Aide Program sample [n = 16], these patterns are merely suggestive and not conclusive" (p. 163).

In addition to these measures, the authors also interviewed key program informants. Program informants reported a high level of client satisfaction with the program. As well, an examination of termination reports indicated that parent aides and child protection workers considered that 77% of the families had partially or completely accomplished the goals that had been set. The authors also calculated the costs of the program and provided an analysis of the cost per case. Using 1983–1984 Canadian dollars, they calculated the cost per case served as $1,030.93 over an average case length of seven months. This cost per case was found to be quite low compared to seven other family support program approaches that the authors assessed at the same time.

Cameron and Rothery (1985) evaluated a similar Homemaker Program in which paid homemakers were hired by a child welfare agency to work with families. Like the Parent Aide Program, the Homemaker Program staff worked with an agency supervisor and the family to develop specific, short-term goals for working with the family. Homemakers had two to three cases at a time. Nearly 80% of families received services for six months or less, indicating that the service was mostly a short-term intervention. The families served were also similar to the parent aide families: mostly poor, young mothers with limited formal education, and many with young children. However, unlike the Parent Aide Program, the Homemaker Program families included adolescents, and there were not as many single-parent families.

The results for this program were less promising than for the Parent Aide Program. The Homemaker families ($n = 16$) showed no significant differences between a comparison group of families from the same region that received normal child welfare services ($n = 125$) on any of the variables that showed change for the Parent Aide families. In a cost analysis, the Homemaker Program was found to be less expensive than the Parent Aide Program, costing $748 (1983–1984 Canadian dollars) per case episode. The authors concluded that:

> [T]he best that can be said from this analysis of case results for the Homemaker Program sample is that some support may be provided to high problem families in periods of high stress. There is no indication of a lower rate of child placement than the comparison groups. (p. 187)

Cameron and Rothery's (1985) studies demonstrated the difficulty in making generalizations regarding the parent aide model. While a casual examination might have shown the two programs to be highly similar, there were in fact marked differences in presenting problems, client characteristics, level and duration of involvement, program interventions, and program administration. The authors felt that these could be important factors in determining the somewhat contradictory outcomes of the two studies.

The present review of the literature found no convincing assessments of parent aide programs. The studies that have been conducted typically involved very small samples, making it difficult to draw conclusions about the relevance of the outcomes to the larger child welfare populations. The time periods covered by the studies were generally of short duration and provided no information about the longevity of changes. Finally, few of the studies included information regarding service content or the structural dimensions of service provisions—variables that may have a significant impact on the outcome of these programs.

The parent aide model may prove to be a significantly different and useful approach to the protection of children and the support of disadvantaged families. As with other models, its effectiveness will likely depend on the situations in which the program is used and whether it is of adequate intensity and duration. However, the information available in the literature is presently of little help in supporting or disproving these expectations.

Our review found many descriptive reports that held that these programs may be beneficial, as well as some outcome studies providing very modest evidence that parent aide programs can result in improvements on a number of indices such as parent-child relationships, parental functioning, and home management. These studies generally failed, however, to demonstrate that these programs were instrumental in reducing child maltreatment or child placement. The one exception was Zimrim (1984), who reported a substantial drop in abusive behavior of parents from program involvement but noted that gains in reducing child abuse soon disappeared following the withdrawal of the home visits. This suggests that involvement with an appropriate parent aide program may temporarily deter child maltreatment and child placement; however, a parent aide program should not be perceived as a substitute for ongoing supports.

SUMMARY: PARENT AIDE PROGRAMS

Parent aide programs characteristically have been created by child welfare agencies to supplement the work of child protection personnel. These programs used paraprofessionals as home visitors. These paraprofessionals were paid for their work and received specific training for their home visiting roles. The rationale for the use of paraprofessional home visitors, who often were chosen to have social, cultural, and economic characteristics in common with the families visited, was that the diminished social distance between helpers and families resulted in increased trust and less stigmatization. Parent aides did not assume legal child protection responsibilities and were described as being less threatening to families than child protection workers.

Parent aides supported parents. Parent aides were involved in teaching and modeling parenting and homemaking skills, assisting with household chores and child care, informing family members about community resources, and providing emotional supports to parents. Some programs reportedly used parent aides to provide crisis supports to families. Parent aides were usually supervised by child protection staff and cooperated with child protection workers in setting goals for their work with families. Parent aides generally worked with two to six families at one time. Services typically lasted between three and seven months (range: three months to three years). The evaluated programs reported between thirteen and thirty-five hours a month of work per case (how much of this time was face-to-face contact was not clarified). There were great differences in the types of family situations in which parent aides intervened. This variability in the ways parent aides were used and in the structural dimensions of parent aide service delivery make it difficult to draw conclusions about this program model.

There are research reviews that suggest that paraprofessionals visiting can be profitably used to support troubled families. Generally, paraprofessional helping has been used to supplement rather than replace professional help-ing. Paraprofessional helping may also be a comparatively inexpensive way of supporting families. However, the research on parent aide programs tells us little. No rigorous evaluations were found in this review. The results from the small number of weak-design studies reviewed generally showed few markedly superior benefit for families from their involvements with parent aides. The literature provided limited insights into how parent aides or para-professional home visitors should be used to support disadvantaged families or the kinds of benefits for families that can be reasonably expected from involvement with parent aides.

NOTE

1.   This section is based substantially on information that has been updated from Bidgood and van de Sande (1990).

Parent Training Programs in Child Welfare   8

INTRODUCTION

For the majority of adults, the job that requires the most time with the least training is parenting. The inadequacy of parenting abilities has been considered by many in child welfare as one of the primary causes of child abuse and neglect (Whiteman, Fanshel, & Grundy, 1987; Wolfe, Sandler, & Kaufman, 1981). Many parents are seen as having insufficient knowledge about child development, as lacking the skills to deal with the challenges of their children's difficult behaviors, and as being unable to handle the frustrations that are part of all child rearing. As a result, numerous programs have been developed to teach parents how to be a parent in the hopes that increased parenting abilities will result in decreased incidence of child abuse and neglect. This chapter reviews what has been published about the effectiveness of parent training programs for child welfare populations. Only studies that have sound research designs, that report outcomes of specific programs, and that focus on child welfare have been included.

The parent training approach explicitly breaks from psychiatric approaches which are seen as seeking the cause for abuse in the psychopathology of the parent. The primary theoretical model supporting the parent training approach is rooted in the principles of behaviorism. More specifically, social learning theory suggests that the maltreating parent has been unable to learn the kinds of skills necessary to raise children in a nonabusive manner. Rather, the parent has learned many abusive parenting strategies and these are reinforced by the ongoing interactions between parent and children. This viewpoint also has been referred to as social situational theory or social interactional theory (Egan, 1983), perspectives that highlight the importance of the context and interactions in precipitating and maintaining patterns of abusive behavior. Brunk, Henggeler, and Whelan (1987) also have suggested that ecological theory supports the use of parent training. They emphasized the importance of viewing problem behaviors in a family in a larger context including the background of the parents, family relationships with extended family, and the broader cultural values that influence child rearing.

This review of parent training programs revealed two major parent training approaches. One approach focuses on teaching parents skills and techniques to manage their children's difficult behaviors. The assumption of these programs is that parents abuse their children because they do not have the knowledge to parent their children nonabusively. Lacking the appropriate skills, such parents are seen as resorting to abusive behavior when faced with crises such as difficulties with their children or marital conflicts (Wolfe et al., 1981). A second group of programs focuses on teaching parents to handle the stress and anger that, when unchecked, lead to abusive behaviors. Anger has been identified as a frequent antecedent of abusive behavior (Whiteman et al., 1987). While acknowledging the many other factors that lead to child abuse, this approach suggests that, since anger is so closely tied to abusive behavior, it provides an advantageous point at which to intervene.

PROGRAM PARAMETERS

Parent training approaches vary widely in the types of curricula that are used. However, several characteristics of the programs reviewed are fairly consistent. Most of the programs in this review used group training formats. These programs provided regular training sessions—usually once a week—which lasted from four to ten weeks. Each session typically was one to two hours long and contained a number of common elements. Most sessions began with the presentation of a new skill, usually by the group leader. Often this included a review of material that would be assigned to the parents as homework or of reading material from previous sessions. Group discussion of the skill often followed the presentation. Finally, the group would take time to practice the skills in role play situations. Between sessions, parents were often instructed to practice new skills at home, and then report their progress and experiences at the next session. A feature of some programs was that the group leader, or a child protection worker, would visit the parent in the home and provide feedback, suggestions, and monitoring of new skills. As well, workers would demonstrate parenting methods with the children while the parent watched, and then give the parent the opportunity to try. The parent trainers were typically undergraduate or graduate students who had education and work experience in child management and who had been trained specifically in how to train parents and lead groups.

Our review revealed two major variations in the parent training service delivery methods. One variation was where the training was done at an agency and parents would come to the group. The other variation was home-based training. In this approach, parents would be trained individually at home, or in groups at an agency location and then worked with individually at home.

A few programs added elements to support parents in other ways (Barth, Blythe, Schinke, & Schilling, 1983; Brunk et al., 1987). One program emphasized facilitating social interaction among group members and providing structured child care for children while the parents were in the group (Burch & Mohr, 1980). Another program provided "agency based support services," which included child care activities for children and social groups for parents with arts and crafts and other activities (Wolfe, Edwards, Manion, & Koverola, 1988).

RESEARCH EVIDENCE

As mentioned, training programs designed to teach parents how to manage their children's difficult behavior have been offered in homes as well as in agency settings. In some cases, programs have been designed to offer a combination of in-home and agency-based training (for example, Wolfe et al., 1981; Wolfe & Sandler, 1981). Other than the difference in the setting for training, many characteristics of the programs appeared similar; nonetheless, the research evidence for in-home and agency-based training programs in child management will be looked at separately.

IN-HOME CHILD MANAGEMENT TRAINING

One of the earliest studies of the impact of home-based parent training was conducted by Tracy and his colleagues in the early seventies (Tracy, Ballard, & Clark, 1975). Forty-one families were involved, eleven of whom had children identified as abused, and 30 who were identified as being at risk for being abused. Nearly 75% of the children were three years or younger, 30% of the mothers were twenty years or younger, and 65% of the families were headed by a single parent. The program involved family health workers visiting the family at home to teach them techniques for managing their children's behavior using the principles of social learning theory. The workers discussed problem areas with the family and identified behaviors that would be addressed.

For research purposes, the specific behaviors were clustered into concerns, resulting in a total of 129 concerns for all forty-one families. Observations by workers, clinical reports, and verbal reports from others were used to determine the frequency of behaviors. To determine program effectiveness, the various concerns were rated, based on the behavior frequency counts, as worse, same, improved, much improved, or unknown. Of the

129 total concerns, 84% were rated as improved or much improved, and 9% as worse or the same. As well, worker observations revealed that "with few exceptions, mothers of these children improved their techniques of controlling the children using less physical punishment" (p. 399). The authors acknowledged the limitations of the study because of the lack of a comparison group, stating that it was unethical to provide no program for families whose children were at risk of abuse.

Christopherson (1979) reported on the effectiveness of a training program with "high-risk" parents. The Family Training Program (FTP) was designed as an intensive, home-based, family-centered intervention for children with behavior disorders. FTP involved three phases. First, the service provider intervened with the child in the presence of the parents to demonstrate effective behavior management techniques. Next, the parents implemented the techniques while the service provider monitored the parents' performance. In the third phase, the service provider had only occasional contact with the parents in order to assure maintenance of the gains. The authors reported that an earlier study of FTP with a group of thirty-four children with behavioral problems showed that FTP children had greater behavior improvements than children who received clinic-based behavior intervention. These children also showed statistically significant improvements three years after the FTP had ended.

FTP was adapted for abusive families by including additional support services such as financial planning, homemaker services, and advice on food preparation. These families also required more contact time, averaging eighty hours of contact per family over a three-month period, compared to twenty-six hours for the behavior problem children and fifty-seven for a young offender group. The authors found that the "recidivism rate" (not defined in the study) was 18% for FTP families, compared to 30% for families who refused FTP and were referred to more traditional child abuse support groups in the community. However, the use of a comparison group that had refused FTP services opens the door to the possibility that other factors, for instance, greater motivation or an increased willingness to change, were responsible for the observed improvements.

Two studies demonstrated the potential of in-home parent training approaches for reducing aversive behaviors considered to be related to actual abusive behavior (Denicola & Sandler, 1980; Wolfe & Sandler, 1981). Due to difficulties in observing actual abusive behavior, the researchers focused on behaviors that they linked conceptually to abusive behavior. The two studies employed similar designs in which baseline rates of aversive behavior were compared to rates during and after families' participation in training programs.

Small numbers of families participated in the studies ($n = 2$; $n = 3$). All the families had incidents of substantiated abuse. The families were poor, unemployed, and most were headed by single mothers. The families were observed in the home over a number of sessions to determine a baseline of the parents' aversive behaviors. Behaviors were coded and rated according to specified procedures.

Following the baseline assessment, families participated voluntarily in weekly training sessions and home observations for eight to twelve weeks. The training consisted of reading assignments, practicing various child management techniques, reviewing and discussing experiences with a professional, and contracting for specific goals and tasks. The results showed that the rates of aversive behaviors were reduced compared to baseline levels, and that this reduction was maintained at follow-ups of three and twelve months. Although these results seem promising, they are limited by the fact that there was no comparison group. As well, the authors acknowledged that the attention received from the trainers, independent of the actual parent training, may have had an influence on parents' aversive behavior. Finally, the very small sample sizes make it impossible to generalize these findings.

In contrast to these studies, Cameron and Rothery (1985) conducted evaluations of two in-home child management training programs that failed to demonstrate significant impacts. These programs were offered within child welfare agencies and were "considered to be both a complement and an alternative to child protection casework" (p. 251). Both programs involved the use of child care staff who had formal child management training experience, as well as experience working with troubled children and families. The programs were perceived to be preventing out-of-home placements of children. Child care workers carried an average of 10 cases each, but in one program the average caseload rose to 13.5 when resources for mainline child protection services were decreased.

A review of these programs showed that the child management services received very positive appraisals from participating parents and other professionals involved with the program. However, these positive assessments by program informants were not supported by data on a variety of indices of parent and child functioning, or on rates of placement. Compared to samples of similar families who did not receive child management services but did receive regular child welfare services ($n = 116$; $n = 163$), the authors found no significant differences from comparison families on a variety of parent and child indices including inadequate parent-child relationship, antisocial/delinquent child behavior, parental functioning, and child emotional and behavioral problems for the two groups who received the child management services ($n = 21$; $n = 24$). These comparisons also showed no statistically significant differences in the rates of out-of-home placements: in one program 20% of program cases had been placed compared to 27% of comparison cases; in the other program 17% of program cases were placed compared to 25% of comparison cases.

The inability of these programs to demonstrate clear positive impacts compared to traditional child protection services may be due to the lack of substantial differences between the types and levels of services provided by the child management programs and traditional child protection services. Although the goals of the programs were to provide parents with the skills and the intensive, personal support that would enable them to keep their children in the home, the authors noted that, in practice, the assistance provided by the programs was not markedly different from the services offered by child protection workers. For instance, in 45–50% of the cases, the child management workers had the "sole responsibility" for the family; in these cases, the services offered were essentially the same as those provided by regular child protection workers. As well, the average number of hours of direct contact per month, 7.36 hours in one program and 8 hours in the other was quite low compared to the six other types of support programs also assessed by the authors in this study. As the authors concluded:

> [I]t is reasonable to wonder whether any superior positive results should be expected [and] to ask whether the actual helping provided by the child care workers is, in fact, substantially different from the assistance provided by the child protection workers. (p. 240)

A number of studies have suggested that parent training tends to be unsuccessful with socioeconomically disadvantaged mothers. Szykula and Fleischman (1985) described two studies that examined the impact of social learning treatment on placement rates for families suspected of child abuse. Although not explicitly stated, the description of the social learning program suggests that it was a combination of in-home and agency-based training. The social learning training program involved fifteen to twenty-five hours of instruction in which parents were taught to observe and record specific child behaviors, and then were taught how to respond to such behaviors. Components included the use of "timeouts," "shaping," and "problem-solving." Parents' progress was monitored by trainers. Parents were required to practice new skills at home and report their experiences to the trainer. Trainers had undergraduate or graduate education.

The first study was a design in which a baseline was established, then the program was offered for nine months. The parents (number of parents not given) in this study were mostly poor, with half of the families headed by a single parent. The authors found that during the program the level of out-of-home placements dropped 83%, but then returned to previous levels after the program was ended. The authors stated that in this type of design, when a variable shows a marked change at onset, and then reverts to previous levels when withdrawn, "it is appropriate to conclude that the intervention was responsible for the change" (p. 279).

In the second study, parents with children considered to be at risk of out-of-home placement were randomly assigned to receive either the social learning training or regular agency services. Parents were of low socio-economic status, with 68% single mothers. A distinction was also made between "less difficult" and "more difficult" cases. Less difficult cases (*n* = 26) were those which had two or fewer reports of abuse, no serious difficulties with housing or transportation, and where the major problem in the family was considered to be the child's behavior. More difficult cases (*n* = 22) were those which had three or more reports of abuse, had serious problems with unemployment, had inconsistent transportation and housing, and were identified as having major problems in addition to the child's behavior. In the less difficult group, there were significantly fewer placements among training families (one out of thirteen, 8%) compared to control families (five out of thirteen, 38%). However, there was no significant difference between placements for children of the more difficult parents. These results suggest that social learning training may be effective among parents for whom child management is the major problem. However, for families that face a variety of challenges, social learning training by itself may not be as effective.

The work of Wahler and his colleagues also implies that parent training may be less effective with parents confronting multiple problems. Wahler (1980b) conducted a study on the impacts of parent training for eighteen mother-child dyads who were identified as "insular." Wahler defined insularity as "a specific pattern of social contacts within the community that is characterized by a high level of negatively perceived coercive interchanges with kinfolk and/or helping agency representatives" (Dumas & Wahler, 1983, p. 302). All of the mothers had sought professional help for child behavior problems and had expressed a strong desire to improve both their child's behavior and their relationship with their child. The program began with four to six weeks during which program staff—graduate level students who had received specific training—observed parent-child interactions in the home. Following this baseline phase, the program staff then provided service that involved a combination of in-home and agency-based sessions teaching the parent how to deal with the problem behaviors that had been identified during the baseline phase. The follow-up portion of the service involved in-home visits twice per week, during which observations were done, as well as opportunities created for program staff to review the parents' progress and provide additional instruction and encouragement. Service was followed by an eight- to twelve-month research phase in which parent-child interactions were observed. During this phase, program staff did not provide further instructions or prompting, but were available twice a month for advice if the parents asked for it.

Two areas were measured: the amount of insularity, as measured by a scale developed by the authors, and the behaviors of the mother and the child, measured by the Standardized Observation Codes. The results indicated that there was improvement during the service phase; that is, there were statistically significant decreases in the mean number of children's and mothers' aversive behaviors during the treatment phase. However, these gains had disappeared by the one-year follow-up. On the measure of insularity, the results indicated that contact with friends was an inverse predictor of the problem behaviors under investigation. More specifically, on days when there was a higher frequency of contact with friends, there were less parent-child interaction problems. Wahler (1980b) concluded that multiple life stressors and social networks are important considerations in determining both short-term and long-term benefits of in-home parent training.

Following up on the above study, Dumas and Wahler (1983) conducted two similar studies to investigate the relationship between two variables—socioeconomic disadvantage and insularity—and the success of parent training programs. Forty-nine mothers participated in the first study, and eighteen participated in a replication study. Measures of socioeconomic disadvantage and insularity were correlated with the outcome measures for the parent training program. The results showed that treatment outcomes were significantly associated with both socioeconomic disadvantage and insularity. Specifically, it was found that mothers who scored high on either measures of socioeconomic disadvantage or insularity did not show sustained gains (as measured by observations of aversive child and parent behaviors) compared to mothers who scored low on the two variables.

These studies provide evidence that the ability of parent training programs to produce significant and lasting changes for parents experiencing difficulties managing their children are heavily influenced by other variables. The authors claimed that their findings "cast serious doubt about the effectiveness of parent training as a singular form of therapy for the majority of insular/disadvantaged families" (p. 311). Dumas and Wahler's studies strongly suggest that parent training should not be contemplated as stand-alone interventions for populations who are extremely disadvantaged or socially isolated. They concluded that

> it is to be expected that mothers who experience high levels of socioeconomic disadvantage, community isolation and social coercion will tend to fare poorly in parent-training programs designed to improve relationships between themselves and their children. (p. 311)

AGENCY-BASED CHILD MANAGEMENT TRAINING

Reid, Taplin, and Lorber (1981) examined the relationship between aversive behaviors between parents and children and incidents of abuse. They also assessed the effects of a program designed to teach families nonaversive ways of interacting. Families ($n = 78$) who were identified as distressed (not defined) and who had children diagnosed as having conduct disorders were recruited to participate in the training program and were compared to a group of families ($n = 27$) recruited through newspaper advertisements, who were not distressed and had no apparent child management problems. The researchers found that of the seventy-eight families identified as distressed, twenty-seven had incidents of substantiated physical abuse of the child. This permitted comparison among three groups: distressed, abusive families (DA); distressed, nonabusive families (DN); and nondistressed, nonabusive families (NN).

The distressed families participated in four weeks of training and two additional observation sessions after the training. Training consisted of reading, watching video films on child management, presenting and modeling of child management skills by service providers, and group discussions. Parents were taught to identify and record specific behaviors of their children and then instructed to use appropriate consequences in managing the behavior, including time-outs. No information was given on the number or length of training sessions.

Observations were made of the number of aversive behaviors by both parents and by the child, using a coding scheme called Total Aversive Behaviours (TAB). Families were observed in their homes before, during, and after the training program, and periodically during the twelve months after the training program. Comparisons of the TAB scores were made between the families receiving training and the families who received no training.

Parents' ability to successfully stop a child's aversive behavior with a nonaversive reaction differed significantly between the three groups: 86% NN parents, 65% DN parents, 47% DA parents. Preliminary postprogram outcomes revealed statistically significant reductions in aversive behaviors for participating mothers and referred children, but not for fathers. The authors concluded that the overall level of hostility in "DA" families decreased as a function of parent skill training.

Burch and Mohr (1980) conducted an evaluation of Positive Parenting, a child abuse prevention project offered by a family service agency in Omaha, from 1974 to 1977. Positive Parenting was a program that offered a range of activities for parents who had abused their children. This evaluation focused on the program's impacts on three goals: (a) to change feelings, attitudes, and values about parenthood, (b) to increase knowledge of what to expect from children and how to deal with problems, and (c) to change isolation patterns by providing social support in the group (p. 93).

The program consisted of parent groups that met once a week for two hours. The groups were open-ended—that is, participants could come and go as they wished—and the groups were ongoing. No information was given about the number of parents in each group. The program elements consisted of socialization among parents, educational presentations by a group leader on topics related to parenting, and group discussions. While parents were in the groups, structured child care was provided for participants' children. A unique feature of this program was the emphasis on providing structured socialization times, and by intentional nurturing of parents by program staff.

A sample of participants in the parent groups was selected to complete a questionnaire twice over a four-month period. A random sample of families with perceived child maltreatment concerns was also drawn from a child protection agency and these parents also completed the instruments twice over a four-month period. These comparison families received regular child protection services.

There were statistically significant differences at the first evaluation times on most of the outcome test items between a group of experienced program participants ($n = 45$) and two other groups: a control group ($n = 41$), and a group of first-time program participants ($n = 20$). The authors argued that there were enough similarities between the three groups to suggest that the more favorable knowledge and attitude scores for the experienced program group resulted from the program involvement. In addition, comparisons were also made between the test scores over a four-month period. Of the forty-five program participants who took the first test, twenty-one were in attendance when the second test was taken; for the control group, ten families of the original forty-one were available for the second test. The average number of errors on the test dropped from 9.00 to 7.70 for the program group, a difference that was statistically significant, while there was no significant difference between the first (11.40) and second (11.25) tests of the control group. The researchers concluded that "the data show that Positive Parenting participants had a statistically significant change in their attitudes, perspectives, and knowledge about child care and development over the four-month period" (p. 98).

Wolfe et al. (1981) conducted a study that demonstrated that social learning training improved parents' ability to manage their children. Sixteen parents who were receiving child protection services because of substantiated incidents of abuse participated in the study; the first eight referrals received the Child Management Program services (CMP), while the remaining eight received regular child protection services. Most of the families were headed by single, poor women. The CMP provided group training and individualized home-based training over a period of eight weeks. Group training involved weekly two-hour parent groups in which graduate level students provided instruction in child management, problem solving, and self-control. The home-based training complemented the group training with weekly visits by a graduate student to demonstrate and to practice the skills learned in the group sessions.

To measure improvement in parents' child management skills and in the children's behavior, independent observations and child protection worker ratings were made on each family before the program, after the program, and ten weeks after the program had ended. Parents' behaviors and skills were measured using the Parent Child Interaction Form (PCIF), and children's behavior was assessed using the Eyberg Child Behaviour Inventory (ECBI). In addition, at the one year follow-up, agency records were also examined for reports of child abuse among both groups.

The results showed that, compared to the control families, the CMP families had a larger increase in PCIF scores (+73.5 compared to −5); a larger decrease in number of child behavior problems as measured by the ECBI (−9.8 compared to −1.7), and a larger decrease in child protection worker ratings of families' service needs (−10.9 compared to +2.0). As well, at the ten-week follow-up, the CMP parents maintained their gains in both child management behavior and number of childhood problems. One year after the program, none of the CMP families had a reported case of child abuse, compared to one reported case in the control group. The authors argued that the CMP program was cost-effective compared to routine child welfare supervision because it accomplished these goals with only 16 hours of group time and an average of 8.9 hours of individual training time in the home. They concluded that their findings "lend support to the social learning hypothesis that abusive parents have not learned (or do not perform) even minimal levels of appropriate child management skills and experience a great deal of difficulty controlling their children" (p. 639).

Wolfe et al. (1988) followed up on this study by investigating the impact of the child management training program offered in addition to agency-based family support services. The authors "theorized that agency-based family support services would have a greater impact on 'high-risk' families if they were accompanied by training in child management" (p. 41). Thirty parent-child dyads participated in the study. Parents were included if they scored within the 'at-risk' range on the Child Abuse Potential Inventory; most of the mothers were single, poor, and young. All families received agency-based family support services in which the children attended child care activities while parents attended group meetings twice per week (two hours each). The parent groups engaged in social activities, arts and crafts, and informal discussion of topics related to health and family.

In addition to these family support services, half the parents were randomly selected to participate in the child management training sessions. Parents were taught in groups of eight to ten by graduate students in psychology. The training involved teaching parents skills in managing their children's difficult behavior, as well as activities to promote their children's development and adaptive behavior. Parents learned and practiced skills, watched themselves on videotape, and also learned relaxation and stress management techniques. The average number of family support sessions attended by both control and parent training groups was twenty. Parent training participants attended an average of nine sessions.

A variety of measures were used to assess the parents' risk of abusive behavior, their child rearing methods, and the children's behaviors. The results showed that the parent training group had fewer parenting risk problems after the training program than the control group. However, there were no significant differences between the groups in their child-rearing methods, with both groups showing some improvement in their ability to provide appropriate and stimulating home environments for their children. The parent training children also showed fewer and less intense behavior problems than the control children, but both groups of children showed similar improvements in development and adaptive behavior. The authors concluded that "the diverse needs of families at risk of maltreatment are best addressed through a coupling of family support and individually tailored assistance in effective child management" (p. 46).

Brunk et al. (1987) compared the efficacy of two approaches to addressing child abuse and neglect: the parent training approach and multisystemic therapy. The authors suggested that multisystemic therapy was based on an ecological theory, in which child maltreatment results from a variety of factors influencing the family. Families who were court-ordered to receive services because of substantiated abuse or neglect were offered participation in the research project as one option. Thirty-three families chose the research project and were randomly assigned to receive either the parent training or the multisystemic therapy.

The parent training was based on the program developed by Wolfe et al. (1981); however, the competency-based component where parents had the opportunity for feedback and practice in their homes was not included. The multisystemic therapy included a variety of clinical techniques such as joining and reframing, and most families also received informal education in child rearing, coaching and emotional support, and advocacy and linking within the social, educational, and health services system.

Through parent self-reports and observations by the researchers before and after the programs, children's behaviors, parental effectiveness, family functioning, and parental stress were examined. The authors pointed out that the research design did not conclusively show that the improvements were caused by the programs, since there was no control group. However, the results suggest that the multisystemic therapy was more effective than the parent training approach in improving the relationship and interaction between parents and their children, in improving parents' ability to manage their children's behavior, and in reducing children's noncompliance. However, parents who received the parent training approach reported a greater decrease in social isolation. The authors suggested that this may be due to the fact that the parent training was conducted in groups. The authors concluded that "although parent training is clearly an effective treatment in many situations, it may present certain limitations when applied as the primary therapeutic intervention for 'multi-problem' maltreating families" (p. 177).

Egan (1983), in a study design similar to Brunk et al. (1987), compared the effectiveness of training parents in child management techniques and teaching parents strategies to cope with stress. Families who had reported incidence of abuse and were clients of a child welfare agency were randomly assigned to one of four groups: child management training ($n = 11$), stress management training ($n = 11$), a combination of both child and stress management training ($n = 9$), and a control group that received regular child welfare services ($n = 10$).

There were no significant demographic differences among parents who participated in each program group. Parents were not highly educated (mostly high school education), and less than half were employed. Of the forty-one participants, fifteen were fathers and twenty-six were mothers. The format for each of the three program groups was similar. In each program, parents were in small groups (four to six) in six weekly sessions of two hours each. The components of each program condition included learning about the skill area, coaching, modeling, rehearsal, self-evaluation and feedback. In the stress management program, parents were taught progressive muscle relaxation and cognitive restructuring skills to reduce stress. In the child management program, parents were taught skills in observing and modifying their children's behavior. In the stress and child management combination, parents spent three weeks in each of the two areas, since the groups were all running during the same six-week period. Finally, in the control group, parents were told that the groups were full and there would be a six-week waiting period after which they would be offered the opportunity to join a program group. During the waiting period, these families received regular services from the agency, including weekly contact with their social worker.

Using a combination of parent self-reports, behavioral observations, and a structured role play observation, all parents were assessed before and after the program on measures of family functioning, child behavior management, parent child interaction, stress, and anxiety. The results showed that the stress management and the child management groups each had statistically significant impacts on different variables. The parents in the stress management group reported less negative affect about negative life events, less conflict among family members, more parent positive affect, more child positive affect, and more verbal commands delivered by parents to their children. The parents in the child management group were more responsive in a disciplinary situation, were more likely to reinforce compliance of their child to a command, and the children showed less positive affect. Parents who received the combined program showed no greater impact on any of the variables than either of the other two program groups. Thus, the different program approaches each had impacts in areas related to the program content, leading the author to conclude that, "it is not obvious from this study which treatment component is better for the abusive parent" (p. 298).

STRESS MANAGEMENT TRAINING

Some parent training programs teach parents to manage the stress that they feel. The child management approach suggests that parents abuse and neglect their children because they do not have the skills to manage their children in a nonabusive way. In contrast, the stress management approach assumes that parents abuse their children—even if they have the appropriate skills—because they cannot handle the stress and the anxiety that they are feeling and, as a result, lash out at their children.

Egan (1983), in the study described above, found that six weekly two-hour sessions of stress management training were successful in reducing the anxiety and stress felt by abusive parents. These parents reported that negative events of the past six months were less upsetting to them, and that there were fewer disagreements in their families. They also tended to show an increase in positive verbal statements, and both parents and children showed more positive affect for one another. There were no reported incidences of abuse among those who received the training or among those who did not, possibly because the six-week time frame was too short. Nevertheless, Egan argued that the success of the parent training approach in decreasing parental and familial stress and conflict may be linked to reducing actual abusive behavior.

Barth et al. (1983) evaluated a group training program with parents that focused on managing the stress and anger that often precipitates incidents of child abusive behavior. The program was designed to address two perceived correlates of child maltreatment: parental stress and poor child management skills. Six families were referred by the state child protective service to participate in the group training, and were compared to a comparison group (n not given), which was recruited from a well-baby clinic. Program parents had lower education than the comparison group (an average of 11.2 years in school compared to 16.8 in the control group). All of the control group children were under five, compared to the program group, which had children ranging from preschoolers to teenagers.

Parents in the program attended the group training sessions led by graduate-level social work students twice weekly for eight weeks in an agency setting. The training focused on teaching parents methods of self-control, reducing anxiety and stress, and relaxation. As well, parents were taught communication skills that would help them to manage their children's behavior more effectively. An additional focus was on encouraging social interaction between group members by extending the communication skills beyond just parent-child communication (for example, in marital and work situations) and by providing time for socializing through coffee and refreshments after each group session.

Both comparison and program groups completed various evaluation instruments before and after the eight-week training sessions, which measured anger level, stress level, parent-child conflict, and marital relationships. In addition, parents' performance in managing stressful situations with children was assessed by having independent observers rate parents in role-played parent-child interactions. Finally, parents gave evaluations of the program during and after the intervention, and completed evaluations three months after the program had ended.

Program parents showed a statistically significant greater decline in anger levels and experienced a significant decrease in their feelings of nervousness and irritability than comparison group parents. Parents in the training group also showed less parent-child conflict, but this difference did not reach statistical significance. Finally, there was no difference in marital relationships between the groups. Program parents showed a greater use of positive self-talk, calming statements and praise than control group members. In the role play observations, program parents showed greater use of "I-statements" and less blaming statements, greater use of effective commands, and a higher ratio of effective to ineffective commands. In the follow-up evaluations at three months, parents stated that they were still using the skills that they had learned in the group, that they continued to practice the relaxation, breathing, and positive self-statements skills, and overall felt better about their life, including their relationships with friends and relatives and, for those working, their colleagues. As well, group members stated that they continued to enjoy the relationships which they had formed in the groups.

Schinke, Schilling, Kirkham, and Gilchrist (1986) reported on an evaluation of a parental stress management training program very similar to the one described by Barth et al. (1983). Twenty-three parents (thirteen mothers, ten fathers) participated in ten weekly two-hour training group sessions led by social workers. Comparisons on a variety of variables were made between the training group parents and a comparison group (no information is given about how many or how they were selected) at pretest, posttest, and six months following the completion of the group training program. The variables measured parents' attitudes toward their children, their anger control abilities, their coping responses, and their child disciplining interactions. The results showed that program parents were statistically significantly better in all areas at the posttest. However, by the six-month follow-up, many of the differences were no longer statistically significant.

Whiteman et al. (1987) designed a study to investigate the effectiveness of a program to address parental anger. They argued that "situationally tied" anger—that is, anger that is directly tied to interactions with children—is a factor leading to abuse. The study assessed the impact of the program on three areas: (a) parent's anger toward the child, (b) parental child-rearing attitudes and behaviors, and (c) the relationship between anger and child-rearing attitudes and behavior. Fifty-five parents were selected from two child welfare agencies and randomly assigned to either a control group or one of four different programs. All of the parents had either a substantiated incidence of abuse or were judged by social workers to be at risk of abuse. Most of the parents (91%) were female, over half were receiving public assistance, and only one-third were employed outside the home.

Each of the four programs was similar in two areas. First, they focused on learning as a process involving gradual skill development, practice, and reinforcement. Second, an emphasis was placed on developing a sense of control over anger by using the newly learned skill as way to "stop and think." The authors identified a number of factors that emerged from the literature regarding parental anger and child abuse that shaped their interventions. The four program interventions, offered in six weekly sessions by doctoral social work students, were as follows:

1.   Cognitive restructuring: Parents were taught to change the way they perceived their children's behavior, particularly in seeing their children's behavior not as intentional provoking but as expected childhood behavior.

2.   Relaxation: Parents were taught techniques to reduce the stress they felt when dealing with their children.

3.   Problem-solving: Parents were taught strategies to deal with their children that would replace their hostile responses.

4.   Combined package: Parents received training that included all three of the above strategies.

The control group received no specific training, but continued to receive regular child protection services from the agencies.

Participation in the combined program was significantly correlated with both adult ($-.54$, $p < .01$) and child anger ($-.46$, $p < .05$; the negative correlation values indicate low anger scores for program families compared with control families). Compared to the control group, parents from all program groups showed significant correlations with two areas of child rearing: parents' ability to be empathic toward their children ($-.36$, $p < .01$), and parents' irritating behavior ($.25$, $p < .05$); the program groups showed higher empathy and lower irritating behavior scores than the control group. This study demonstrated that a combination of different anger and stress management strategies was most effective at reducing parental anger and improving parents' child-rearing attitudes and behaviors.

SUMMARY: PARENT TRAINING PROGRAMS

Whiteman et al. (1987) acknowledged that "child abuse undoubtedly is multidetermined," but argued that "significant as these [other] influences are, they are relatively removed from the abusive act itself" (p. 469). Parent training programs endeavor to focus on parent behaviors and parent-children interactions that immediately precede acts of child maltreatment. Parent training programs also are based on social learning theory, which suggests that maltreating parents have been unable to learn the kinds of skills necessary to respond to children in a nonabusive manner. This review revealed two major parent training approaches: (a) teaching parents to manage their children's difficult behaviors and (b) teaching parents to handle the stress and the anger that can lead to abusive behaviors.

Most of the parent training programs assessed used small group sessions to teach parents. Many programs supplemented these group sessions with several in-home training sessions in order to reinforce the skills that had been learned in the group sessions. A few programs relied exclusively on individualized in-home training. These parent training programs focused on specific behavior change goals with parents and generally followed predetermined curricula in their training. The typical program group met parents once a week for two hours over six to ten weeks. Training procedures usually involved presenting new skills, modeling the new practices, allowing parents time to practice the new behaviors, providing feedback to parents on their learning, and often observing parents interact with their children in natural settings and then providing feedback and demonstrating alternative ways of interacting with children. A few programs offered child care support during program times and a couple encouraged mutual support and socializing between parents. While there were differences in the training content, most of the parent training programs reviewed were very similar both in their teaching principles and in their service delivery procedures.

The review uncovered twenty evaluations of parent training programs. Although the sample sizes for many of these studies were very small, a few studies did use credible experimental and quasi-experimental designs. While the range of outcome measures used was quite limited, many of these studies used comparable outcome measures to determine program effectiveness. Most important, while the individual studies had limitations, there was substantial agreement between the findings of most of these studies. This consistency of research outcomes and the similarities in parent training program content and procedures permits more clarity about the strengths and limitations of parent training programs in child welfare.

The Range of Supports Available: These parent training programs provided quite specific kinds of information and educational support to parents—generally concentrating on parenting methods, child development and, sometimes, on stress and anger management. Modest amounts of encouragement and emotional support were available to participating parents.

The Level of Support Available: These parent training programs generally involved parents once a week for about two hours. Some programs included an additional weekly individual contact.

Availability in a Crisis: The Parent Training Programs reviewed had no provisions to respond to emergencies in participating families' lives.

Motivation and Skill Requirements: Most of the parent training was done in groups and participation generally was voluntary in all programs. This suggests that parents need to be willing and able to attend group meetings. A basic openness and ability to learn the program concepts and methods also seems necessary.

Focused Technical Expertise: A strength of parent training programs is their ability to provide specialized information on parenting and stress management and expert training in applying this information.

The Length of Time Supports Available: Parent training programs are of short duration—usually from six to ten weeks.

Reciprocity and Social Integration: Group training did permit a modest level of emotional support and reciprocity between members in some programs. However, this was limited by the brief duration of the groups. These parent training programs did not emphasize participants doing for themselves or being helpers of others in similar circumstances or developing connections with peers.

Anticipated Program Impacts and Rationales: Gains in the parent training programs reviewed were closely linked to training content: less aversive parenting behaviors, better parent-child interactions, and better stress and anger management by parents. Some studies suggested that these gains became less evident after program involvement ended. Only a few of the studies examined program impacts on incidents of child abuse and neglect or on out-of-home placement rates for children. Those which did look at placement rates generally did not find fewer child placements for parent training participants. Three studies suggested that the benefits of parent training were less evident where parents were coping with high levels of stress and multiple difficulties in their lives. Several others suggested that parent training is more effective with disadvantaged families when joined with other supports and services.

Informal Helping ————————————————————— 9

INTRODUCTION

Informal helping refers to assistance received through positive interactions with friends, relatives, peers, neighbors, co-workers, or others in one's social network. Understanding of the importance of informal support is not new, but only recently has informal helping been used explicitly in support programs for disadvantaged families (Seagull, 1987). Mutual aid/self-help refers to reciprocal support between members of informal networks or groups created for specific populations. While mutual aid/self-help programs have been used with good effects with many populations coping with serious challenges, mutual aid has been largely ignored as a helping strategy in child welfare (Cameron et al., 1992).

This chapter reviews the available literature on informal helping and mutual aid for families coping with multiple difficulties. Although the focus will be mainly on child welfare, our review is limited by the fact that programs emphasizing informal helping/mutual aid for disadvantaged families are remarkably absent from the child welfare literature. For this reason, some examples of informal helping/mutual aid with other populations also will be described in order to illustrate the potential of these approaches. Despite the many reasons for optimism about the potential usefulness of informal supports/mutual aid, exploiting these benefits to support families coming to social service agencies for help remains conceptually and practically a relatively unexplored challenge.

RATIONALE FOR INFORMAL HELPING[1]

Albee (1959) predicted that there will never be enough professionals to respond to the problems experienced by children and families. The Ministry of Community and Social Services (1990b) released a report documenting the status of children's services in Ontario. The outcomes were not entirely positive: existing services were overtaxed, waiting lists were exceedingly long, program costs were high, and services failed to reach marginalized groups. Inevitably, this imbalance between the system's capacity to supply services and the requests for assistance means there are children and families who are not receiving the assistance that they require. For example, one in six children in Ontario were projected to have psychiatric, behavior, or school problems, but only one in six of these children have access to professional help (Ministry of Community and Social Services, 1986). While there is a need for more effective use of limited professional resources, there also is an argument for taking greater advantage of the potential of informal helping.

Informal helpers often are more accessible and more acceptable than professional helpers. Parents and children are surrounded by potential help from friends, extended family members, members of peer groups, and colleagues. Many of these people are able to provide an immediate response to a call for help. At the same time, the nature of informal relationships may increase the likelihood that a helper will witness signs of impending distress and thus be in a position to offer assistance before child maltreatment occurs. This preventive property of informal helping has been acknowledged by several researchers (Bertsche, Clark, & Iversen 1982; Cohn, 1991; Seagull, 1987), who argue that families will seek out informal, as opposed to formal supports at earlier stages of difficulty. Thus, at least potentially, informal helping may reduce the need for professional involvement after child maltreatment problems already have occurred.

Many authors have identified social isolation or inadequate social integration of caregivers as a common characteristic of disadvantaged families and as a significant contributing factor to child maltreatment (Bertsche & Clarke, 1982; Borman & Lieber, 1984; Breton, 1980; Cameron et al., 1992; Cameron & Rothery, 1985; Howze & Kotch, 1984; Kempe & Helfer, 1972; Lieber, 1984; Lieber & Baker, 1977; Meyers & Bernier, 1990; Polansky, Chalmers, Buttenweiser, & Williams, 1979). Informal strategies address this problem by providing parents and children with opportunities to interact with supportive peers on a regular basis.

The availability of emotional support and problem-specific guidance from informal helpers has been associated with an improved ability to manage many different challenges and potentially buffers the recipients from the adverse effects of stressful circumstances. Positive social integration (e.g., successful social role performances, close friendships, being embedded in larger and diverse social networks) is an essential ingredient in the development, maintenance, and reconstruction of a positive social identity and sense of psychological well-being (see Chapters 3 and 4 in this volume for a discussion of these benefits of informal support and social integration). It is also very evident that access to useful informal support and positive social integration is seriously deficient for many families using child welfare and other social services (Cameron et al., 1992).

Despite the obvious potential of informal supports, this type of helping has not been accepted broadly as part of the helping repertoire in child welfare. There are various possible explanations to account for the lack of interest, and even resistance, on the part of professionals to using informal supports to greater advantage in protecting children and supporting families. For example:

> [I]nformal methods of providing assistance are based on paradigms, explaining the nature of the problems facing many child welfare clients and the appropriate responses to their difficulties, that are different from those used by most child welfare service providers. There is also little doubt that many social support, social network, and self-help interventions do not accord formal child welfare service providers the central role in the helping process to which they have become accustomed. (Cameron, 1990b, p. 145)

However, many proponents of informal helping claim that informal strategies complement, and even improve, the effectiveness of formal child welfare services, and are not intended to replace professional services (Cameron, 1990b; Gaudin, Wodarski, Arkinson, & Avery, 1990–1991; Halper & Jones, 1981; Whittaker, 1983).

THE RELEVANCE OF MUTUAL AID PROGRAMS AND CREATED NETWORKS[2]

When presented with the rationale for social support, many professionals legitimately query how they can be expected to create social networks, friendships, or valued social roles for clients who have serious social integration deficiencies, some of whom lack the social skills needed to sustain such relationships. The argument has been made that created rather than embedded relationships may be more practical ways for professionals to exploit the potential of informal ways of helping:

> Perhaps one of the fundamental differences in the character of informal helping hinges on whether help is exchanged between those who have an existing relationship or involves people whose relationships were initiated by an agency. . . .
> Embedded relationships help fewer people per helper. . . . Such relationships are slow to develop and, because of their idiosyncratic nature, time is required to identify the helpers and the culture of the networks. . . .
> Created relationships, since they are designed and initiated by the agency, can be targeted on the desired populations. Since they are more open and egalitarian, they can be useful for isolated individuals or families. Created relationships may be more compatible with the nature of formal agencies and professional workers. They also present an opportunity for people to develop

new helping roles, skills and values. On the other hand, created relationships require a heavier investment of agency resources to initiate and maintain. Created supports may initiate shorter relationships and provide fewer basic supports. The recipients may find them less satisfying than embedded relationships. (Froland et al., 1981, pp. 51–53)

Mutual aid organizations are relatively well-known vehicles for creating supportive relationships for a range of struggling populations. Cameron described their potential for a child welfare constituency in the following terms:

Considering the social isolation of many child welfare clients, and their stigmatized status in the community, it seems probable that informal social supports created specifically for these groups may prove to be more accessible than such supports available within the general community. The creation of mutual aid organizations specifically for various groupings of child welfare clientele may be a promising and practical way of actualizing some of the benefits of informal social supports.

One of the great strengths of the mutual aid model is its potential to provide a broad range of social supports. Such groups can also be flexible enough to provide benefits to participants for brief or for extended periods of time. As a model, child welfare mutual aid organizations have the theoretical potential of producing many of the main effects, as well as the buffering effects, of social support. However, the benefits of participation in a mutual aid organization—as with all family support programming—will depend on the levels and types of involvements a particular self-help organization is able to provide. (1990b, pp. 159–160)

PARAMETERS OF INFORMAL HELPING PROGRAMS

The diversity of informal helping strategies makes it difficult to formulate an encompassing characterization for these approaches. The array of available informal helping activities goes far beyond the few informal strategies that are sometimes accessed by professional helpers. For example, Cameron (1990b) provided the following partial list of informal program strategies, which he argues are both promising and underutilized in child welfare:

1. social and recreational programming, preferably with high levels of participant responsibility for development and implementation;
2. peer groups or social networks of similar people that encourage contact outside of scheduled activities;
3. dyadic contacts between service users, and/or other status-equal people, in the hope of creating enduring relationships (e.g., by developing buddy systems);

4. opportunities for participants to become recognized givers as well as receivers of help through opportunities to be volunteers, participation in group projects, and so on;

5. mutual aid or self-help organizations for various child welfare and other populations;

6. opportunities for participants to take on new social roles and responsibilities through participation in self-help organizations, in community organizations, through employment or education involvements;

7. cooperative service projects for babysitting, recreation for moms or kids, and so on. (p. 159)

The types of helpers who have provided informal supports have varied as have the types of assistance they have provided. Anyone who does not receive payment to provide assistance may be considered an informal helper. This group has included friendly visitors, colleagues, friends, relatives, neighbors, members of churches and community associations, members of social and recreational groups, people in key community positions such as hairdressers, fitness instructors, and members of self-help groups. Informal helpers have been recruited not so much for their educational training or their employment history, but rather for their personal experiences and attributes (Bertsche et al., 1982). According to Alexander and Kempe (1982), informal helpers in child welfare often have been mothers whose own parenting experiences had been positive, whose lives were stable, and who were compassionate, open to different styles of parenting, and available to families on a long-term and regular basis.

The duration and intensity of informal supports provided to families has also varied. The length of time supports were available ranged from a one-time offer from a friend or relative of an evening of respite, to participation in a mutual aid group over a number of years. The intensity of support varied from a neighbor who was asked to provide a few food items, to involvement of parents in weekly group meetings, to contact with parent aides who assisted families daily.

There have been very few descriptions of programs emphasizing informal helping in the child welfare literature. This review uncovered three basic informal helping program models: lay home visitors, mutual aid groups, and community living networks. Lay home visitor support programs resemble the home health visitor and parent aide programs described in Chapter 7, except that they use volunteer visitors. They tended to visit families one to several times a week over several months to a year. A few mutual aid groups specifically for child welfare families (e.g., Parents Anonymous, Parent Mutual Aid Organizations) have been evaluated. They fostered contact between members once to several times a week from a few months to several years. Community living networks have been developed to support potentially maltreating families and other populations for whom institutional placement was an imminent risk. They provided members with access to frequent and ongoing supports from peers (e.g., support groups, friends, sometimes shared accommodations, drop-in centers, etc.) in their own community.

EVALUATIONS OF INFORMAL HELPING PROGRAMS

Over the past two decades informal helping has been used, albeit infrequently, to support families considered at "high-risk" for child maltreatment; however, little research evidence exists to support the usefulness of these helping strategies (Auslander & Litwin, 1987; Cameron, 1990b; Cameron et al., 1992; Seagull, 1987). As Rothery (1990b) pointed out, "[T]he literature on 'multi-problem' families does not deal extensively with the importance of informal as well as formal helpers, and this may be a major gap in our theory and practice respecting this population" (p. 23). In addition, Cameron and his associates (1992) argued that part of the difficulty encountered by researchers who wish to investigate informal helping strategies is the fact that standard methods and tools of assessment are not always appropriate. Research may be challenged by confidentiality issues, changing group memberships, the self-selected membership of many groups, the lack of standard program duration or content, varying levels of participation, the great difficulty of randomly assigning participants to program and comparison groups, difficulty in finding suitable comparison groups, and the need to involve participants in designing the research.

Based on a review of social support theory and research, Cameron (1990b) postulated some expected impacts of one type of informal helping with child welfare populations, namely parent mutual aid organizations:

1. members should report less social isolation and more friends and peers to whom they can turn for support and help in coping with problems;
2. members should require less support from child welfare agencies and more cases should be closed by the agencies;
3. fewer of the members' children should require placement and less time should be spent in care;
4. there should be fewer reportable incidents of child abuse and neglect among group members;
5. because of savings in expenditures on care and professional services the self-help groups should have the potential to cover all or most of their costs if they were sponsored by the child welfare agencies;
6. members should be more optimistic and confident in their abilities to deal with a range of problems. This should be evident in higher self-esteem and more positive conceptions of their social identities. (p. 165)

As shall be seen, some of these expectations are resonable for informal helping strategies other than mutual aid and are examined in the studies described in the following sections.

INFORMAL HELPING WITHIN COMPREHENSIVE SUPPORT PROGRAMS

Informal strategies have sometimes been included as components of comprehensive support programs. The types of informal approaches utilized varied and may have included lay visitors, homemakers, and/or peer or mutual aid groups. One of the significant findings that emerged from Cohn's (1979) review of eleven comprehensive child abuse service demonstration projects was that programs that included lay helpers were more effective and less expensive than approaches that relied exclusively on professional services. The results of Berkeley Planning Associates' (1983, cited in Cohn & Daro, 1987) evaluation of nineteen demonstration programs supported Cohn's (1979) conclusions. Evaluations of other comprehensive support programs that included informal helping (e.g., Callard & Morin, 1979; Halper & Jones, 1981; Irueste-Montes & Montes, 1988; Lutzker & Rice, 1984; Stephens, 1979; Wieder et al., 1988) also reported positive outcomes. However, these studies did not isolate the program effects that were due to informal helping (see chapter ten on comprehensive strategies for a more detailed description of informal helping in comprehensive support programs).

LAY HOME VISITING

The use of lay home visitors is one of the more common ways informal helping has been used by child welfare agencies. This strategy linked the family with a volunteer who was available to provide supports such as companionship, help with housework, transportation, and a sympathetic ear.

Pallone and Malkemes (1984) presented a detailed description of an intensive, comprehensive, informal helping program for families with children under the age of twelve for whom reports of abuse had been substantiated. This program, called SCAN (an acronym for Stopping Child Abuse Now), incorporated Parents Anonymous groups and parent education groups; however, most of the supportive services were provided on a one-to-one basis by "lay therapists" in the families' homes. The SCAN volunteers reportedly were available to families twenty-four hours a day and seven days a week. Volunteers helped with such things as housework, changing diapers, arranging for reliable child care, locating suitable housing, taking family members to appointments or out shopping, and organizing recreational activities. The volunteers were intended to act as role models, educating parents about child development, teaching them how to set appropriate limits for their children, and intervening when parents were at risk of abusing their children.

"The SCAN program was evaluated in three communities over a three-year period as part of a national child abuse and neglect demonstration effort from 1974 through 1977" (Pallone & Malkemes, 1984, p. 58).[3] Results of the aggregated evaluation of three SCAN programs indicated that parents who participated in the programs for six months or more and who received informal supports such as lay therapy or self-help group services were more likely to demonstrate increased self-esteem, enhanced anger management skills, reduced stress, and better communication skills. These positive outcomes were attributed by the researchers to the quantity and intensity of support provided through lay visitors and group services. In addition, the lay visitor and group models included in the overall evaluation were found to cost about half as much as intervention strategies based on individual counseling provided by professionals. Finally, the evaluation showed that SCAN was able to "reduce the use of foster care more significantly than other programs, both in terms of total number of children in care and length of time spent in foster care" (Pallone & Malkemes, 1984, p. 59). Children placed through SCAN spent an average of six months out of home, as compared to the national average (U.S., 1984 data) of thirty-four months in care.

Lines (1987) reported on a parent aide program that was established in 1978 and operated out of a children's hospital in Adelaide, Australia. The program involved matching volunteers with physically and/or emotionally abusive mothers. Twelve experienced mothers (all with telephones and cars) were selected and were required to make a two-year commitment to the program. They received fifteen hours of initial training, as well as ongoing training and supervision from agency social workers. Lines outlined the duties of the parent aides as follows:

1.   To nurture and provide mothering experiences for abusing mothers.
2.   To be flexible about parenting.
3.   To respond to the client whenever the client makes contact.
4.   To visit the client's home.
5.   To focus on the mother, not the child.
6.   To meet regularly with the primary care worker. (p. 508)

Each parent aide was matched with no more than two mothers on the basis of geographic proximity, occupation, personality, and so on. Mothers selected to participate in the program were screened by a child protection panel, which normally made decisions about referrals to various child welfare services. Early in the relationship, parent aides visited mothers in their homes approximately twice a week. However, the frequency of contact was reduced over the duration of program involvement.

The six parent aides for whom evaluation data were available spent an average of 22 hours per month with each mother that they were assigned to assist, though the intensity of contact ranged from just over 15 to just under 37 hours per month. More than half of the hours spent with a mother were devoted to personal or in-home counseling (average of 11.5 hours/month). The remaining time was typically divided among telephone contact with a mother (2.5 hours/month), meetings with the primary care worker (1.4 hours/month), attending ongoing training (4.8 hours/month), and other activities on behalf of a mother (1.5 hours/month). No information was provided about how many months parent aides spent with the mothers.

Outcome results were available for thirty-one of the thirty-six cases opened during the first five years of the demonstration project. Based on the judgments of the mothers, the parent aides, and the primary care workers, ten mothers successfully completed the program. Successful resolution was based on the following criteria: "(a) the abuse had stopped, (b) the mother viewed the child more favorably than before intervention, (b) the mother was able to seek appropriate assistance when necessary, and (d) the mother had reasonable confidence that she could deal with future crises" (Lines, 1987, p. 510). Another ten mothers discontinued their relationships with their parent aides, usually because they moved. According to the South Australia Child Abuse Register, none of these mothers had engaged in further abusive behavior, though this conclusion is valid only if incidents of maltreatment were reported and the family did not move to another state. At the end of the evaluation, six mothers continued to be involved with a parent aide. Since the review, all six mothers have completed the program with no subsequent reports of reabuse. In four instances, mothers asked their parent aides to withdraw. Though this request was considered premature in all four cases, there were no reports of subsequent maltreatment in any of these families. Only one mother engaged in abusive behavior while involved with the program; her child(ren) was removed from the home. While program outcomes were not recorded for the remaining five families, the state register contained no reports of maltreatment for any of these families. Consequently, the researchers claimed better than 97% success rate for cases in which a parent aide was assigned to a mother. However, despite the comparison to the 8% reabuse rate for all cases referred to the child protection panel during the same five-year period, it is difficult to accept such strong assertions about the program's effectiveness without a research design using a credible comparison group.

Zimrim (1984) described a short-term research project conducted in Israel in which low-socioeconomic, physically abusive mothers were matched with young women in the same neighborhoods with similar socioeconomic backgrounds. The parent aides "spent three hours a day, three days a week, over a period of three months with the mothers in the mothers' homes. The contact between them and the mothers was of a social nature, with some help with housework" (p. 478).

The main goals of the project were presented as follows: "(a) to help the children who, without the research, would have remained untreated, and (b) to examine possibilities of providing treatment in cases in which professional personnel is not available" (p. 476). Related to these two project goals was the primary evaluation objective, namely, to investigate "whether a mere human contact, which is not accompanied with any definite treatment goal or technique, can bring about a change in the behaviour of abusing mothers, and what are the elements of treatment in this 'not doing anything'" (p. 477).

The researchers divided a sample of forty mothers identified as physically abusive according to severity of abuse, educational level, and ethnic origin, and then randomly assigned the members to the experimental group (twenty women) or to the control group (twenty women). The mothers in the experimental group were assigned a parent aide. The women in the control group received no intervention.

The evaluation design involved a pretest, posttest, and three-month post-intervention follow-up to assess the stability of program gains. Information on the mothers' behaviors was collected at each of the three intervals from two independent sources: (a) a descriptive and evaluative report written by a nurse at the well-baby clinic, and (b) a psychosocial report written by a social worker at the welfare agency. Mothers who were assigned a parent aide were also asked to participate in a structured interview where they were asked to comment on the overall intervention, the women who visited them, and any changes in their behavior.

At the end of the intervention period, nine of the twenty mothers who had been linked with a parent aide showed positive change in their abusive behavior. In contrast, only one mother in the control group demonstrated positive change. "Four out of nine [program] mothers whose behavior changed indicated that the intensive contact itself served as social control and the mother changed her behaviour in order not to expose herself" (p. 480). Nine mothers associated an increase in self-confidence, an enhanced self-image, and reduced stress with the attention that they received from their parent aides. In addition, four mothers attributed the positive change in their behavior to the help that they received with housework. According to Zimrim, "this new situation lowers the need to abuse the child"

(p. 481). Regrettably, these positive outcomes do not seem to persist after the intervention ends. At three months postintervention, only one mother who was matched with a parent aide continued to demonstrate positive behavior change. All other mothers reverted to their former abusive behavior patterns. Given these findings, Zimrim concluded that human contact can be an effective intervention strategy if the relationship continues for as long as the mother and/or the family is experiencing difficulty.

SELF-HELP/MUTUAL-AID STRATEGIES

Self-help or mutual-aid organizations are probably the best known methods of informal helping. Typically, these organizations are made up of small, voluntary groups of people who share similar histories and/or interests, and who wish to learn from others' experiences (Borman, 1984). These groups are designed to extend peer support and to decrease isolation, and to provide members with opportunities for mutual helping, access to valued social roles, and a framework through which they can learn to change their behaviors (Stavrakaki, 1985).

Breton (1980) reported on a child abuse demonstration project created in 1976 by the East Branch of the Children's Aid Society of Metro Toronto. To counteract the impact of social isolation on mothers' abusive behaviors, a small group approach was adopted. Initially, the group consisted of seven voluntarily participating mothers, all of whom were emotionally, economically, and socially deprived, and who had also been physically abusive toward their child(ren). While their children were being cared for in their homes, the women met weekly for about four hours in the morning. A small apartment had been rented in the mothers' neighborhood for this purpose. While funds were available, program activities mainly involved hairdressing (a nonthreatening and socially acceptable activity) and sharing a meal. For the first eight months, leadership of the group fell to several nurturing women including the hairdresser, a caterer, and two social workers. Over time, as the professionals and other outside lay helpers withdrew from the group, leadership shifted to the mothers, who, with support from two volunteers, continued to meet.

Approximately three to four years after the program began, a small qualitative evaluation was conducted. Breton did not indicate how many mothers participated in the study; however, she did mention that some of the original members were still involved in the group. Mothers were asked for their opinions of various aspects of the group through a series of open-ended questions. When asked if they had a clear idea of why they joined the group, all of the mothers answered Yes, citing reasons such as to talk about their problems, to get away from their children, to get out of the house, and to relax. In response to the question, "How has the group changed?", most mentioned that leadership for the group had shifted from professionals to self-direction. Questions about group processes prompted the majority of women to report that the group was more open-minded than when it began; all of the women said that they had made friends in the group and felt a part of the group. When asked to rate the significance of the group, all but one of the mothers stated that the group was just as important as their families. Reflecting on how the group had affected their lives, the majority of mothers said they had learned better child management skills and felt more self-confident, and all of them said they felt more independent and less isolated.

Based on the mothers' comments, Breton concluded that if abusive parents are provided with nurturing supports in the beginning of group development a basic helping network evolves within the group. However, Breton also points out that the *initial* costs of providing these supports were high. Operating the mothers' group involved retaining the services of both professional and lay helpers, renting the apartment, purchasing food, and providing child care. Breton concluded:

> that the massive investment necessary to attract deprived and isolated individuals, whether they are abusing parents or simply non-coping parents will have a high return in the long run, as these individuals take advantage of their newfound social network to get the support they need without resorting to professional or social welfare funded services. (1980, p. 81)

Cameron et al. (1992) assessed three parent mutual aid organizations (PMAO) for child welfare families in three medium-sized southern Ontario cities. They provided the following summary of the Parent Mutual Aid Organizations in Child Welfare Demonstration Project: [4]

> The hybrid model created for this project was based on several areas of understanding. First, the project was firmly grounded in the daily realities faced by child welfare families. These include multiple problems touching on individual, family and social factors, which more often than not also represent long-term needs. Secondly, the project pieced together experience from existing family support programs. The picture that emerged highlighted the importance of providing high levels of direct contact through multiple services and supports rather than single, time limited interventions. Finally, the project tried to pull together current knowledge on mutual aid and social support. Mutual aid groups that work seem to have several characteristics: members share a common experience, membership is voluntary, equality among members is stressed, members meet regularly, and leadership is provided by members themselves. . . .

One of the first challenges facing the project was to create a practical program model that reflected this knowledge about families using child welfare services, family support programs and mutual aid. The following organizing principles became the starting point for each of the mutual aid organizations.

1.   Allow participants access to high levels of direct contact per week (2–5 times in scheduled activities and between meeting contacts among members).

2.   Provide access to a variety of helping strategies and activities (for example, parent relief, information, personal development courses, emotional support, concrete resources).

3.   Provide a safe place to be and to facilitate access to a positive network of peers.

4.   Help members become friends with each other and to contact each other outside of scheduled meeting times.

5.   Facilitate members becoming helpers as well as receivers of assistance.

6.   Facilitate members assuming responsibility for running and maintaining their own organization.

7.   Encourage members to take part in a broader range of social involvements and to support them in new successful social roles (for example, group leader, student, employee, volunteer). . . .

A unique aspect of the PMAO was the broad array of program activities and experiences in which members participated. Over time interesting patterns emerged with respect to the kinds of activities that were emphasized. In the early stages of development recreational activities predominated, while later activities focused on members' program management responsibilities. Throughout the project, however, the importance of having fun and celebrating events and accomplishments was highlighted. As well, many of the social activities incorporated elements of skill building and health improvement, e.g., cooking, fitness, sewing, etc. Diverse educational opportunities focusing on personal growth issues relevant to member needs were also offered. These ranged from the use of cosmetics to information on sexual abuse. However, topics of greatest interest stressed parenting, academic and employment skills, and building members' abilities to manage their own organization. In addition, a regular feature of each PMAO was an activity called "check-in" where members informally talked with one another about issues of personal importance. [Members of the PMAO participated in program activities on average two to three times a week. Members also tended to contact each other outside of the PMAO by phone or in person two or more times a week. The average duration of involvement was six months to one year.] . . .

Both quantitative and qualitative methods were employed in documenting the implementation of the program and its impact on participants. Individual interviews were conducted with members of each PMAO as well as a comparison group of child welfare clients receiving regular child protection services at the three host agencies. These interviews occurred at three separate time periods throughout the life of the project. As well, focus groups were conducted with PMAO members during the first and third years of the demonstration project. Interviews were also conducted with the PMAO program development workers and other professionals involved at the sites. Program attendance data for the PMAO members was also recorded. . . .

Quantitative data were collected via a measurement package consisting of descriptive and demographic questions, several standardized instruments, and open-ended questions developed by the research team. Both program [$n = 96$] and comparison groups [$n = 60$] completed these instruments which gathered data on: the daily living realities of child welfare clients; the perceived availability of social resources; self-esteem; parental attitudes towards their children; marital satisfaction; perceived life stress; and, various dimensions of group involvement. Data were also collected with respect to out-of-home placement of children and use of regular child welfare services. [Data were gathered from agency records and in face-to-face interviews with the primary caregivers three times over a fourteen month evaluation period.] . . .

All PMAO members were asked to participate in the study. Comparison group members were selected to have children of the same age as the program sample. However, despite the efforts of the research team, it was not possible to obtain a random sample of comparison group members at individual sites. Therefore, the comparison sample cannot be assumed to be representative of the broader population of child welfare clients. It is worth highlighting, however, that there were indications that child welfare workers were excluding "higher risk" families from the comparison sample. This being the case, the data indicated that PMAO participants initially represented a "higher risk" group on a number of indicators than the comparison sample. . . .

Between 20% and 60% of all child welfare families referred to the PMAO attended program activities more than twenty times. And, between 13% and 40% attended more than forty times. These levels of direct contact were substantially higher than those available through most family support programs in child welfare. The variation in participation patterns among the three mutual aid organizations was largely accounted for by the support resources available and how well integrated each PMAO was into the host child welfare agency. . . .

There were consistently significant differences in out-of-home placement of PMAO and comparison samples. The PMAO sample used care one-half to one-third as frequently as the comparison group sample. Further, it appeared that PMAO participation was preventing use of care as a short-term and medium-term intervention. While significantly fewer PMAO members had children placed, the ones who were placed tended to be in care on average four to eight weeks longer than the average comparison group case. . . .

At two out of three sites and for all time periods, the PMAO members had statistically significant lower levels of involvement with child protection workers than the comparison group sample. Perhaps even more importantly, they showed a far greater percentage decline in the levels of contact with child protection workers. These patterns did not occur at the third site because agency policy required PMAO members to have regular contact with child protection personnel. . . .

The PMAO sample consistently showed statistically significant positive change on most [personal and family functioning] outcome indicators over the evaluation time period, while the comparison group sample demonstrated very little change on any indicators. The PMAO sample showed higher levels of social involvement (most of it centred on the PMAO), improved access to social support, improved self-esteem, improved parenting attitudes, and improved confidence in ability to cope with daily stress. In addition, there was some evidence of higher levels of positive change for PMAO members in terms of their ability to cope with limited finances, home management responsibilities and family health problems. . . .

Basic cost estimates suggested per case cost advantages for the PMAO sample of between $420 and $869 per year. If forty families were served by the PMAO over a year, this would result in annual savings to the agency of between $16,800 and $34,760. . . .

[Cameron, Hayward and Mamatis (1992) considered that] the outcomes from the evaluation of the PMAO were very encouraging and compare favourably with those from other intensive family support program models in child welfare. While it may not be suitable for all clients, the PMAO can be a useful compliment to professional ways of helping. . . .

At the same time, the program development requirements of the PMAO model were found to be quite formidable. Thus, while the benefits to participating families and to the sponsoring agencies indicate the value of continued expansion of mutual aid methods in child welfare, there is also a need to approach this undertaking with respect for the effort and the commitment that will be required to succeed. . . .

It was beyond the scope of the Demonstration Project to determine what would be required to implement the PMAO model in a general fashion across the child welfare system. However, our experience in this project suggests the question is worth pursuing. The lack of progress made by comparison group members receiving regular child welfare services was striking and points to a clear need for more effective service delivery models. Moreover, the positive impacts associated with participation in a PMAO indicates this program model may be an important compliment to the service delivery system in child welfare. (pp. 2–8)

Cameron and Rothery (1985) assessed a self-help program with groups in Kapuskasing and Cochrane in northern Ontario. Organized by the local Children's Aid Society, these self-help groups involved families with very similar presenting problems to many of the families in the study's total sample of 547 child welfare cases. Cameron and Rothery (1985) provided the following general description of the self-help program:

The Self-Help Program is organized around two groups working independently of each other in two different municipalities. About 20 women are active participants in each self-help group. Besides activities for participating mothers, each group has organized a parent-assisted day care service for their children. The philosophy of the program emphasizes an approach to program planning and implementation in which the women decide on priorities and "own" the group. The groups explicitly provide social support to these women and encourage mutual aid and socializing. These are not treatment groups. Neither are the groups organized around a predetermined educational curriculum. Rather, activities have been varied including undertakings as diverse as camping, recreation and sports, giving community dinners, presenting a play, inviting guest speakers, social events, visiting community services, fund-raising, as well as following a parenting and life skills course. The women were proud of their accomplishments and expressed their loyalty to their self-help group. The groups are places where they can feel at home. Participants in the program have definite long-term social support requirements. (pp. 68–69)

Participants in the self-help group ($n = 22$) were compared to randomly selected samples of cases from the same agency ($n = 30$) and the same region ($n = 91$) as well as other cases from the study sample with similar aged children and the total nonprogram study sample ($n = 547$). Ratings were made by workers of family functioning at case opening (done retro-spectively) and at the time of the first evaluation interview. Approximately six to eight months later each worker reviewed a brief questionnaire for each case requesting follow-up information on that family.

The review of this self-help program was very encouraging and demon-strated (a) low unit costs; (b) very few children going into care, less time being spent in care, and good success at returning children home from care; (c) a clear positive impact on case closures and client independence from the agency; (d) high member satisfaction and pride in their group accom-plishments; (e) increased social connectedness and access to problem-solving resources; (f) improved personal functioning of adult participants; and (g) a better public image for the agency. Due to limitations of this study's design, these results were considered by the researchers to be suggestive rather than conclusive.

An investigation of Parents Anonymous (Lieber & Baker, 1977)[5] demon-strated favorable outcomes for the members involved in the group. Parents Anonymous is a mutual aid group for parents who feel that they are at risk of abusing their children and focuses on developing support networks through peer counseling, confidence building, consciousness raising, formal teach-ing, and mutual support among members (Lieber & Baker, 1977; Comstock, 1982; McCarthy, 1976; Murphy, 1980; Nix, 1980; Powell, 1979). Profes-sional support is usually available to the organization.

This evaluation process was overseen by Parents Anonymous staff, board members, group members, and representatives of the funding agency. In total, 613 questionnaires were analyzed. The characteristics of the Parents Anonymous members participating in the study indicated many similarities with the members of the child welfare group studied in Cameron and Rothery (1985). The results from this investigation also were very encouraging: (a) the members expressed high levels of satisfaction with their membership in Parents Anonymous; (b) there was a substantial decrease in the frequency and severity of physical abuse almost immediately after entering Parents Anonymous; (c) there was a sizable decrease in the level of verbal abuse and this increased with the length of participation; (d) there was a positive relationship between participants' self-esteem and their length of involvement; (e) members developed feelings of greater personal competence as well as an increased ability to deal with stress; (f) there was a reduction in social isolation and a greater willingness to seek help that became more evident over time in the group; and (g) there was a positive impact on the parents' understanding of child behavior and development and this increased over time. However, the lack of a comparison group and the gathering of data at one point in time are limitations in this particular study.

A separate investigation of Parents Anonymous by the Berkeley Planning Associates (1977) echoed these positive conclusions. These researchers found that, for families troubled with child abuse, Parents Anonymous or peer group therapy was "the treatment modality of choice," both in terms of relative costs and lasting positive impacts upon families.

Participation in mutual aid organizations has also been beneficial for persons outside child welfare, such as the elderly, teenagers of alcoholic parents, and widows. For example, an evaluation of SAGE (Lieberman & Gourach, 1979)[6], a mutual aid group that emphasizes a variety of personal change strategies with elderly members, found that its members (two groups of thirty) had significantly lower depression and anxiety scores, lower anomie and parental strain scores, and higher life satisfaction scores than a control group of thirty nonmembers. Similarly, Berkowitz, Waxman, and Yaffe (1988) reported positive results with a resident mutual aid model among the elderly. The program was designed to reduce isolation and loneliness, increase social skills, and enhance mental and physical well-being. Residents were trained as volunteers to sponsor social events and weekly self-help group meetings, and make referrals for needed services. Although the mutual aid model was modest, residents involved in the program demonstrated greater perceived control, social involvement, and self-esteem, as compared to a control group of residents who did not have access to the program.

A study of Alateen (Hughes, 1977), a mutual aid group for adolescents who have alcoholic parents, revealed positive changes in self-esteem for members ($n = 25$) in contrast to a control group ($n = 25$) of adolescents who had an alcoholic parent but were not members of Alateen. Alateen members also had fewer problems at school or with law enforcement officials. Similarly, Alcoholics Anonymous has demonstrated its effectiveness in maintaining its members' sobriety over periods of time (Alford, 1980; Gartner & Riessman, 1977).

A two-year study of widows' mutual aid groups revealed that nonmember widows showed greater immediate postbereavement depression and preoccupation with the past compared to group members. Also, group members showed substantially better socialization twelve months after the loss of a partner than the control group (Vachon, Lyall, Rogers, Friedman-Letafsky, & Freeman, 1980). Another study reported that THEOS, a mutual aid group for the widowed, positively affected the well-being of its members. Active members of THEOS experienced less depression, increased self-esteem, and less use of medication as compared to members who were not very active (Todres, 1982).

COMMUNITY LIVING NETWORKS[7]

Gaudin et al. (1990–1991) reported the results of a demonstration project designed to reduce neglectful parenting through interventions to strengthen individuals' informal networks. Neglectful families were identified through the Department of Family and Children's Services, and were randomly assigned to the Social Network Intervention Project (SNIP) ($n = 34$) or to the control group ($n = 17$). Comparison group members received the regular casework services offered by the Department.

The SNIP model involved five steps:

1. assessment of the family's network;
2. assessment of the family's psychosocial functioning;
3. identification of barriers that prevented families from developing healthy and supportive network linkages;
4. goal-setting based upon the barriers and problems;
5. interventions that included the social network interventions and professional casework/case management activities.

The social network interventions included:

1. personal networking, which involved attempts to strengthen the family's existing social networks;
2. creating mutual aid groups for parents, facilitated by SNIP social workers, which met weekly for two hours for a six-month duration, and groups for children;
3. linking volunteers to families to provide parent-aide services and assist with the groups;

4. identification of existing neighborhood helpers in the SNIP families' communities;
5. social skills training in the mutual aid parent group.

Assessments of the families in both the program and control groups were completed prior to participation, six months after participation was initiated, and twelve months after participation was initiated. The period of program involvement varied considerably, ranging from two to twenty-three months. Ten months was the median length of involvement for the families served through the project. The assessments of the families included a determination of the size, composition, and supportiveness of the mother's support network, using the Social Network Assessment Guide, developed by Gaudin. As well, the level of neglect was measured by three rating scales (Childhood Level of Living Scale, Child Neglect Severity Scale, and Indicators of Caretaking Environment for Children Scale). Lastly, the Adult-Adolescent Parenting Inventory was used to indicate attitudes that have been associated with maltreating parents (Gaudin et al., 1990–1991).

After six months, the SNIP families were found to score more positively on the three measures of parenting adequacy than the comparison group families. As well, improvements were made on the Adult-Adolescent Parenting Inventory, indicating that the SNIP families had significantly more appropriate expectations for their children. Furthermore, improvement in the SNIP families' supportive networks were reported. After twelve months of participation, SNIP families reported highly significant changes on the three measures of parenting adequacy. No significant changes were reported on these same measures for the comparison group families. This same pattern was noted for the Adult-Adolescent Parenting Inventory, that is, improvements were noted for the SNIP families, but no significant changes were noted for the comparison group families. Furthermore, at the twelve-month retest, the SNIP families reported significant increases in the size and supportiveness of their informal networks. The comparison families' networks remained essentially the same. Finally, at the time of termination of the project, 59% of the SNIP families had their cases closed, compared to 23.5% of the control group families (Gaudin et al., 1990–1991).

Recovery Inc., the Association of Nervous and Former Mental Patients, provides a social network for formerly hospitalized psychiatric patients. Raiff (1984) studied 393 former psychiatric patients after they had joined Recovery Inc. She found that these members consistently improved on all measurements of medical utilization. In particular, although 50.6% of the study's sample had been hospitalized at some time in the past, only 17.6% of this group was hospitalized after joining the organization. In addition, although 32.3% of the sample had experienced electroconvulsive therapy (ECT) at some time in the past, only 3.3% of this group experienced ECT after joining

Recovery Inc. Furthermore, 92% of the members replied positively to the question of how happy they felt with "the way things are these days."

The Community Network Development (CND) program created a self-help organization for psychiatric patients, which helped members enhance their social networks and develop life and leadership skills. A Peer Mutual Aid Network was initiated in the hospital, and patients were assisted in developing peer self-management techniques. Once patients were discharged into the community, they joined the CND. The CND was described as a "community-based, patient-managed leadership and support program which prepares patients for the transition from residential treatment to community life" (Todres, 1982, p. 42). Edmunson et al. (1984) conducted a controlled evaluation of this network. Individuals ($n = 80$) discharged from a nine-week intensive treatment unit were randomly assigned to either the CDN or to a control group. There were no significant demographic or psychiatric differences between the two groups prior to the intervention. The evaluation was very positive:

> At an average follow-up interval of 10 months, one-half as many patients in the CDN group had required hospitalization as compared with the control group (17.5% to 35%) and CDN members' average total days of hospitalization was lower (7.0 days vs. 24.6 days). Finally, a significantly greater percentage of CDN members were able to function without any mental health system contact (52.5% to 26%). (p. 201)

In another investigation, Froland and his associates (1981) reviewed the informal helping strategies used by a variety of social agencies. They concluded that interventions that enhance or create personal networks or build mutual aid networks resulted in a demonstrable reduction in institutionalization and greater independence from formal services.

SUMMARY: INFORMAL SUPPORT PROGRAMS

Informal helping comes from constructive exchanges with friends, relatives, peers, neighbors, co-workers, and others in a social network. It is unpaid helping and is often characterized by reciprocity between the helping partners. Personal attributes and willingness to participate rather than formal training are the strengths of informal helpers.

The literature suggests that there have been few attempts to use informal helping in child welfare. Nonetheless, the limited number of studies uncovered on informal helping with disadvantaged families were encouraging about the usefulness of informal helping. The review found three informal helping program models in use with families considered at risk of child maltreatment: lay home visitors, mutual aid organizations and community living networks. The research findings for the mutual aid and community living network approaches, in particular, suggested their value for disadvantaged populations. However, what is clear is that more experimentation with informal helping in child welfare and other service sectors is required in order to properly understand its potential.

Lay home visitor programs provided one-to-one visiting in the families' homes. The visitors were community volunteers, often from similar backgrounds to the visited family, who received little formal training for their roles as visitors. Families were visited two to three times a week and the length of program involvement ranged from three months to almost two years. Mutual aid organizations were created specifically for parents using child welfare services. These mutual aid organizations offered program activities a few times a week and members often got together socially outside program activity times. Members were encouraged to share their experiences and to help each other and member responsibility for managing the mutual aid organizations was encouraged. The duration of involvement could legitimately be long-term, but there was substantial variation in the length of participation in these programs. The community living networks shared many of these characteristics with the mutual aid organizations. They often included mutual aid groups as part of a broader array of informal helping strategies and community supports. They too offered members chances to connect with each other and encouraged mutual aid among members. Network participation could be long-term and frequent access to other members was possible.

The Range of Support Available: Lay Home Visitors helpers provided emotional supports, concrete assistance, and some information and modeling about appropriate behaviors. Mutual aid organizations and community living networks provided a broad array of supports including emotional supports, concrete assistance, social and recreational activities, instruction, some crisis support, friendships, and opportunities for new types of responsibilities.

The Level of Supports Available: All three informal helping approaches offered face-to-face contacts in program activities at least twice a week. Mutual aid organizations and community living networks facilitated additional friendly contacts between members outside scheduled program activities.

Availability in a Crisis: None of these approaches were designed as rapid response, twenty-four-hour-a-day programs. The more intensive lay home visitor programs would be available to family members during periods of high stress. The mutual aid organizations and community living networks would give members access to other members who they might call upon when they were feeling overwhelmed.

Motivation and Skill Requirements: Lay home visitors actively reached out to families. Mutual aid organizations and community living networks appear to make relatively high motivation and skill demands upon participants compared to the other support program models reviewed. Participants in both approaches were self-selected.

Focused Technical Expertise: Lay home visitors are not intended to bring professional expertise to families. Some mutual aid organizations with a specialized focus acquire a good deal of expertise in confronting particular difficulties. The same would likely be true of some community living networks. However, the level of expertise available to members varied greatly from program to program.

The Length of Time Supports Available: Lay home visitors tended to be involved with families from a few months to two years. Mutual aid organizations and community living networks can quite legitimately create opportunities for members to participate for years. Duration of participation would vary substantially from family to family in mutual aid organizations and community living networks.

Reciprocity and Social Integration: Mutual aid organizations and community living networks were the strongest of the support programs reviewed in encouraging participants to do for themselves and become helpers of others in similar circumstances. They provided members with access to a stable social network of peers and facilitated the development of friendships between members. Members were also supported in assuming new responsibilities and roles. Lay home visitor programs did not facilitate these kinds of involvement for family members.

Anticipated Program Impacts and Rationales: There was some evidence that the more intensive lay home visitor programs reduced child maltreatment and child placements as well as produced improvement in parenting behaviors. However, there were reasons to suspect that these gains disappeared when program supports were withdrawn. The more intensive and longer-term mutual aid organizations and community living networks clearly reduced institutional and foster care placements. Participants reported greater self-confidence and perceived abilities to cope with difficulties. For many members, there was a dramatic increase in the size and supportiveness of their social network and in their positive social involvements. Because of these connections and the levels of informal support available, mutual aid organizations and community living networks were the only support program approaches reviewed that lessened reliance on professional helpers and closed cases at service agencies. When mutual aid organizations focused on particular personal difficulties, then improvements in these areas often were noted.

NOTES

1.   The theoretical and empirical rationales for the importance of informal support and positive social integration are discussed in Chapters 3 and 4 of this volume. They will not be repeated here. Rather, this discussion focuses specifically on the use of informal support programs in child welfare and related service sectors.

2.   This summary in this section was adapted from Cameron et al. (1992, pp. 23–24).

3.   This national evaluation was conducted by Berkeley Planning Associates (1977).

4.   Adapted from Cameron and Birnie-Lefcovitch (1992).

5.   This review of Lieber and Baker (1977) and Berkeley Planning Associates (1977) was adapted from Cameron et al. (1992, pp. 54–55).

6.   The following reviews of Lieberman and Gourach (1979), Berkowitz et al. (1988), Hughes (1977), Alford (1980), Gartner and Riessman (1977), Vachon et al. (1980), and Todres (1982) were adapted from Cameron et al. (1992, pp. 58–59).

7.   Summaries of community living network interventions were adapted from Cameron et al. (1992, p. 55–58).

Comprehensive Support Programs _____ 10

Many share the belief that child maltreatment is a multifaceted challenge that requires packages of services and supports as a response (Cameron et al., 1983; Garbarino & Gilliam, 1980; Gaudin, 1993; Geismar & Krisberg, 1967; Halper & Jones, 1981; Helfer, 1982, cited in Cameron et al., 1983; Jones, Magura, & Shyne, 1981; Jones, Neuman, & Shyne, 1976; Lutzker & Rice, 1984; Rothery, 1990a; Rothery & Cameron, 1985; Sinanoglu, 1981, cited in Cameron et al., 1983; Whittaker & Garbarino, 1983; Wodarski, 1981a, 1981b). The premise is that a focused intervention would not be effective in eliminating maltreatment in families coping with multiple difficulties because it would respond to only certain elements precipitating abuse (Cohn & Daro, 1987; Daro, 1988; Pallone & Malkemes, 1984; Wodarski, 1981a, 1981b). For example, a support program that offers only parenting training may be disregarding the daily living realities of poverty and isolation, which can also contribute to maltreatment (Dumas & Wahler, 1983; Wahler, 1980b). A comprehensive support program, on the other hand, might offer individual counseling to the parent in combination with other supports such as vocational skills training, access to transportation, a parent socialization group at a neighborhood drop-in center, child care, and recreational activities for the children.

PARAMETERS OF COMPREHENSIVE STRATEGIES

There were few standard defining features for the comprehensive programs reviewed other than that each intervention combined several helping strategies. Some programs offered a standard package of services/supports, while in others the family received individually tailored services/supports. Consequently, as Bidgood and van de Sande (1990) pointed out, "the degree of variance across programs makes it impossible to describe a general program model" (p. 121). Nevertheless, it is possible to outline some common patterns described in the literature.

Comprehensive programs often incorporated both formal and informal approaches, through there tended to be an emphasis on formal (paid) help. Services drew on the skills and resources of multiple helpers, including professionals, paraprofessionals, and volunteers. Several authors emphasized the need to coordinate the efforts of the various helpers (e.g., Greenley & Robitschek, 1991; Whittaker & Garbarino, 1983; Wieder et al., 1988). Rothery's (1990b) review of the literature suggested that service coordination was best accomplished if one of the helpers involved with the family was appointed as the case manager. This primary helper would be instrumental not only in coordinating services, but also in providing the family with access to someone who was familiar with their circumstances. There was also some indication that the primary helpers in comprehensive programs had smaller caseloads compared to regular child protection workers, permitting increased levels of contact between helpers and families (Stephens, 1979).

Coming up with an effective blend of program elements requires creativity as well as a sound knowledge of helping alternatives. A number of authors have offered their own formulas for working with disadvantaged families. Wodarski (1981a, 1981b) favored a support program comprised of child management training, marital enrichment counseling, and the development of vocational and interpersonal skills. Rothery (1990a) advocated an approach that provides emotional and educational supports, addresses concrete needs, and works to reduce social isolation. According to Gaudin (1993), "multiservice models that use family counseling, parent groups, and trained paraprofessionals to supplement skilled professional problem-solving counseling offer the best chances of success" (p. 86). The range of supports described by Cameron and his associates (1983) included skill development, counseling, concrete assistance, informal supports, and efforts to reduce social isolation. While several authors recommended the concurrent delivery of services and supports (Helfer, 1982, cited in Cameron et al., 1983; Rothery & Cameron, 1985), the provision of concrete resources and helping with immediate "survival concerns" (Rothery, 1990b) often were given priority. As explained by Rothery (1990b) and Geismar and Ayres (1958), a family is better able to work on skill development, family interactions, and other personal concerns if they do not have to worry about meeting their survival needs, such as food, physical safety, child care, and decent housing.

Many comprehensive programs were described as systems-oriented rather than parent-focused. Service packages often offered services and/or supports to a variety of family members and focused on both personal and environmental factors. For example, a package might have included a mutual aid group for parents, an afterschool program for the children, family counseling, and assistance in locating suitable housing.

In the studies reviewed, most provided little information about the intensity or the duration of program involvement. However, in those projects where participation patterns were described, involvement lasted from four months to several years with several programs offering a year or more of participation. Once a week was a minimum level of contact, with many programs providing opportunities for involvement twice a week or more.

OUTCOME STUDIES OF COMPREHENSIVE PROGRAMS

Descriptions of comprehensive program models are considerably more abundant in the literature than outcome studies. Bidgood and van de Sande (1990) have attempted to explain this gap in the literature by pointing out the methodological challenges associated with assessing complex program models. When evaluations have been done for comprehensive support programs, researchers frequently have focused on global program effects, such as a lower reincidence of abuse, and reduced risk factors associated with child maltreatment, rather than the specific impacts of the various program components. This chapter examines available outcome evaluations of comprehensive support programs used with child welfare populations.

REVIEWS OF MULTIPLE COMPREHENSIVE SUPPORT PROGRAMS

This section reports the findings from several reviews that summarized the research evidence for the effectiveness of a number of comprehensive support programs in different settings. These reviews focused on broad indicators of effectiveness (e.g., decreased incidence of child maltreatment, fewer child placements, cost savings) and several examined programming characteristics correlated with better outcomes.

To examine the effectiveness of short-term multicomponent treatment programs, Cohn (1979) reviewed the eleven different abuse/neglect projects that made up the National Demonstration Program on Child Abuse and Neglect. To study the different service packages, Cohn used a multiple comparison group design, that is, the families receiving one type of program were compared to families receiving different service packages. Participants in this study were the 1,724 parents who received at least one month of services from one of the eleven projects during the two-year period between January 1975 and December 1976. This large group of parents was heterogeneous in nature, incorporating cases of substantiated abuse as well as parents considered to be at high risk of maltreatment, and both voluntary and court-mandated participants. Approximately 30% of the parents received a package consisting of lay services (e.g., parent aide counseling, Parents Anonymous), individual counseling, and case management. Another 12% of the participants were offered group service packages that combined group therapy or parent education classes with other services. Individual counseling was the only service given to the remaining 54% of participants. Instrument packages, completed by case managers trained to complete the forms, requested information on the nature and severity of maltreatment, the types and amounts of services received by parents from a particular project or on a referral basis, recurrence of abuse/neglect during service, and workers' judgments regarding parents' abusive behavior in the future.

Cohn (1979) reported that the data did not suggest a single best method of service delivery. While the review revealed that the most effective service packages included lay service, only 53% of those receiving this component demonstrated a reduced propensity for maltreatment. However, less than 40% of the parents receiving any other mix of services demonstrated benefits from their involvement. Cohn offered various reasons why lay services may have been somewhat more effective than the other services: (a) the difference in case load size (one to three families for a lay counselor; twenty to twenty-five families for a full-time service worker), which permitted lay counselors to spend more time with each family, (b) the different role expectations, which allowed lay counselors to become the family's friend, (c) the fact that the "stigma of authority" was not attached to lay counselors, and (d) the ability of mutual aid groups to provide parents with supportive environments in which they learned to deal with their problems and to respect themselves.

Lay service packages also were found to be less expensive than either professional group therapy or individual counseling models. The annual cost per case for lay service packages was given as $1,400 (U.S., 1979 rates) compared to $1,700 for professional individual counseling. Factoring in the higher "success" rates for lay service models provided further support for the cost-effectiveness of this approach. Programs incorporating lay services cost approximately $2,600 per successful case, compared to professional group services at $4,000 per successful case, and $4,700 per successful case for professional individual counseling. However, regardless of the type of intervention package, Cohn states:

> [A]lthough it clearly costs a program money to keep a client in treatment for any length of time, this study found that the likelihood of reduced propensity is significantly increased and it is more cost effective if a client is in treatment for six months to a year. (p. 517)

Cohn and Daro (1987) later combined the results of the National Demonstration Program on Child Abuse and Neglect presented above (Cohn, 1979; Berkeley Planning Associates, 1977) with three other studies. One of the additional studies was Abt Associates' (1981) evaluation of twenty programs funded by the National Center on Child Abuse and Neglect (NCCAN). A total of 488 families took part in this investigation. Another study was White's (1981) assessment of twenty-nine service improvement grants, also funded by NCCAN. For this study, data were gathered from 165 families. The final study was Berkeley Planning Associates' (1983) evaluation of nineteen programs. One thousand families were involved in this study. In sum, Cohn and Daro's (1987) review spans over ten years of research on eighty-nine demonstration treatment programs, involving 3,253 families.

Each of the four evaluations used the multiple-comparison group design described earlier (see Cohn, 1979). The choice of data collection methods was not consistent across the studies; however, all measures were restricted to workers' judgments rather than direct measures of families' behavior. As in the Cohn (1979) study, the studies' participants varied in family characteristics and perceived risk of child maltreatment, but similarities were noted regarding their major presenting problems.

The study by Berkeley Planning Associates (1983) corroborated the Cohn (1979) study's findings suggesting that service packages incorporating lay services resulted in more positive participant outcomes and were more cost-effective than any other service combinations or singular interventions. On the other hand, Abt Associates' (1981) evaluation found no significant correlation between a particular blend of services and positive client outcomes. Cohn and Daro (1987) concluded:

> [T]he latest child abuse and neglect demonstration projects made more progress in reducing the propensity for future maltreatment and in improving client functioning than those funded a decade ago. . . . *Expansions in the service package* and the better targeting of services to specific child maltreatment subpopulations are among the factors which have most likely contributed to these successes. (p. 439; italics added)

MULTIPLE-COMPONENT PROGRAMS

The programs discussed in this section were characterized by multiple program components but appeared not to have any central core of program elements that participants received. Services often were individualized for families.

Childhaven (Durkin, 1986; Sheehan, 1984, cited in Miller & Whittaker, 1988) was a multidisciplinary program operated out of a private child care agency in Seattle. It offered individualized service plans consisting of therapeutic day care in conjunction with transportation and other concrete services, education, parent support groups, referrals to health and social services, and health, developmental, and psychological services for children. The evaluation of this program involved the 142 families that were referred by Child Protective Services. On average these families remained in the program for thirteen months. The measures used to evaluate the effects of the program included child behavior assessments, reports of abuse or neglect, clinical assessments of both parent and child improvement, and the discontinuation of Child Protective Services' involvement with the family. Upon leaving the program, 69% of families had improved in all identified problem areas, including reincidence of abuse. The results also indicate a positive relationship between the duration of families' contact with the program and goal achievement. Unfortunately, the study did not include any comparison group or follow-up information.

Comprehensive Emergency Services (CES), a demonstration project that was offered by the Children's Bureau of the Department of Health Education and Welfare, Nashville, Tennessee, endeavored to coordinate the services available to families with an identified child maltreatment problem (Hawkins, 1979). The primary goal of CES was to develop an extensive network of services available to children and families at risk. The CES system operated on the basis of three assumptions:

> [(a)] *any system serving children and their families should seek to maintain and strengthen that family and avoid whenever possible separation of children from their parents,* . . . [(b)] services would seek to respond to crisis situations involving families . . . [and, (c)] families in crisis must be offered rescue and must be assisted in assessing the alternatives available to them so they can make decisions regarding their lives. (Hawkins, 1979, pp. 105–106; italics added)

CES incorporated seven main service components, though other types of resources were sought when necessary. A twenty-four-hour/seven-days emergency intake service provided families in crisis with a face-to-face response within one hour of a referral. Emergency caretakers were available, on a time-limited basis, to care for children in the family home when temporary guardianship was necessary. An emergency homemaker service also helped to maintain children in the home when a parent could not assume routine responsibilities. Children who were not able to remain in the family home could be cared for in emergency foster homes. To avoid the use of detention centers, emergency shelters geared to meet adolescents' needs were available to teens in crisis. When a crisis placed an entire family out of home (e.g., fires, evictions), alternative accommodations were acquired to keep parents and children together. Finally, ongoing counseling, assistance, and resource brokerage were offered through outreach and follow-up services.

Hawkins (1979) provided few details about the CES program and its evaluation. For example, information about CES service providers, the duration of involvements, and the mixtures of service components was not available. Particulars of the evaluation such as the research design, sources of information, and data collection procedures also were not available. However, the study's outcomes are reported. Substantiated cases of maltreatment decreased more than 55% from 602 cases in 1969–1970 to 266 in 1973–1974. A corresponding increase was noted in the number of families in which reports of suspected abuse or neglect were unsubstantiated upon investigation: 770 cases screened in 1969–1970 compared to 2,156 screened in 1973–1974. In the same time period, the number of children under six who were placed into institutional care dropped dramatically, from 180 cases to zero. A similar reduction in placement rates was noted for children entering noninstitutional care settings. Whereas 353 of these children were removed from their homes in 1969–1970, only 174 were placed in 1973–1974, a decrease of 51%. The percentage of recidivist cases also experienced a decline of 88%, from 196 cases in 1969–1970 to 23 in 1973–1974. Finally, despite the fact that referrals increased 92% from 1969 to 1974, there was a net savings of $68,000 (U.S., 1979 rates) between the old system and Comprehensive Emergency Services. Hawkins concludes that "a solution was achieved in which *effectiveness increased* while *cost decreased*. (p. 111; italics added).

Halper and Jones (1981) assessed Special Services for Children (SSC), a prevention demonstration project offered to disadvantaged families in the Bronx, New York. Despite the researchers' cautions that the information gathered from comparison group cases was limited, incomplete, and not of the best quality, this study had the strongest evaluation design found in the literature on comprehensive support programs. The research goals were to determine if intensive comprehensive services provided to families at risk of dissolution could help avert placement and improve the quality of children's lives in their families. Special Services for Children's mission was

> to provide services and opportunities that would help the parents develop
> confidence and competence in dealing with all aspects of their lives, especially
> with their parental responsibilities and where indicated, to provide supplemen
> tal care and stimulation to the children to maximize their developmental
> potential and enable them to better cope with their environment. (p. 22)

Program families were referred, sometimes involuntarily, by their caseworkers because of family dysfunction considered to be serious. The criteria for acceptance included: the family resided in the Bronx; program services had not been received in the past three years; the safety of the child could be assured if she/he remained in the home; at least one child under fourteen was at risk of placement; no court cases were pending; no child in the family had been in care for at least three years; one parent who has had contact with the child since birth or in the previous three years had accepted service; the child did not have any serious mental or emotional problems, and the primary caregiver was not psychotic or addicted to drugs.

Each service provider with SSC was responsible for eleven to twelve families. Comparison group workers, on the other hand, maintained average caseloads of eighteen families, though some of these workers were found to be responsible for up to thirty-three cases at one time.

A range of program components was available to program and comparison group families twenty-four hours a day, seven days a week. The types of assistance offered included counseling, homemaking, day care, chore service, babysitting, recreational/cultural enrichment, emergency children's services to meet after-hours needs, foster care, tutoring, vocational counseling/job training/placement, housing assistance, psychological/psychiatric evaluation, psychological/psychiatric treatment, family planning, medical services, legal aid, public assistance, and summer camps. The specific blend of services differed for each program family based on their identified needs; however, all program and most comparison group families received counseling and most reportedly concentrated initially on instrumental needs. Three additional services were open to demonstration project cases, but not to comparison group families: the twenty-four-hour hotline, emergency financial assistance from the project, and family assistants or special friends.

The investigation of the enriched SSC program was conducted over two years, from February 1978 to February 1980. A total of 120 families were randomly assigned to either the enriched services program group (sixty families), or a comparison group (sixty families) that received the regular complement of services offered to families. Analysis of baseline variables showed no significant differences between the two groups of families. The majority (93%) of families accepted for the project were protective service cases referred to SSC because of neglect (about two-thirds of the families), abuse (about one-third of families), or both (6% of cases). The remaining 7% of families were connected with SSC through voluntary requests for placement or homemaker services.

Service figures indicated relatively heavy use of the three enrichment services by experimental families: 23% of these families used the twenty-four-hour hotline, 47% made use of financial assistance from the program, and 35% of the families requested a family assistant or special friend. Of the eighteen remaining SSC services, only four were used as much or more by comparison group families when compared to program families.

Experimental families used SSC services from two to twenty-five months, with a median duration of fourteen months. Comparison group families tended to be involved with the program from one month to two years, with a median length of eight months. Results showed statistically significant differences between the two groups of families with regard to the number of in-person and telephone contacts. On average, families with the service enrichment options engaged in five times as many personal contacts and twelve times as many phone conversations with SSC workers than comparison group families. Even when the assessment period was limited to one year for each group, the enrichment program families still had three times the number of in-person contacts than comparison families (39 versus 12.5 contacts, respectively), and eight times as many phone calls (25.4 versus 3.4 calls, respectively).

A statistically significantly greater proportion of children receiving enriched services (98%) than children in the comparison group (90%) were living with their parents or other relatives at case closure or the end of the data collection phase. Furthermore, significantly fewer experimental children (4%) than comparison children (17%) were placed into care during the intervention period. When experimental children were placed in a foster home, they spent substantially fewer days in care (the six experimental children who experienced a placement spent a total of 685 days in care, or on average 114 days each; the twenty-two comparison group children spent 3,150 days in care for an average placement of 143 days).

Compared to children who received regular SSC services, children who were given the enriched service program were rated as having significantly better physical and emotional living arrangements. Though twice as many family functioning problems were identified for experimental families than comparison families, by the end of the evaluation period "the experimental group far outstrips the control group in the proportion of functioning problems that are believed to be 'better' by the end of the evaluation period. Conversely, a greater proportion of the problems for the control cases were 'worse'" (Halper & Jones, 1981, p. 125).

A total of nine experimental families (15%) were reported to the Central Registry for child maltreatment at some point after referral to SSC; seven cases were substantiated incidents and two were unsupported. Eight of the fifty-five comparison families for whom information was available were reported to the Central Registry; five cases were verified, two were unsubstantiated, one was pending decision.

Halper and Jones (1981) also included a cost-effectiveness analysis in their report. Over a three-year period, the projected cost of enriched services was $250,000, or between $3,000 and $4,000 per family, per year. Based on a rate of $25 per day for each child placed into foster care,

the enriched service resulted in a savings of $61,625 in foster care expenditures during the life of the project itself and $404,225 in anticipated expenditures over the next 4½ years, for a *total projected savings of $465,850 in foster care expenditures* attributable to the project. (p. 143; italics added)

CORE INTERVENTION PROGRAMS

The following programs had a core program element or combination of elements that every family received. However, there were also additional program components available to family members as needed.

Project 12-Ways (Lutzker & Rice, 1984; Lutzker, Wesch, & Rice, 1984) was described as an in-home service for the "treatment and prevention of child abuse and neglect." Emanating from the belief that child abuse is a problem with multiple contributing factors, Project 12-Ways attempted "to assess and treat as many contributing variables as possible when serving families under state child protective service because of indicated child abuse or neglect" (p. 64). The overall goal of the program was to reduce the propensity for future maltreatment by parents. Project 12-Ways incorporated fifteen different services: parent-child training, stress reduction and assertiveness training, multiple-setting behavior management, self-control training, social support, basic skills training, leisure time counseling, health maintenance and nutrition, home safety, marital counseling, alcoholism treatment and referral, pre- and postnatal prevention services for young and unwed mothers, job placement, and money management. In the majority of cases, families received more than one project component. Services were provided in multiple settings (e.g., clients' homes, schools, foster care settings, day care centers) and were delivered primarily by pairs of graduate students.

Lutzker and his colleagues (Lutzker & Rice, 1984; Lutzker et al., 1984) conducted an evaluation of Project 12-Ways. The design of this research involved a one-time, postintervention collection of data pertaining to two time periods for randomly selected groups of program and comparison families. Information on substantiated occurrences of abuse was gathered using records supplied by the Illinois State Control Registry. Fifty families receiving Project 12-Ways were compared with forty-seven families, matched on geographic area, who were receiving conventional child welfare services. All ninety-seven families were protective service clients with a history of at least one confirmed incident of abuse or neglect, or were considered at high risk for child maltreatment.

Results revealed significantly fewer reports of abuse and neglect during program involvement for Project 12-Ways families (one incident) in relation to the comparison group sample (five incidents). There were also significantly fewer reports of repeated abuse in program families (no cases) than in the comparison group (three cases). However, there was no significant difference between program and comparison group cases on their overall recidivism rates (four children were abused/neglected in program families after their program involvement ended; five comparison group children were maltreated after services were terminated). This last finding brought into question the project's ability to effect lasting change.

Lutzker and his associates were forthright in identifying the limitations of their study. First, other than their area of residence, no demographic information was collected on the comparison group families. Similarities and differences between the services provided to the two groups were not investigated. Likewise, the duration and frequency of contact were not studied. The extent of the gains comparison group families made during their contact with child protective services was also not reported. In addition, data were not available to determine if the two groups of families differed on the severity, frequency, or type of maltreatment. These limitations restricted the study's ability to predict the effectiveness of the program. Furthermore, in the absence of a cost-effectiveness analysis, the researchers were unable to determine whether Project 12-Ways was a more or less expensive approach to supporting families than conventional service strategies.

Parents and Children Together (PACT) (Callard & Morin, 1979) was another home-based demonstration project serving low-income families who had or were considered at risk of having a child placed into care because of abuse or neglect. PACT's primary goal was to keep parents and children together by averting placements or by returning children who were already in care to their families. Counselors worked with families to improve the conditions that were considered to precipitate a child's placement. Attention was directed at improving parenting and home management skills, though a range of service components was offered: counseling, skills modeling and demonstration, parenting workshops, re-education, linking to community resources, child care, surrogate siblings, surrogate parents, mental health consultation, and concrete assistance such as moving services, furniture and clothing donations, and home repairs. PACT services were coordinated and delivered by two-counselor teams trained in child development and family relationships that shared a caseload of not more than twelve families. When necessary, faculty from various departments at Wayne State University in Michigan (PACT headquarters) provided consultation regarding issues such as nutrition, housing, and consumer affairs. The combination of helping strategies was individually tailored to meet the specific needs of each family. Families participated on a voluntary basis and were selected for this program because they had expressed a desire to maintain custody of their children. Though not specifically stated, the duration of intervention seemed to range from two months to four months.

The evaluation of PACT looked at the 108 families, including 422 children, who were served between June 1977 and September 1978. No comparison group was used in the study. When the research concluded in September 1978, 60 cases had closed after an average of six months of service. The remaining 48 families (representing 214 children) remained as open cases, with 190 or 89% of the children in care or at risk of placement.

Several child placement rate outcomes are reported. Of the 324 children (representing 99 families) who had received at least two months of PACT services between June 1977 and September 1978:

[(a)] 197 (92%) of the children initially at home and indicated at risk remained at home, [(b)] 17 (8%) of the children initially at home and indicated at risk were placed into foster care, [(c)] 51 (46%) of the children in foster care were returned to their natural parent(s), and [(d)] 59 (54%) of the children [in foster care remained in their placements], although for many, return was imminent. (Callard & Morin, 1979, p. 63)

However, the lack of a comparison group indicates a need for substantial caution in interpreting these findings.

Callard and Morin found no significant differences between initial and terminating scores on the Child Social Adjustment Scale, the Inventory of Home Stimulation, or the Parent Interview measures. However, the dependent variables evaluated using the Monthly Assessments, which measured the status and seriousness of family problems, showed significant change. More specifically, upon case closure, parents demonstrated improved child management skills, positive parent-child interactions, an ability to provide a safe and stable home environment, and better use of personal and community resources. The reductions in number and severity of family problems were most pronounced after two months of treatment, with a ceiling effect occurring during the final two months. Callard and Morin claimed that this leveling off of program gains raises the question of the optimal duration of a family's involvement with PACT.

Stephens (1979) provided information about a third in-home demonstration project. The Polk County branch of Iowa Children and Family Services offered a wide spectrum of helping alternatives to help disadvantaged families cope with their many challenges. The families considered for this voluntary program had at least one adult and one child under eighteen living in the same home, and had at least one child considered to be at risk of placement. Service packages were coordinated by workers with undergraduate training in social work or psychology. These family workers generally provided supportive counseling, parenting skills training, and advocacy. Auxiliary services such as homemaking, marriage and family therapy, tutoring, and day care were provided by other helping agents. Each worker carried a caseload of approximately four to five families, each of which received about six hours of direct service per week. The intervention commenced with a two-week observation period during which the primary worker assessed the family's problem-solving abilities, defined treatment goals, and developed a suitable service package.

Stephens offered little information about the research design or methods used in the evaluation of the Polk County Children and Family Services Demonstration Project, though some data about placement rates and cost effectiveness were available. These findings are based on a study of a small sample of twenty-six "high-risk" families containing forty-three adults and eighty-nine children who were served by the project between June and December 1977. No comparison families were involved in the study.

Initial assessments suggested 46% of the families (i.e., twenty-six children in twelve families) were considered at risk of at least one of their children being placed. At the end of the six-month period, six children had been placed into either institutional or foster care. In terms of costs, Stephens estimated that in-home services for the twelve families with children at risk of placement would amount to $48,000 (U.S., 1979 rates), or $4,000 per family per year, assuming a full year of service was required. He compares this figure with the estimated expense of $332,000 for keeping all 26 children in care for one year. However, as the research on Intensive Family Preservation Services presented in Chapter 6 shows, the presumption that all of these participating children would have been placed without program involvement is far from credible.

Irueste-Montes and Montes (1988) compared the effects for voluntary and court-ordered participants in Project Respite and Remediation. This project had three primary components (day care, parent groups, and home treatment) in an integrated service plan aimed at helping families rather than only parents. Therapeutic family-style day care was provided for children ages one through six in groups of five for thirty-two hours a week by licensed child care workers. Two-hour parent group meetings were held once a week, during which family trainers and a child psychologist met with six to eight parents to work on parenting skills and to discuss their own personal development concerns. Family trainers also conducted weekly in-home sessions with entire families to demonstrate appropriate behavior and to provide feedback to help parents integrate the skills learned in the parent group meetings.

Over the three years Project Respite and Remediation was in operation, sixty-five families with substantiated histories of child maltreatment were referred by the El Paso County Department of Social Services in Colorado Springs, Colorado. Only forty-two of these families participated in the program and are represented in Irueste-Montes and Montes's (1988) study. To be considered for the program, several criteria had to be satisfied: the family had to include at least one abused/neglected child between one and six years old (could not be a situation involving sexual abuse); the abused/neglected child(ren) had to be in the home or able to return home; there could be no pending criminal charges against the parents other than for maltreatment; the children could not exhibit physical or mental disabilities; and, the parents could not be psychotic or have substance abuse problems. Twenty-four families were court-ordered to participate in Project Respite and Remediation and eighteen families participated of their own volition. Both groups received the same services.

The evaluation used a time-series design that compared the two program groups. No comparison sample was included in the study. Baseline measures were taken prior to the family's involvement with any program components. To collect these data, parent-child interactions were observed for approximately fifteen minutes on up to three occasions. The observer, who was usually the family trainer, recorded the types of behavior exhibited by parents and the corresponding reactions of the children. On average, there was an 83% interrater reliability level between family trainers' observations.

Evaluation findings showed similar outcomes for the mandated and voluntary clients. Both groups demonstrated significant increases in their use of praise and descriptive praise. Parents' criticism of their children significantly decreased from baseline to program end. There was some indication that parents had reduced their "attention to 'buggy' behavior" (from 19% at baseline to 15% at program end for voluntary parents, and from 12% at baseline to 9% at program end for mandated parents); however, these changes were not statistically significant. "Both groups of parents exhibited very low levels of physical aggression before and after treatment, although the court-ordered group displayed higher levels of occasional spanking, pinching, hair pulling, and arm twisting" (Irueste-Montes & Montes, 1988, p. 36). The increased severity of maltreatment in court-mandated families is also demonstrated in the finding that "three court-ordered families (and none of the voluntary families) lost permanent custody of their child during the first weeks of treatment" (p. 36).

EARLY INTERVENTION PROGRAMS

These programs focused on providing supports to families with young children before serious concerns with child maltreatment developed. They provided intensive and multiple supports to parents and sometimes to children.

The Yale Child Welfare Research Program (Rescarla, Provence, & Naylor, 1982; Seitz, Rosenbaum, & Apfel, 1985; Trickett, Apfel, Rosenbaum, & Zigler, 1982; for a synopsis see Heinicke et al., 1988), housed in a multidisciplinary agency providing social work, educational, and health care services, provided a combination of home visitors (primarily social workers), day care, extended pediatric care, developmental exams for children, support for mothers' education or career training, and family planning information. Services were provided to severely impoverished first-time parents (usually single mothers) from the onset of pregnancy until the child reached two-and-a-half years of age. Evaluation data indicate that over the course of the intervention each family had contact with the program on approximately 300 occasions (28 home visits, 13–17 well-baby examinations, 7–9 developmental examinations, and 13.5 months of day care). The interdisciplinary team of professionals delivering the program focused on strengthening the problem-solving skills of the family to achieve the goals of enhancing (a) mothers' adaptation, (b) the quality of mother-child relationships, and (c) children's development.

A ten-year follow-up investigation of eighteen matched pairs of families showed positive outcomes for program participants based on measures of maternal education, socioeconomic status, and parenting style, and on assessments of children's IQ levels, academic achievement, school behavior, and adjustment. At thirty months, children who were part of the Yale Child Development Research Project had higher language development scores than same-age comparison children. Also, at the end of the intervention period, program mothers, in relation to comparison mothers, reported higher developmental expectations of their children and were more likely to think that their children were experiencing problems. As the children reached seven-and-a-half years of age, program and comparison group families were again investigated. The results showed that program families attained higher socioeconomic status and had fewer children than nonprogram families. Furthermore, in families receiving project services, mothers were more likely to be employed, and children had higher IQ and academic scores and demonstrated better school attendance. The results at the final follow-up interval (child age ten) were again more promising for families that had experienced the Yale Child Welfare Research Program. Heinicke et al. (1988) summarize the ten-year follow-up findings in three sections:

> 1. [Program] mothers completed more years of education, waited longer to have a second child, were more frequently a part of a nuclear family, were more frequently self supporting, more frequently initiated contacts with teachers, and made greater use of remedial and supportive services.
> 2. [Program] mothers showed a better relationship with their child, who was seen as pleasing them and giving them pleasure.
> 3. Children [from comparison group families] were more frequently absent from school, made greater use of remedial services, and were more frequently described as disobedient, not getting along with other children, and as unhappy, sad, or depressed. (pp. 127–128)

Wieder et al. (1988) investigated the Clinical Infant Development Program (CIDP), "a community-based comprehensive service model, designed to respond to the needs of infants and families through an early intervention and prevention approach" (p. 6). CIDP intervention teams consisting of two primary workers provided families with three main services: (a) assistance meeting basic needs including food, shelter, medical care, and education, (b) supportive relationships, and (c) specialized services to mother and child. Pregnant mothers, with at least one child, who were experiencing difficulties caring for themselves and their families, were offered services. Typically the first focus of intervention was meeting instrumental needs. The authors presented findings from a five-year follow-up of thirty-two "high-risk, multi-problem families" (headed by nineteen adult and thirteen adolescent mothers) that received CIDP's intensive service package (initial assessments were conducted on forty-two families). Similar to many other evaluations of comprehensive programs, the CIDP study did not include a comparison group.

Clinical assessments at the onset of the mothers' contact with the program "revealed a population of severely fragmented and depressed women, some with impaired reality testing and/or very low adaptive functioning, and all seriously compromised in their ability to provide protective environments, develop intimacy, and read and respond to their infants' cues" (p. 8). A distinctly different picture emerged through the results of a follow-up investigation of more than three-quarters of the program families. Wieder et al. (1988) claimed that the gains from program participation became apparent after involvement concluded. Five years after the intervention ended, 31% of the adolescent mothers had completed high school (none had done so upon entry into the program), 77% were employed, and none were receiving social assistance. While the adult mothers did not increase their educational level, they did receive job training and three times as many of these mothers had jobs at follow-up compared to program entry, and only half as many were on social assistance. Improvements were also observed in the mothers' interpersonal relationships. A decrease in spousal/partner abuse was observed for adult mothers (from 60% at program entry to 5% at follow-up) as well as for teenage mothers (from 50% to 18%). A parallel finding was noted in terms of older mothers' physical abuse patterns. Whereas almost half of these mothers were physically abusive toward their children prior to treatment, none had abused since. A general conclusion drawn from the research was that longer intervention periods resulted in better outcomes for adult mothers.

Positive changes were also noted for the children who received early intervention. "The overall emotional, behavioral, and cognitive status of [these] children suggests that [they] developed good ego functions; they are intelligent, achieve in school, show good impulse control, are engaged socially, and evidence warmth, closeness, and a wide range of affect" (p. 10). Such qualities were contrary to the characteristics observed in the parents and siblings of these children.

SUMMARY: COMPREHENSIVE SUPPORT PROGRAMS

The defining features of these comprehensive support programs were that they provided multiple forms of support for families using multiple helpers. Participant involvement tended to be intensive (e.g., two times a week or more) and moderately long-term (e.g., six months to a couple of years). Some programs offered a standard package of services/supports, while others provided individually tailored packages of services/supports. Comprehensive support programs often incorporated formal (paid) and informal (unpaid) helping, though the emphasis was upon paid helpers. Many programs had a primary helper responsible for service support coordination as well as for providing direct assistance to family members. These primary workers worked with substantially fewer families at one time than comparison service providers. Programs often offered a combination of counseling, education, and concrete assistance to families. Service packages frequently offered services/supports to a variety of family members and focused on both personal (e.g., self-esteem, parenting skills) as well as environmental (e.g., food, child care, peers) factors. Most of the comprehensive support programs reviewed were designed to involve families who had maltreated, or were considered to be at risk of maltreating, their children. However, several of these programs focused on reaching parents with infants or young children prior to the risk of maltreatment becoming immediate.

Eleven reviews of the research or individual program assessments were examined about comprehensive support programs. There are some clear cautions in drawing conclusions from this research. While some studies had substantial samples, others drew conclusions from relatively small numbers of participants. Second, the absence of control or comparison groups in most studies made it difficult to determine if the observed changes were a function of program involvement or other factors in the families' lives. There was also a great deal of variation in the definitions of child maltreatment and the criteria for admittance into these programs. In addition, the studies often did not report details about program participation patterns (e.g., what services were received, duration of involvement, frequency of contacts). There was no attempt to discern the discrete contributions of various program components; rather, outcomes were reported for the programs as a whole. On the other hand, there was substantial consistency in the findings across all of the studies reviewed. In addition, the studies with stronger designs tended to support the conclusions of the weaker assessments.

Many of these comprehensive support programs were assessed ten to twenty years ago. If reports in the literature are a reliable indication, these multifaceted support program models seem to have fallen out of favor as attention has switched to more focused support programs such as Intensive Family Preservation Services, home health visitors and parent training programs. Unfortunately, this apparent neglect of comprehensive or multifaceted support approaches does not seem warranted either by available evaluation research or by current theory about working with disadvantaged families. While particular comprehensive support program models may be dated, many of the helping principles motivating these earlier efforts continue to be relevant.

The Range of Supports Available: A strength of these comprehensive support programs was that they provided families with multiple helpers and a variety of types of support. The programs appeared able to respond in a flexible fashion to families. A minimum for most programs was providing counseling and emotional support, information and instruction around specific topics (e.g., parenting, child development) and access to concrete supports (e.g., transportation, help with housekeeping, child care). Many programs had, in principle, a range of other supports available to families upon request. There was great variation in the types and the number of supports available across programs.

The Level of Support Available: Comprehensive support programs tended to involve family members at least once or twice a week in program activities. Some offered substantially higher levels of participation.

Availability in a Crisis: These were typically not rapid-response programs; however, several comprehensive support programs were described as having crisis support components. Providing high levels of support during periods of high stress was a basic intervention principle for many programs.

Motivation and Skill Requirements: These motivation and skill requirements varied a great deal across programs and across different program components for particular comprehensive support programs. For example, program elements stressing group participation and skill learning would have higher requirements. However, most of these programs stressed actively reaching out to family members and many included an in-home component to their services. Referral criteria for many programs excluded more resistant or very distressed families.

Focused Technical Expertise: The research provided few details about the content of the services provided. Nonetheless, it seems reasonable to presume that many of these programs brought considerable expertise to focus on particular areas of family life (e.g., parenting, child development, conflict). On the other had, there would have been considerable variation in focused expertise across different comprehensive support programs.

The Length of Time Supports Available: Program involvements lasted between four months and several years. Many programs provided supports for at least one year.

Reciprocity and Social Integration: Many programs did include support groups for parents as part of their helping repertoire. A few provided child care for children. The descriptions of participation in the comprehensive support programs did not emphasize participants doing for themselves or being helpers of others in similar circumstances or developing ongoing connections with peers. Generally, it appeared that reciprocity and social integration opportunities for participants in these programs were fairly limited. However, some programs did encourage and support parents returning to or staying in school or employment. Also, when children had access to quality child care experiences, the social integration benefits to these children would have been substantial. There may have been a great deal of variation in reciprocity and social integration opportunities for participants from program to program.

Anticipated Program Impacts and Rationales: The research evidence suggested that participants in comprehensive support programs often had lower reported rates of child maltreatment and out-of-home placement than baseline or comparison groups. These results were likely due to the broad range of supports available and the relatively high levels of weekly involvement of participants in program activities. All of the studies that included cost analyses suggested that, because of averted placement costs, the comprehensive support programs, despite relatively high direct program costs, either covered their program costs or saved money when compared to traditional child welfare services. When such outcomes were assessed, positive changes in variables such as parenting and parent-child relations were also reported. This was likely due to the capacities of some comprehensive programs to provide good levels of emotional support and instruction around specific difficulties. In particular, the early intervention programs, consistent with the evidence on home health visitor programs, reported clear positive changes in parenting and child management as well as on various long-term indicators of child and parent personal development. There were also notably fewer incidents of child maltreatment, out-of-home placements and other family breakdowns for early intervention program participants. Overall, these comprehensive support programs did not report greater social involvements or social integration for participants (with the exception of a few programs focusing on these areas and perhaps the early intervention programs) nor a lessened dependence on professional services (with the possible exception of the early intervention programs). There was some evidence suggesting that comprehensive support programs that allowed for longer participant involvements (e.g., one year or longer) and that incorporated lay helpers (e.g., paraprofessionals, peer groups) produced better outcomes for families as well as greater cost-savings. There was agreement between service providers and participants that the provision of concrete supports was an important component of these comprehensive support programs.

The two tables that follow give an overview of the support programs reviewed in Part II. In general, the patterns of relationships between the structural dimensions and outcomes of these programs lend credence to the principles contained in the Support Program Impact Assessment Framework developed in Part I. For example, the support programs that demonstrated a capacity to prevent child abuse and neglect and to reduce out-of-home placements of children in precarious families had high levels of contact with families and made a variety of supports available. They also often had a capacity to respond rapidly and with high levels of support during family crises. The only programs that lessened families' reliance on professionals and increased participants' confidence in their ability to manage on their own enmeshed participants in informal networks that provided frequent contacts and multiple supports. Changes in specific aspects of personal or family functioning (e.g., parenting skills) were noted when these aspects were the focus of specific program elements (e.g., parent training). However, programs that provided only focused expertise with modest levels of contact with family members frequently did not produce encouraging benefits if participants were confronting multiple stressors in their lives.

For some program models, better outcomes for families and superior cost-savings for agencies were clearer when program participation was of relatively long duration (e.g., one year or more). Intensive, long-term, and early interventions with new mothers considered to be at high risk of child maltreatment demonstrated many positive changes for both mother and child, and lessened the use of professional services over time. Many of the most effective support programs made active efforts to reach out to families and to reduce the barriers to program participation.

There are many promising approaches to supporting distressed families that were not assessed in Part II: adolescent afterschool programs, family resource centers, child care programs, return to school and employment programs, social and recreational programs, health and nutrition programs, programs that combine health, education, mental health, and child welfare services, and so on. In addition, for the five groupings of support programs reviewed, no single program approach emerged as clearly superior for all families. Children and parents can benefit from access to the helping elements of all of these programs under appropriate conditions. This means that there are still choices to be made about which program elements should be incorporated into a particular service setting and how the various program elements might be linked together to benefit families.

In the final analysis, it is more useful to understand the helping principles built into these programs and their connections to program outcomes than it is to know the details of different support program models. Having an ability to make informed use of a Support Program Impact Assessment Framework allows more informed decisions to be made about the relevance of particular program elements and program models. Equally important, having a general way of understanding support programs for disadvantaged families assists in the synthesis of diverse program elements into powerful ways of helping that are appropriate for particular populations and settings.

There is a need to beware of a "program trap." When support program models are seen as indivisible wholes, then a false choice is created between model A or model B. In addition, there are clear limits to the number of stand-alone programs that can be supported by any agency. Perhaps the focus should not be on creating new programs. The real challenge is bringing promising ways of protecting children and supporting families into everyday ways of working in the social services. It would be better to think about building capacities into service organizations and delivery systems to be able to respond in diverse, intense, and flexible fashions to families.

Yet this perspective poses tremendous challenges to how child welfare services and other services are organized. Certainly without a fundamental shift in thinking about how children are best protected, few of these more promising ways of helping can become practical realities. As suggested earlier, the undertaking may be "to stand the system on its head", away from investigation and litigation toward investing a much greater proportion of resources into helping methods that will be welcome in the lives of most of the families coming through the doors of child welfare, and many other, agencies. Part III begins the discussion of the organizational issues emanating from a adopting a support perspective in child welfare as well as other related service sectors.

Table 11.1. Anticipated Performance on Structural Dimensions of Support Programs

Program Type	Range of Support Available	Level of Support Available	Availability in a Crisis	Motivation and Skills Requirements
Intensive Family Preservation Services	◆ counseling, emotional, and concrete supports ◆ focus on case management may increase the range	◆◆◆ high level of direct contact with family members (5–10 hours per week) potential increased access to external supports	◆◆◆ rapid response to crises and high level of time spent with family during crises	◆◆◆ in-home services and flexibility increase participation of "hard-to-serve" families
In-Home Programs: Home Health Visitors	◆ mainly information and education, with some attention to emotional supports ◆ range limited by reliance on single helper	◆ moderate (2–4 contacts per month) in the more intensive home health visitor programs may be supplemented by links to additional community services	◆ programs designed to prevent, rather than respond to, crises focus on early contact before child abuse occurs	◆◆◆ in-home services provided in nonstigmatizing ways seem to be effective in reaching "hard-to-serve" families

(continued)

Legend: ◆◆◆, high performance; ◆◆, medium performance; ◆, low performance.

217

Table 11.1. (Continued)

Program Type	Range of Support Available	Level of Support Available	Availability in a Crisis	Motivation and Skills Requirements
Parent Training Programs	◆ specific kinds of education and training about parenting are provided, but often with moderate or little other supports	◆ parents typically received training for 2 hours once per week ◆ some programs included a few additional individual contacts	◆ no provisions to respond to crises	◆ most programs were voluntary and required relatively high motivation ◆ also required ability and willingness to learn and practice concepts
Comprehensive Support Programs	◆ multiple helpers and a variety of supports	◆ moderate levels of contact (1–3 times per week), depending on the specific types of supports received	◆ not typically crisis response, but many programs provided some level of crisis support	◆ many programs made efforts to reach undermotivated parents ◆ provision of in-home services and flexibility of support increased motivation in some programs
Informal Support: Mutual Aid/ Community Living Networks	◆ concrete, emotional, educational, and social integration supports are available but vary depending on the type of program	◆ high level of supports available (minimum of twice per week)	◆ crisis response not built into most programs, but access to crisis support often available through personal relationships between members	◆ demands for participation require relatively high levels of motivation and skill

Table 11.1. (Continued)

Program Type	Length of Time Support Available	Focused Technical Expertise	Reciprocity and Social Integration
Intensive Family Preservation Services	◆ short-term crisis intervention (4–8 weeks) ◆ few graduation procedures developed	◆ ◆ intended to provide professional expertise focused on a few priority areas	◆ little emphasis on participants becoming helpers of others, fostering positive social integration, or encouraging independence
In-home Programs: Home Health Visitors	◆ ◆ ◆ effective home health visitor programs provided services for 1–3 years, giving support to families during early years of children's lives	◆ ◆ ◆ specially trained home visitors, particularly nurses, brought strong expertise in parenting, child development, nutrition and health, and infant care	◆ little emphasis on participants becoming helpers of others, fostering positive social integration, or encouraging independence
Parent Training Programs	◆ most programs are of short duration (6–10 weeks)	◆ ◆ ◆ specific, focused expertise by trained professionals provides specialized information and expert training on parenting and stress management	◆ little emphasis on participants becoming helpers of others, fostering positive social integration, or encouraging independence ◆ limited connections encouraged among members of some parent training groups

Legend: ◆◆◆, high performance; ◆◆, medium performance; ◆, low performance.

(continued)

Table 11.1. (Continued)

Program Type	Length of Time Support Available	Focused Technical Expertise	Reciprocity and Social Integration
Comprehensive Support Programs	◆ ◆ support ranges from 4 months to several years, but most lasted about 1 year	◆ ◆ some programs have considerable focused expertise, usually in areas of parenting, life skills, and home management	◆/◆ little emphasis on participants becoming helpers of others, fostering positive social integration, or encouraging independence ◆/◆ some connections among members in peer groups
Informal Support: Mutual Aid/ Community Living Networks	◆ ◆ potential opportunity for long-term involvement (6 months to several years), but dependent on the program and the participant	◆ ◆/◆ generally, high levels of expertise not available unless there is a specific focus (e.g., Alcoholics Anonymous)	◆ greatest opportunities for participants to be helpers of others and to do for themselves ◆ provide access to stable social networks and development of positive peer relationships ◆ create opportunities for participants to occupy new social roles

Legend: ◆◆◆, high performance; ◆◆, medium performance; ◆, low performance.

Table 11.2. Anticipated Impacts and Rationales of Support Programs

Support Program Type	Anticipated Impacts and Rationales
Intensive Family Preservation Services	if truly focused on "high-risk" families, can reduce both frequency of out-of-home placements and the amount of time children spend in out-of-home care, resulting in substantial cost-savings results are likely attributable to broad range of supports, intensity of services, and high crisis availability impacts may disappear because of the lack of ongoing supports
In-Home Programs: Home Health Visitors	when helpers establish relationships with mothers during pregnancy and early infancy, and when services are provided intensely for one or more years, can result in improved mother-child interactions, improved parenting behaviours and attitudes, decreased health risks for babies, and increased developmental gains for babies the most intensive programs can also reduce incidence of child abuse and neglect, and may improve mothers' lives in areas of employment, education, and use of community resources and result in less need for professional services over time; this may result in long-term cost savings from the program investment results appear to be due to the provision of timely information and education coupled with emotional support as well as service intensity and duration and the focus on important development points in child and family lives
Parent Training Programs	results can be expected which are directly linked to training content: less aversive parenting behaviours, better parent-child interactions and decreased parental stress and anger evidence suggests little impacts can be expected on child abuse and neglect or out-of-home placement with families coping with multiple difficulties parent training appears to be most effective when combined with other supports impacts are likely to disappear because of lack of ongoing supports

(continued)

Table 11.2. (*Continued*)

Support Program Type	Anticipated Impacts and Rationales
Comprehensive support Programs	can be expected to reduce rates of child abuse and out-of-home placement, probably because of broad range of supports available, the high levels of involvement, crisis supports, and long-term involvement
	positive changes in parenting behaviour and skills, and parent-child relations are also sometimes evident, likely because of emotional supports and specific training in these areas.
	generally, longer program participation and use of several key helpers produced better outcomes and clearer cost-savings
	impacts are likely to attenuate because of lack of ongoing supports
Informal Support: Mutual Aid/ Community Living Networks	decreased incidence of institutional and other out-of-home placements for more intensive programs and with longer participation
	dramatic increases in size and supportiveness of social networks and positive social involvements
	reduced reliance on professional helpers
	when focused on specific difficulties, such as parenting or substance abuse, resulted in improvements in these areas as well
	involvement can legitimately be long-term and benefits may be maintained because of this ongoing support for some participants

Much has been learned over the past twenty years about the characteristics of interventions that are promising in protecting disadvantaged children from poor outcomes and in supporting distressed families. In this volume, we have uncovered similar helping principles and programming parameters at work with diverse populations and in multiple settings. A basic premise undergirding the work in Parts I and II is that it is possible to abstract useful guidelines from the available program literature and research for assessing and for constructing promising programs. There is a need to be more conscious and deliberate in our decisions about investing in programs for disadvantaged children and families. The purpose in Parts I and II is to provide a beginning conceptual and empirical basis to inform such choices.

Despite the positive views presented so far in this volume, it remains clear that these promising programs have had little impact on how everyday helping is approached in child welfare or most other social services used by disadvantaged populations. There are good reasons for this lack of influence. The barriers to the diffusion of different helping principles are formidable. In addition, almost no attention has been devoted to the complex challenges of translating these promising programs into everyday ways of working in these settings. It is time to begin addressing the issues of organizational and delivery system transformation. The challenges to existing ways of working emanating from this support perspective touch the heart of our helping efforts. We need to do our business differently. Not to do so means that ways of helping that produce better outcomes for children and families, make superior economic sense, and are more acceptable to participants will remain on the margins of our social services.

What would a child welfare organization incorporating a support perspective be like? What is involved in moving from here to there? We now turn our attention to these questions. However, these are very difficult issues to resolve in a clear fashion. In addition, very little work has been done focusing on the nature and the requirements of such a transformation. At this point in time, we can only highlight the importance of these considerations and begin a discussion of suggested changes. Inevitably, our efforts must raise more issues than are put to rest. Our hope in Part III is to stimulate thinking and to encourage initiatives in these vital, yet unexplored areas.

Part III incorporates two distinct sections. In October 1994, an invitational conference was organized focusing on the practical relevance of the material in Parts I and II and the organizational challenges in implementing these ideas. Chapter 12 summarizes the themes emanating from the discussions at this conference. Most conference participants were frontline service providers, administrators and government policymakers in child welfare. Their responses represent a microcosm of the reactions to be expected if we propose a wider adoption of a support perspective and promising programs. Chapter 13 concludes the volume with our speculations about organizational changes in child welfare that would be consistent with a support perspective. While our focus in this discussion is upon child welfare, these considerations have broader relevance in the social services.

Incentives and Obstacles in Adopting a Support Perspective in Child Welfare

12

The helping principles reflected in the support perspective and in the promising programs reviewed in this volume raise difficult questions about how child welfare should be organized. Identifying promising program models and a general framework to guide creating better ways of helping disadvantaged children and families is only part of the challenge facing us. How do these approaches fit into existing service delivery systems? What needs to change in order to take advantage of the promise of these programs? What obstacles stand in the way of making these changes? This chapter begins an examination of these issues.

This volume is a product of a larger research and development project. A component of this larger project involved familiarizing representatives from child welfare and related service sectors with a support perspective and with information about promising programs for disadvantaged children and families. The purpose was to solicit their comments about the relevance of this material to their work and to engage in a dialogue about the challenges inherent in adopting a support perspective in child welfare. This chapter presents the findings of our consultations with these child welfare and community representatives.

RESEARCH METHODOLOGY

Representatives of four child welfare agencies and the Ontario Ministry of Community and Social Services participated in the design and implementation of this project. The purpose was to search for more promising ways of helping disadvantaged children and families. At the onset of the project (summer, 1993), separate group discussions were held with representatives of each participating child welfare agency as well as with people representing the ministry. At this point, their concerns about the implications of an expanded support perspective in child welfare were solicited.

The material from Parts I and II was condensed into seven summary bulletins. An invitational two-day conference for 115 participants was hosted at Wilfrid Laurier University in October 1994. All participants received in advance of the conference the seven summary bulletins and each participating organization as well as a few other participants received copies of Parts I and II of this volume. A set of discussion questions for the conference was circulated and each participating organization was encouraged to hold one or more group discussions among its delegates prior to their attending the conference. The conference included plenary sessions as well as small group meetings focusing on the conference discussion questions. All sessions at the beginning of the project and during the conference were audiotaped. These were then analyzed to identify major themes relevant to adopting a support perspective in child welfare.

Most of the participants in the preliminary discussion groups and the conference were frontline service personnel from the child welfare agencies. Child welfare supervisors and managers were also well represented. The government representatives were primarily the planning officers responsible for child welfare in the areas served by the four child welfare agencies. About ten people from related service sectors or from universities also attended the conference. About eight conference participants were users of child welfare services. One of the limitations of these data stems from the mix of people participating in these discussions. In particular, if more community representation and child welfare services users had been included, the themes emanating from the conference and the attitudes expressed toward a support perspective may have differed from these findings in important ways. These discussions also were influenced by the particular local circumstances being lived in these four agencies. Nonetheless, these data are helpful in that they do alert us to the complexities of trying to carry the lessons from promising programs into everyday work in child welfare.

MAJOR THEMES

Not surprisingly, there were great differences of opinion expressed about the relevance of a support perspective to child welfare. Opinions ranged from enthusiasm about adopting these new approaches to outright rejections of the appropriateness of these ideas. Most participants were sympathetic to a support perspective and cautiously curious about trying more promising ways of working. But they had many questions about how these approaches fit into child welfare practice and whether meaningful organizational changes were possible at this time. While interested, they worried about once again investing their hopes in "something too good to be true." Emotions sometimes ran high during discussions. Some participants were excited and wanted to move ahead; others expressed anger at perceived criticisms of their work and what they saw as wrong messages about what to do; some were afraid; many were interested in what they were hearing and wondered what it might mean for their work.

CATALYSTS FOR CHANGE

A dominant reality for the child welfare system at the time of these discussions was adjusting to substantial reductions in public funding. While great concern was expressed about the potential damaging impacts of these cuts, some participants felt that these economic pressures were pushing child welfare personnel to consider worthwhile service alternatives that they would otherwise have ignored. As one participant said, "I think the biggest motivation has probably been shrinking resources. This has forced us to be creative." Another participant added:

> The desperation in terms of how to cope with the funding situation right now and understanding the need for change to occur I think is great. There seems to be more willingness to look at adventurous ways of doing things and changing things in sensible ways than [we] ever would have done otherwise.

A common lament was the increasing pressures on personnel because of increased referrals combined with fewer staff and other resources. Some expressed the futility of trying to do their work with children and families in the same ways as in the past but with much reduced resources. Others saw this as an opportunity to try something new: "I'm excited. I think that this is a wonderful opportunity for us to look at what we're doing as an agency."

A few participants were of the opinion that current approaches to helping were inadequate, even with prior levels of funding and welcomed the search for promising alternatives:

> A mother calls for help, but child welfare cannot help because she did not bash the kid. Two years later the worker gets called back and has to remove the kid because the mother bashed him! Why are we closing the doors on these people when they come to us the first time?

> We need a shift in thinking. If you have the focus of "I'm going to help this family and try to support this family" rather than on the focus of just following all the child abuse guidelines—you have to do the investigation stuff, but you could go into it with the approach of having a primary function of helping the family, and not just to carry out the investigation. I don't think it's a matter of one or the other, I just think it's a shift in thinking and emphasis.

DETERRENTS TO CHANGE

Many participants considered that the climate of fiscal restraint required a narrowing of the scope of child welfare activity—usually giving priority to the investigation-apprehension-litigation-care nexus. These participants were skeptical or hostile to a greater adoption of a support perspective in child welfare:

> It is difficult to measure prevention in the short term. This causes problems getting funding. When there are these money pressures then we can only provide some of the mandated services.
>
> I think one of the concerns is that with constraints and with the tight fiscal situation, that the mandatory is carried out, but the nonmandatory falls away.
>
> In the last fifteen months or so, since the funding reductions began to bite on us a year ago, we have stopped serving many of the clients who would be, yeah, they've got child welfare problems, but they're not bad enough as yet.

Legislative mandates give child welfare personnel the authority to intervene into the lives of distressed families. Many participants thought that these legal mandates, and the accompanying regulations defining how practice should be done, were too restrictive to allow for a broad adaptation of a support perspective in child welfare:

> There is an investigative role there because society is confronting the fact that abuse is very real in this country. By legislation, by statute, by standards, by guidelines, workers are being forced to apply those regulations, standards, and this entails investigations.
>
> That is the dilemma we are facing because we have the government saying these are the child abuse standards which we must follow. . . . Governments tend to prescribe, and we get a framework that isn't flexible.

Some felt that the use of the legislated authority to investigate families and to apprehend children was the only effective way to protect children at risk of abuse or serious maltreatment. Others expressed concern about using the support perspective in situations of extreme family difficulty:

> For some children it is a crisis situation. Some kids are at immediate risk, and despite all the philosophy and "good news" [of the support approach], you've got to make a decision based on the degree of risk to the children right then.
>
> A support perspective is not the way to go with hostile people.
>
> We have a significant amount of sexual abuse cases, physical abuse and the proliferation of spousal violence and substance abuse cases. The moment, for example, the child is in physical jeopardy—they don't fit so nicely into [support] models.

A few participants spoke strongly against the idea of incorporating a support perspective into child welfare. They argued that the support approach is inconsistent with the traditional mandate to protect children. These workers felt that the investigation, apprehension, and legal requirements of child welfare make it impossible to build supportive relationships with families. They thought that supportive work would be best done by other organizations:

> [Child welfare] has kind of a core of services that are unique to them around the protection area. . . . Then there's a whole range of things that they do, that actually anybody else could do, like prevention programs in the communities and community development, group work around parent teen conflict. And so you kind of have a question of do you need to do that? How much do you need to do that? How much does that support your mandate?

> You can do what you want to change definitions, and you can say that the broken bone cases, if we caught that earlier, could have been prevented, but that doesn't stop the broken bone cases from coming in the door.

> I've got to feel okay about that, that it is okay in our world, our community, that somebody, namely me, has that particular responsibility in certain situations [i.e., authority to remove children from a family]. I don't think people will ever—and this is sort of my personal feeling—will ever not be afraid of that.

A frequent lament was that child welfare workers have more than enough difficulty meeting current work demands, without considering how to incorporate new approaches into their work:

> I think the fear comes from the perception that there may be a request to do more and already the feeling like geez I've got to get all this done already, and that's where the fear comes from, of whether there will be the time to do everything that's necessary.

> The reality is we can't do what you want us to do even now. We can't spend any more time planning, we've got to do some work.

> There's a lot of workers that are quite frustrated when you have the families come in on your caseload and the families identify their needs and we have ideas of what their needs would be in order to have them live the standard of living that would be acceptable and healthy, . . . and they just can't seem to do it because of time and numbers and all these other variables.

Clearly, the suggestions of adopting a support perspective in child welfare raises quite contradictory reactions. Many are less than satisfied with existing ways of working and want to use the current time of change to try more promising approaches. But the forces of inertia and resistance are strong with many participants identifying strongly with the investigation-apprehension-litigation-care mode of protecting children. In such a climate, the process of change to increase the use of a support perspective in child welfare would be difficult and require skillful guidance.

DOES A SUPPORT PERSPECTIVE BELONG IN CHILD WELFARE?

The prevailing opinion expressed was that support approaches need to be available but cannot replace the functions played by investigation-apprehension-litgation-care services. An appropriate balance needs to be found. An investigation focus would be available, "in the background possibly," but more supportive approaches should usually be attempted first. The conception was of a continuum of service from supportive to apprehension and care. In this understanding, support programs, staff, and resources would be added to existing child welfare operations:

> Front line workers like to have these programs available. They like to know that there is a parent aid or volunteer or family preservation worker. We're doing more of that and I think we should be doing more of that. We need to put more of that kind of support in. We will always have to investigate and meet the guidelines, we're always liable for lawsuits, we know that. I'm optimistic to believe that people should do both.

> To start with [we] would include that consultation stuff, training of informal resources, working closely with them, the client mutual aid [which] blends with neighbourhood family support . . . . And we will always need to have in the background a very high quality system of the response system, that still does a case approach to child abuse investigations and still provides residential care for kids who can't be cared for in their family or in community kinds of situations.

A few participants felt that adding support programs to existing child welfare services was insufficient. They were of the opinion that child welfare required a new philosophy, structures and ways of working:

> We have to take a close look at children's agencies and how they're structured because many of them are structured the way they were forty or fifty years ago.

In contrast, some participants felt that child welfare agencies already adequately supported families and protected children:

> I think there are lots of examples [in what we do already] of components of what was presented today. . . . I think there needs to be some recognition that even though we don't have hard data, there are probably all sorts of examples where our work is effective.

Many participants expressed a need for more information to guide decisions about how to improve services to children and families. They expressed interest in the support perspective but also caution about its implications and what should be done:

> I hope that we can learn about different interventions that are more effective than what we're doing now.

> We know that there's all sorts of different ways of intervening and they fall into some broad categories and none of us really knows which one is the most effective for what circumstance.

> I think it's time that we start taking a step back and looking at what we're doing and trying to figure out how to do things a bit more efficiently and effectively. . . . And to break ourselves of a mind set that we've had for many years that this is the way we do things because we've always done things this way. I think we need to evaluate.

LEGISLATIVE AND FUNDING OBSTACLES

A common perception was that child welfare agencies were receiving mixed messages from their government funders. Public rhetoric encouraged a search for more effective and efficient ways to help children and families. On the other hand, as the comments by a government representative suggests, there was real pressure to focus on a narrow interpretation of legislative mandates:

> I'm not willing, as one individual working for the ministry, to allow one of the two agencies that I supervise to do something different than what it says in [legislation and regulations] they should do, in case it turns out wrong. I don't have the authority to let them do that anyway, I mean my job is to monitor, supervise and inspect as to what the legislation says they're supposed to do.

The desire to avoid the consequences for employees of a wrong decision in protecting a child was a common theme in these discussions. Before trying something new, many workers want to know what will happen to them if something goes seriously wrong. The observation was made by several participants that fear drives workers and agencies to be conformist rather than innovative:

> [A child welfare agency's] question will be, if they make a shift and a child goes unprotected, and it hits the press, where are we [i.e., government] going to stand? Are we going to leave them out there, and leave the worker on their own?

> What has happened to agencies where the child has died? What has hap-
> pened to the lives of the directors, the supervisors, the workers? The ministry's
> response was "we will give you some structures, we will give you very clear
> expectations, and if you follow those we'll be behind you. If you don't follow
> that, you swing."

Families may prosper with appropriate support and less dependence on
professionals, but child welfare agencies are funded on the basis of how
many open child protection cases they have and how many children they
have in out-of-home care. Some participants noted that agencies are being
rewarded for being more intrusive with families and that current funding formulas are a disincentive to adopting a support perspective in child
welfare:

> It is not right that agencies seem to get rewarded by receiving funding for
> having greater numbers of children in care.

> If you take a kid into care and stick him in a [home] and you run a deficit
> because of that, the ministry will come in and say, "Okay, that's legitimate,
> your numbers went up, you couldn't control that, therefore you get your
> dollars," as opposed to saying, "Was that really the best decision?"

There was a general consensus that current legislative and financial incentives discourage innovation and weigh heavily against broadening the
support perspective in child welfare. As fiscal and political conservatism
increases, child welfare personnel may increasingly find themselves struggling to balance their desire to be more supportive of children and families
with the need to sustain the financial viability of their agencies. Clearly,
changes to these legislative and financial guidelines would be required if a
process of seriously trying to learn from promising programs with disadvantaged children and families were to begin.

RESISTANCE FROM FRONTLINE PRACTITIONERS

More enthusiasm was expressed for adopting a support perspective by
child welfare agency managers and directors than by frontline child protection workers. While frontline protection workers were far from unanimous
about the relevance of the support perspective, they did voice some particular concerns. Perhaps not surprisingly given the nature of their work, and in
contrast to their frustrations with the work pressures they lived with, the identification with the investigation-apprehension-litigation-care model of child welfare practice was strongest among frontline child welfare practitioners.

Many frontline workers perceived an incompatibility between a supportive approach and an investigative one. While they valued the support per-

spective, many had little confidence that it could prosper within the context of their current mandate to protect children:

> People are sort of wondering how you can really help people if you're holding a big stick over them.

> There is a fundamental piece of role conflict between the mandate to find out if there are reasons for a protection case, and then develop the case against this parent, as opposed to someone who is coming in to help.

> Wherever you go there's always that piece: at the very back, if push comes to shove, you can take their kid away, and they all know it.

In addition, many frontline participants expressed feelings of being extremely vulnerable in their work and of tremendous pressure to adhere to legal regulations and procedures in order to protect themselves:

> There is a subconscious element that really is having a strong impact. When you and I read the [newspapers] and you read about the child who has returned home and ended up dead and we have these strong reactions wondering how they could have possibly left this child within this environment and we get angry about the fact that this child was not protected. Any common sensed person would conclude that that was the wrong place for the child. I'm not sure how you get past that but I think that really fosters a better safe than sorry—immediacy of danger response. We want the Royal Commission to burn whoever made the professional judgement that caused this child to die. That's very strong and it's a difficult thing to talk about even within the child protection support network. That's a very strong reality.

> If you listen to people [i.e., frontline workers], what they seem to be saying is the major driving force that directs their work is compliance with ministry expectations, compliance with what they believe the public wants to see, what the courts order, and it's sort of fear that if we don't do all of that, we're going to screw up, we're going to be on the front page of the paper and we're exposed to a whole lot of risk.

> The bottom line is that Thursdays I'm in court and I've got to get up with the Judge and say, "This is what we did. This is how we did it." If there's one part of the job that takes priority over everything else it's being prepared for that day.

> [Workers are] very caught into compliance, they must do this list of things in order to make sure that they've done everything that they're supposed to do and they then move to the next list and the next list and the idea of going in and building on family strength and supporting has to be reinforced and reinforced.

> I'm going to make sure I keep very clear notes as to what I did and why and when and how it all happened. . . . So it is going to depend on our management backing us up at the front line level, that if things go awry, that we're all in it together.

I think there is a commitment to [adopt a support approach] as a part of delivery of services, but that has approached to "What will the judge say if something goes wrong?"

There's a whole admission-into-care kit that we fill out, and that follows, again, the legislation. We have to have all these questions answered. We write some things over six times I'm sure.

Saddled with more authority and responsibility than perhaps they would like, and coping with declining resources and increasingly difficult family situations, it is not unexpected that many frontline child welfare practitioners would view the adoption of a support perspective with disbelief and mistrust. But there also is an attraction, perhaps distant for many, for frontline practitioners in a support perspective as well. It promises greater job satisfaction and a belief that their work might be appreciated and considered helpful by families:

I think by adding more of the supportive systems the plus for the worker is that they actually become a social worker again. They can get that commitment back to their ideals and working with their families.

I think there are a lot of incentives for people to get involved. It will provide more job satisfaction, I mean, I think the people who are doing the family preservation are having more fun, probably, than the other workers.

OVERVIEW OF THEMES

A recurring pattern in these discussions among child welfare and community representatives has been the struggle between competing visions of child welfare—one focused on investigation-apprehension-litigation-care services and another orientation favoring the inclusion, or perhaps even the primacy, of more supportive initiatives for distressed children and families. There will be no simple resolution of these differences.

Most participants considered the inclusion of a support perspective to be necessary in their work with children and families and a majority thought that supportive options needed to be within the continuum of child welfare services. But there was great disagreement about an appropriate balance between supportive and investigative modes of child welfare practice. However, respondents did agree that the obstacles to implementing a more substantial support perspective in child welfare were formidable. Much would have to change for supportive approaches to be accepted and implemented successfully.

The barriers to adopting a support perspective in child welfare are indeed daunting and there are a few places to which we can turn for guidance. Nonetheless, it may be useful to speculate, based on the support perspective elaborated in this volume, about how the child welfare delivery system might be modified in order to bring more of these promising resources to disadvantaged families. This is the focus of the final chapter of this book.

Organizational Issues in Adopting a Support Perspective

13

If we want to reduce child abuse and neglect, support distressed families, lessen reliance on costly and intrusive interventions, and produce better outcomes for disadvantaged children and families, we will have to respect the principles and methods associated with promising programs for disadvantaged populations. In addition, these new ways of helping will have to be brought into the heart of the ways that child welfare and other social service agencies respond to families. It will not be enough to simply add a range of small programs to existing ways of working. However, current legislative mandates and regulations, methods of payment, types of service personnel, standard work methods, as well as agency structures make experimenting with these ideas exceedingly difficult. Notwithstanding these obstacles, in the final analysis, a support perspective suggests a rethinking of how the work of child welfare and related service sectors should be organized.

As we have investigated promising programs and clarified a support perspective over the past ten years, it has become apparent that these methods bear little resemblance to how helping is organized in child welfare. While individual programs can be exciting in their potential, the practical challenge emanating from a support perspective is to transform how we invest resources and deliver help to distressed children and families. As long as an overwhelming majority of personnel and money are invested in helping methods that do not reflect promising program principles with disadvantaged populations, we will not produce better outcomes for children and parents, greater independence from paid service providers, or substantial cost savings. Yet, the organizational changes suggested by a support perspective seem daunting in their complexity. What is needed is a place to start and some ideas to guide our efforts.

We begin by examining a series of implications for service organization that follow from the material in Parts I and II. Our reflections draw primarily upon our experiences with child welfare services in Ontario between 1983 and 1995. However, this discussion will be relevant for other settings and other service sectors. We also will offer a few ideas about how we might begin to experiment with adapting a support perspective to everyday ways of working. However, it is important to remember that conceptually and empirically this is unexplored territory. Our offerings in this section are speculative. Our intent is to stimulate reflection and discussion of these issues and, hopefully, efforts to put these principles into practice that will inform the many who are searching for better ways of helping.

LANGUAGE TRAP: PROTECTION

There are several language conventions that make it very difficult to consider alternatives to current ways of working. These biases in our language need to be recognized if we hope to think clearly and to act differently. For example, the distinction between protecting children[1] and supporting families is a false one. Most of the helping principles that are germane to supporting disadvantaged families are identical to those useful in protecting their children. However, the idea of protecting children has become tightly bound to particular ways of working (i.e., individual cases-investigation-apprehension-courts-care) that are not the only approaches worthy of consideration and often not the best ways of helping many of these children and families. We need to disconnect our efforts to protect children from the ways that we already do our work. They are not identical. We need to redefine what we mean by protection based on what is in fact most needed, most helpful, and most acceptable for children and families. We need to become comfortable with the idea that supporting families is usually not different from nor less important than protecting children.

PUTTING THE CART BEFORE THE HORSE

Most families coming to the child welfare system are *not* in immediate danger of seriously hurting their children nor of having their children placed in care, yet child welfare organizations are organized and resources are allocated as if all families must be investigated. It is true that some children are facing critical risks to their safety and well-being and it is essential that child welfare systems be able to respond quickly in these circumstances, but the consequences of making these concerns *the* core organizing principle in child welfare means that most families are not responded to appropriately and resources are used inefficiently.

It would be preferable if service priorities would reflect what the majority of children and parents actually need. This would require allocating most resources to supporting families in a positive fashion as the best way of protecting children. Investigation-apprehension-litigation-care services would remain important but specialized components of a child welfare organization, which could be marshaled quickly when needed, but they would not be the first nor the most common response to families. They would cease to represent the essence of child welfare in the public mind. In addition, these specialized services would make extensive use of the agency's supportive resources to complement their work with those families for whom these more intrusive measures were unavoidable. What we need to experiment with is finding an appropriate balance between supportive and investigation-apprehension-litigation-care resources in child welfare and how they might work together constructively.

QUALITY CONTROL BLOCKS QUALITY

Methods of organizing child welfare resources have become more standard and less flexible as service quality controls ensure that work is done in predetermined ways. For example, an emphasis has been placed on hiring graduate social workers with clinical training and upon regulations that control the procedures and timeframes used in a neglect or abuse investigation. Behind these efforts is an established vision of what child welfare should be; over time, these types of controls drive child welfare organizations to become more like themselves and each other. That is, they incorporate a standard set of policies, administrative controls, as well as service delivery procedures. However, we have presented evidence suggesting that existing work procedures and organizational structures do not allow for the best work to be carried out with disadvantaged children and parents, and they place a great deal of pressure on staff providing direct services. In particular, these quality controls make it almost impossible to experiment with new and promising ways of helping as everyday ways of assisting children and parents. Innovations have remained on the margins of the child welfare delivery system, having minimal influence on the core concepts and methods of protecting children.

We need to disconnect our idea of good child welfare practice from images that standardize agencies and often make their efforts more expensive and less productive. We need to find a balance between system maintenance and creating credible vehicles for well-conceived experiments to proceed and be assessed. For example, procedures could developed for a child welfare agency, or a group of related agencies, to make the case for exemptions from existing controls in order to try promising innovations in their core operations. At this point in time, demonstration organizations or service delivery systems may be more important than demonstration programs.

LANGUAGE TRAP: PROGRAMS

There is no "one-size-fits-all" program. As we have seen, all support programs have their strengths and limitations. Thinking in terms of discrete programs is limiting. It creates false choices between one helping approach and another. For example, the extensive marketing of Intensive Family Preservation Programs (see the discussion in Chapter 6) over the past decade has had the unfortunate consequence of freezing out consideration of other valuable helping options and making it difficult to consider the strengths and weaknesses of this particular program option. It is also true that individual agencies can only create a small number of stand-alone programs with separate staffing and administration.

The support perspective suggests that we need to investigate how to incorporate a variety of key ways of helping into child welfare organizations and how to use these resources in a flexible fashion to help children and families. The evidence in Parts I and II suggests that both an appropriate range of assistance and a consistent and intensive pattern of involvement with this assistance are prerequisites for good outcomes with multiply disadvantaged populations. It will not be enough to have a range of options available; we will need to find ways to bring these supports together in powerful concurrent and sequential packages for particular children and families. In a sense, it would be preferable to think of the child welfare organization as the program. In this vein, it may be that the concept of coordinated resource centers for children and parents has its place in child welfare system design.

EXPANDED CONCEPT OF HELPING

We need to learn how to work with "whole" children and parents. It is not effective to single out concerns with inadequate parenting when participants do not understand basic nutrition and good health practices, are lonely, or have difficult peer relations, when school and employment are chaotic, and so on. It is not enough to think only about professional modes of helping. For example, conferencing and coordination of work between formal service providers will not be sufficient. In addition, in practice, referrals to formal services are too often ways of ensuring people do not get the help they need because of waiting lists and because too many formal services are providing a similar range of helping options to the same populations. In the end, what matters is that children and parents get the assistance they need. We are suggesting loosening our self-imposed constraints on what we consider appropriate types of helping in child welfare.

However, a single organization cannot do everything and choices will still be required about what to incorporate into a child welfare organization. A definitive answer to this question is hard to provide, but it is possible, based upon our review of promising programs, to identify some promising program components worthy of serious consideration for inclusion: rapid response crisis supports, social networks and mutual aid organizations, nutrition and physical health education and support, a drop-in/resource facility, parenting and life skills education, social and recreational programming, parent relief opportunities, quality child care, referral and service coordination services, school and employment supports, transportation supports, individual and group emotional and educational support, as well as specialized treatment and investigation-apprehension-litigation-care services.

This is clearly a different vision of child welfare than the one currently in place. Some will argue that we are not talking about child welfare at all. In addition, it is not yet clear how appropriate our vision is for child welfare or how many of these elements can be practically incorporated into a child welfare organization. On the other hand, if we do not try to learn from promising programs, our helping interventions will continue to be very expensive as well as unsatisfying for many program participants and frustrating for staff wanting to do good work.

VARIED STAFFING/VARIED WORK

Organizations are limited by the talents and preferences of the people working for them. The support perspective points clearly to the need for more varied staffing profiles in child welfare. There is a greater role for paraprofessionals, for people skilled in child management and parent education, for crisis workers, for group animators, for community/program developers, and for problem and treatment specialists. It will also become necessary for services/support personnel to be able to do more things. Individuals' jobs will become more varied. The current pattern of organizing the total organization around professional, individualized work is a very expensive, limiting, and ultimately ineffective structure for child welfare.

Changing the staffing profiles of child welfare organizations will be very difficult. There will be substantial resistance and the process needs to be slow and considered. Organizations can change only at the pace at which the values and abilities of the people within the organization change. Varied staffing also will introduce the strains of balancing the requirements and ambitions of different groups of employees. Notwithstanding these obstacles, if we wish to benefit from what we have learned about promising programs, we need to rethink who should be working in a child welfare organization and how they can work together in more flexible and powerful combinations.

FIRST RESPONSE IS WELCOME

For the support perspective to be implemented, child welfare organizations have to become places where family members feel comfortable coming for help. Currently, this is seldom the case. At best, families approach child welfare services with ambivalence and often with trepidation. For example, in Better Beginnings, Better Futures, a primary prevention program for disadvantaged children in twelve communities across Ontario, service organizations and local residents were to work together to improve the life chances of children and families (Ministry of Community and Social Services, 1990a). However, child welfare organizations were seldom part of these coalitions and, in two communities, although the child welfare agencies' representatives wanted to participate, they were asked to withdraw (Cameron, Vanderwoerd & Peters, 1995). For this attitude to change, the initial reception for most families should be, "Welcome. How can we help?" The focus of intake units would change primarily from investigation to greeting, assessment, and support, unless there is clear evidence of the need for investigation-apprehension-litigation-care service involvement. It may also prove counterproductive for many families to pass through a formal intake and assessment process to connect with the supportive resources available through child welfare organizations. Some families may just drop in or connect directly with support groups or networks. Of course, it makes little sense to modify the initial connections with family members in these ways if the balance of the child welfare enterprise is not modified to make diverse helping resources available to families in a flexible fashion.

REDEFINING SPACE

Child welfare organizations are unequivocally professional space. Offices, common space, and equipment reflect the needs of the employees of the organization, who can be very territorial about allowing others even partial control over this space and equipment. As an illustration, when parent mutual aid organizations were introduced into three child welfare organizations and members started to behave as if they had a right to be themselves in parts of this space—instead of behaving as clients who enter quietly and move through the agency in prescribed ways—it proved stressful for some service providers to adjust to this change (Cameron et al., 1992). Agency spaces are seldom places where family members can feel at home or where participants can find each other or find community. They should be. It would open a range of powerful helping options that are presently closed in child welfare.

BREAKING DOWN BARRIERS

The quality of many promising programs is often found in the details of participants' experiences as well as in the programs' basic helping strategies. In particular, it is essential that mechanisms be in place that allow people to participate consistently and frequently if the probabilities of good outcomes are to be maximized. In a supportive child welfare system, this means breaking down the practical and psychological barriers to children and parents coming for the first time and to their consistently participating in helping processes, for example, welcoming and acceptable locations, multiple entry formats, providing transportation to families with young children, having parent relief and child care support available, and actively reaching out to isolated or reticent families.

FLEXIBLE BASES

It would be advantageous to create as *part* of child welfare ways of helping children and parents that provide a good base for adding and deleting program content in an inexpensive fashion. Professional assistance is not always required or desirable; neither is case-by-case assistance. In addition, these types of interventions are seldom enough by themselves. For example, when parent mutual aid organizations were created in partnership with three child welfare organizations, their original focus was on the creation of network and friendship connections for members as well as providing emotional, crisis, and parenting supports. However, when the mutual aid programs achieved adequate size and stability, it became relatively easy and inexpensive to connect members with assistance around topics such as nutrition and healthy life-styles, returning to work or school, sexuality, and addictions, and to link individual members or their children with professional supports. These new opportunities opened because the mutual aid networks existed; otherwise, they would have represented prohibitive investments of time and resources. Indeed, members learned to find many of these resources for themselves (Cameron et al., 1992). Peer groups and networks, mutual aid organizations, and drop-in/resource centers may be practical ways of creating flexible service bases. Case management and linking to formal and informal resources may become important additions to these strategies.

AFTER WE ARE DONE

In Part II, evidence was presented that the benefits from participation in most formal programs attenuate after involvement with the program terminates. In addition, it was clear that little investment was made much of the time in creating effective graduation procedures for program participants or in the long-term support needs of children or parents. From a support perspective, short-term or proximate gains from formal services are seldom enough. Connecting participants to community and to ongoing informal supports and, as necessary, to professional services are essential elements of better outcomes for children and families.

INDEPENDENCE FROM PROFESSIONALS

In a recent assessment of Intensive Family Preservation Services in four child welfare agencies and two children's mental health organizations, there was dramatic evidence that almost all IFPS participants came into the programs with a history of heavy involvement with service professionals and returned afterwards to a substantial dependence upon professional service providers (Hayward et al., 1995). This continuing saga of reliance on service professionals is very common for users of child welfare or children's mental health services (Cameron & Rothery, 1985). Few would argue that this is a healthy outcome for children or parents. What was striking for each of these IFPS programs was that fostering participant independence from professional service was not a goal. It was not considered and, during interviews with program and agency personnel, it was clear that there was little faith that independence was an achievable outcome. Increasing independence from professionals should be a clear priority in most support strategies. If it is, our attention will, of necessity, shift to the value of social networks, mutual aid, and community connections: strategies that have demonstrated success in weaning participants from reliance on professional help.

In an implicit fashion, most child welfare interventions presume that the people who come to the agency for help are not competent and are not likely to become competent or responsible. Nonetheless, our conviction is that the potential for competence and responsibility among many parents and children is far higher than our ways of working encourage. We need to create more opportunities for people to learn, for participants to do for themselves and others, for participants to connect with each other and others in the community, and for them to access the resources that they need to manage their own lives and to prosper. If we truly believe in the value and the potential of the people coming to our agencies for help, and in their need to be disconnected from ongoing reliance on professional services, and if we are committed and persistent in our efforts, more children and parents will be liberated from lives full of too many helping professionals.

HAVING THEIR SAY

We should work hard to make service participant influence in child welfare a basic value and a practical reality. This can only be accomplished with persistent effort and with some deep changes in how professionals view child welfare practice and in their images of the people coming to these agencies for assistance. With conviction, determination, and skill, respectful and productive partnerships have been created between disadvantaged families and professional service providers (Cameron, Peirson, & Pancer, 1995; Cameron et al., 1994; Pancer & Cameron, 1994).

OUTCOMES MATTER

In Part I, our argument was that programs and interventions need to be based upon credible explanations of why good outcomes and bad outcomes happen for disadvantaged children, parents, and families. Also our contention was that programs/interventions needed a plausible and publicly defended rationale grounded in conceptual and empirical evidence explaining why specified outcomes were reasonable expectations from this investment. We need to try to install as a basic value in our work and in our organizations that "outcomes matter." They should be central to our ongoing reflections and debates about what to do. We should encourage a concern with the effectiveness of our work with children, parents, and families and encourage and reward an ongoing search for ways to be more helpful. When we undertake new programs/interventions, we should plan them so that they can be evaluated. We should stress using evidence from formal and informal assessments to inform our deliberations about how we try to help. We should listen to program participants about what they need in their lives and about which of our efforts worked best for them.

CONCLUDING REMARKS

The vision presented in this chapter is very different from the principles currently reflected in child welfare policies, organizations, and practices. Is this vision of child welfare based upon a support perspective desirable? Is it

practical? How can we begin to incorporate the lessons learned from promising programs into our everyday ways of helping disadvantaged children
and parents? Our discussions in this section have been speculative and they
have been partisan. Hopefully they will encourage our consideration of such
questions and encourage experiments with better ways of organizing our
helping efforts.

Part of the difficulty in bringing about change is that we do not want to
devalue what is being done well now as we try to incorporate new ways of
helping. It would also be wise to remember that we have no clear blueprints
to follow in constructing these new realities. There is much to learn as we go
and it would be easy to go astray. It might be best not to attempt to do too
much at one time. For example, it may be practical to focus on specific
populations (e.g., adolescents, young mothers) as a way to experiment with
reorganizing services, or a specific child welfare organization or service
department could be the focus of attention. Also, we would do well to
remember that planned organizational change is a slow and complex process and one where skilled help can be an asset.

These are very big challenges; however, if we cannot begin to think
creatively about these questions and to experiment in an informed fashion,
much of what has been learned about helping disadvantaged children and
families over the past twenty years must remain marginal to the daily work of
child welfare.

As work on this volume concludes, the child welfare system in Ontario is
experiencing substantial reductions in public financial support as have
many other jurisdictions in North America. These constraints are fostering
two opposite tendencies in child welfare. Perhaps the most common reaction has been a retreat toward narrower definitions of the legally mandated
ways of working. It would be ironic indeed if, in the name of fiscal responsibility, child welfare is driven toward its most expensive and least effective
options. The counterreaction has been a growing awareness that many traditional ways of delivering child welfare services are not satisfying either
service providers or service participants and they may not be sustainable
with the reduced financial resources available. Perhaps out of hard times
will come a willingness and the opportunities to begin to adapt what we
have learned about promising programs.

NOTE

1.   A similar case could be made about the detrimental effects of the distinction
between treatment and support in mental health settings and the tight linking of
treatment with particular modes of helping (individual-group-family professional
counseling).

References ─────────────────────────────────────

Abt Associates (1981). *Impact evaluation of twenty demonstration and innovative child abuse and neglect treatment projects* (Vols. 1–2) (DHHS under Contract 105-77-1047). Washington, DC: National Center for Child Abuse and Neglect, Office of Human Development Services.

Adam, B. D. (1978). *The survival of domination: Inferiorization and everyday life.* New York: Elsevier.

Albee, G. W. (1959). *Mental health manpower trends.* New York: Basic.

Alexander, H., & Kempe, R. (1982). The role of the lay therapist in long-term treatment. *Child Abuse and Neglect, 6,* 329–334.

Alford, G. S. (1980). Alcoholics Anonymous: An empirical outcome study. *Addictive Behaviors, 5*(4), 359–370.

Alinsky, S. D. (1971). *Rules for radicals.* New York: Vintage.

Allen, V. L., Wilder, D. A., & Atkinson, M. L. (1983). Multiple group membership and social identity. In T. R. Sarabin & K. E. Scheibe (Eds.), *Studies in social identity* (pp. 92–115). New York: Praeger.

Altman, D. (1971). *Homosexual: Oppression and liberation.* New York: Outerbridge and Dienstfrey.

Antonucci, T. C. (1985). Social support: Theoretical advances, recent findings, and pressing issues. In I. G. Sarason & B. R. Sarason (Eds.), *Social support: Theory, research, and application* (pp. 21–37). Dordrecht: Martinus Nijhoff.

Arch, S. D. (1978). Older adults as home visitors modelling parenting for troubled families. *Child Welfare, 57*(9), 601–605.

Ashem, B., & Kurz, S. (1988). *Parents helping parents: A model to promote child development in a multi-ethnic community.* Paper presented at National Council for International Health Conference, Washington, D.C., May.

Auslander, G. K., & Litwin, H. (1987). The parameters of network intervention: A social work application. *Social Service Review, 61,* 305–318.

Bagley, C., & Thurston, W. (1989). *Family poverty and children's behavioural and learning problems: A review of the evidence* (Monograph No. 7). Waterloo, Ontario: Wilfrid Laurier University, Centre for Social Welfare Studies.

Ballew, J. R. (1985). Role of natural helpers in preventing child abuse and neglect. *Social Work, 30*(1, January/February), 37–41.

Barnard, K. E., Magyary, D., Sumner, G., Booth, C. L., Mitchell, S. K., & Spieker, S. (1988). Prevention of parenting alterations for women with low social support. *Psychiatry, 51,* 248–253.

Barrera, M. E., Rosenbaum,, P. L., & Cunningham, C. E. (1986). Early home intervention with low-birth-weight infants and their parents. *Child Development, 57,* 20–33.

Barrera, M., Jr., Sandler, I. N., & Ramsay, T. B. (1981). Preliminary development of a scale of social support. *American Journal of Community Psychology, 9*(4), 435–447.

Barrera, M. E., Rosenbaum, P. L., & Cunningham, C. E. (1986). Early home intervention with low-birth-weight infants and their parents. *Child Development, 57,* 20–33.

Barth, R. (1990). Theories guiding home-based intensive family preservation services. In J. K. Whittaker, J. Kenney, E. M. Tracy, & C. Booth (Eds.), *Reaching high-risk families: Intensive family preservation in human services* (pp. 89–112). Hawthorne, NY: Aldine de Gruyter.

Barth, R. (1991). An experimental evaluation of in-home child abuse prevention services. *Child Abuse and Neglect, 15,* 363–375.

Barth, R., Blythe, B., Schinke, S., & Schilling, R. (1983). Self-control training with maltreating parents. *Child Welfare, 62,* 313–324.

Behavioral Sciences Institute (undated). *First year homebuilders mental health project report.* Federal Way, WA: Behavioral Sciences Institute.

Berkeley Planning Associates (1977). *Evaluation of the joint OCD/SRS demonstration projects in child abuse and neglect* (Vols. 1–12) (DHEW, under Contracts HRA 106-74-120 and HRA 230-76-076). Washington, DC: National Center for Health Services Research, Office of Assistant Secretary for Health.

Berkeley Planning Associates (1983). *Evaluation of the clinical demonstration of the treatment of child abuse and neglect* (Vols. 1–9) (DHHS, under Contract HEW 105-78-1108). Washington, DC: National Center for Child Abuse and Neglect, Office of Human Development Services.

Berkman, L. (1985). The relationships of social networks and social support to morbidity and mortality. In S. Cohen & L. S. Syme (Eds.), *Social support and health* (pp. 241–262). New York: Academic Press.

Berkman, L., & Syme, L. S. (1979). Social networks, host resistance, and mortality: A nine year follow-up study of Alameda County residents. *American Journal of Epidemiology, 109*(2), 186–204.

Berkowitz, M. W., Waxman, R., & Yaffe, L. (1988). The effects of a resident self-help model on control, social involvement and self-esteem among the elderly. *Gerontologist, 28,* 620–624.

Bertsche, J. W., & Clark, F. W. (1982). *Improving the utilization of informal helping systems by child welfare workers: Final report.* Missoula, MT: Department of Social Work, University of Montana, March.

Bertsche, J. W., Clark, F. W., & Iversen, M. J. (1982). *Child welfare training center program—Using informal resources in child protective services: A self-instructional guide.* Ann Arbor, MI: National Child Welfare Training Center, University of Michigan, School of Social Work, March.

Bidgood, B. A., & van de Sande, A. (1990). Home-based programming for a child welfare clientele. In M. Rothery & G. Cameron (Eds.), *Child maltreatment: Expanding our concept of helping* (pp. 107–125). Hillsdale, NJ: Lawrence Erlbaum Associates.

Blythe, B., Hodges, V., and Guterman, N. (1990). Interventions in maltreated adolescents. In M. Rothery and G. Cameron (Eds.), *Child maltreatment: Expanding* our concept of helping (pp. 35–48). Hillsdale, NJ: Lawrence Erlbaum Associates.

Borman, L. D. (1984). Part I: Self help groups: An overview. In L. D. Borman & L. L. Lieber, Self-help and the treatment of child abuse (pp. 3–18). Chicago: National Committee for Prevention of Child Abuse.

Borman, L. D., & Lieber, L. L. (1984). Self-help and the treatment of child abuse. Chicago: National Committee for Prevention of Child Abuse.

Boyce, W. T. (1985). Social support, family relations, and children. In S. Cohen & L. S. Syme (Eds.), Social support and health (pp. 151–173). New York: Academic Press.

Breakey, G., & Pratt, B. (1991). Healthy growth for Hawaii's "healthy start": Toward a systematic statewide approach to the prevention of child abuse and neglect. Zero to Three, (April)16–22.

Breton, M. (1980). Fostering basic helping networks: Report on a child abuse demonstration project. In B. Z. Shapiro (Chair), Helping networks and the welfare state: A symposium (Vol. 1) (pp. 62–83). Toronto: University of Toronto, Faculty of Social Work.

Bronfenbrenner, U. (1979). The ecology of human development. Cambridge, MA: Harvard University Press.

Brophy, K. (1990). The role of preschool programs in meeting the needs of abused or neglected children. In M. Rothery & G. Cameron (Eds.), Child maltreatment: Expanding our concept of helping (pp. 91–106). Hillsdale, NJ: Lawrence Erlbaum Associates.

Brown, G. W., & Bifulco, A. (1985). Social support, life events and depression. In I. G. Sarason & B. R. Sarason (Eds.), Social support: Theory, research, and applications. Dordrecht: Martinus Nijhoff.

Brown, R. (1986). Social psychology: The second edition. New York: Free Press.

Brunk, M., Henggeler, S., & Whelan, J. (1987). Comparison of multisystemic therapy and parent training in the brief treatment of child abuse and neglect. Journal of Consulting and Clinical Psychology, 55, 171–178.

Burch, G., & Mohr, V. (1980). Evaluating a child abuse intervention program. Social Casework, 61, 90–99.

Callard, E. D., & Morin, P. E. (1979). Parents and children together: An alternative to foster care. Detroit, MI: Wayne State University, Department of Family and Consumer Resources.

Cameron, G. (1990a). Child maltreatment: Challenges in expanding our concept of helping. In M. Rothery & G. Cameron (Eds.), Child maltreatment: Expanding our concept of helping (pp. 277–286). Hillsdale, NJ: Lawrence Erlbaum Associates.

Cameron, G. (1990b). The potential of informal social support strategies in child welfare. In M. Rothery & G. Cameron (Eds.), Child maltreatment: Expanding our concept of helping (pp. 145–168). Hillsdale, NJ: Lawrence Erlbaum Associates.

Cameron, G. (1993). Proposal for a multiple site evaluation of intensive family preservation services. Waterloo, Ontario: Wilfrid Laurier University, Centre for Social Welfare Studies.

Cameron, G., & Birnie-Lefcovitch, B. (1992). *Summary and highlights of parent mutual aid organizations in child welfare administration project.* Waterloo, Ontario: Centre for Social Welfare Studies.

Cameron, G., Hayward, K., & Mamatis, D. (1992). *Mutual aid and child welfare: The parent mutual aid organizations in child welfare demonstration project.* Waterloo, Ontario: Wilfrid Laurier University, Centre for Social Welfare Studies.

Cameron, G., Holmberg, R., & Rothery, M. (Canadian Sociotelic Limited) (1983). *The nature and effectiveness of family support measures in child welfare.* Toronto: Ministry of Community and Social Services.

Cameron, G., Peirson, L., & Pancer, S. M. (1994). Resident participation in the Better Beginnings, Better Futures prevention project: Part II—Factors that facilitate and hinder involvement. *Canadian Journal of Community Mental Health, 13,* 213–227.

Cameron, G., & Rothery, M. (1985). *The use of family support in children's aid societies: An exploratory study.* Toronto: Ministry of Community and Social Services.

Cameron, G., Vanderwoerd, J., and Peters, R. (1995). *Building bridges: Service provider involvement in Better Beginnings, Better Futures.* Kingston, ON: Queen's University, Better Beginnings Research Coordination Unit.

Cameron, J. G. (1983). Defining and measuring effectiveness for the personal social services. Unpublished Ph.D. thesis, School of Social Work, Columbia University, New York.

Carol, N. A., & Reich, J. W. (1978). Issues in the implementation of the parent aide concept. *Social Casework, 59*(March), 152–160.

Christopherson, E. R. (1979). The family training program: Intensive home-based family-centred parent training. *Education and Treatment of Children, 2*(4), 287–292.

Cohen, S., Mermelstein, R., Kamarck, T., & Hoberman, H. M. (1985). Measuring the functional components of social support. In I. G. Sarason & B. R. Sarason (Eds.), *Social support: Theory, research, and applications* (pp. 73–94). Dordrecht: Martinus Nijhoff.

Cohen, S., & Syme, L. S (1985). Issues in the study and application of social support. In S. Cohen & L. S. Syme (Eds.), *Social support and health* (pp. 1–22). New York: Academic Press.

Cohen, S., & Wills, T. A. (1985). Stress, social support, and the buffering hypothesis. *Psychological Bulletin, 98*(2), 310–357.

Cohn, A. (1979). Effective treatment of child abuse and neglect. *Social Work, 24*(6), 513–519.

Cohn, A. H., & Daro, D. (1987). Is treatment too late: What ten years of evaluative research tells us. *Child Abuse and Neglect, 11,* 433–442.

Cohn Donnelly, A. H. (1991). What we have learned about prevention. What we should do about it. *Child Abuse and Neglect, 15,* 99–106.

Collins, H., & Collins, D. (1990). Family therapy in the treatment of child sexual abuse. In M. Rothery & G. Cameron (Eds.), *Child maltreatment: Expanding our concept of helping* (pp. 231–245). Hillsdale, NJ: Lawrence Erlbaum Associates.

Comstock, C. H. (1982). Preventive processes in self-help groups: Parents Anonymous. *Prevention in Human Services, 1*(3), 47–53.

Consortium for Longitudinal Studies (1983). *As the twig is bent.* Hillsdale, NJ: Lawrence Erlbaum Associates.

D'Augelli, A. (1983). Social support networks in mental health. In J. K. Whittaker & J. Garbarino (Eds.), *Social support networks: Informal helping in the human services* (pp. 71–106). Hawthorne, NY: Aldine de Gruyter.

Daro, D. (1988). *Confronting child abuse.* New York: Free Press.

Denicola, J., & Sandler, J. (1980). Training abusive parents in child management and self-control skills. *Behavior Therapy, 11,* 263–270.

Dumas, J. E., & Wahler, R. G. (1983). Predictors of treatment outcome in parent training: Mother insularity and socioeconomic disadvantage. *Behavioral Assessment, 5,* 301–313.

Dunu, M. (1979). Lower eastside family union. In S. Maybanks & M. Bryce (Eds.), *Home-based services for children and families: Policy, practice, and research* (pp. 211–224). Springfield, IL: Charles C. Thomas.

Durkin, R. (1986). The use of therapeutic day care to resolve the legal dilemma of protecting the rights of both children and parents in equivocal cases of abuse and neglect. *Child Care Quarterly, 15,* 138–140.

Edmunson, E. D., Bedell, J. R., Archer, R. P., & Gordon, R. E. (1982). Integrating skill building and peer support in mental health treatment: The early intervention and community network development projects. In A. M. Jeger & R. S. Slotnick (Eds.), *Community mental health and behavioral-ecology* (pp. 127–139). New York and London: Plenum.

Edmunson, E. D., Bedell, J. R., & Gordon, R. C. (1984). The community network development project: Bridging the gap between professional aftercare and self-help. In A. Gartner & F. Riessman (Eds.), *The self-help revolution* (pp. 195–203). New York: Human Sciences Press.

Egan, K. (1983). Stress management and child management with abusive parents. *Journal of Clinical Child Psychology, 12,* 292–299.

Epstein, N., & Shainline, A. (1974). Paraprofessional parent-aide and disadvantaged families. *Social Casework, 55*(April), 230–236.

Fairweather, G. E., Sanders, D., Maynard, H., & Cressler, D. (1969). *Community life for the mentally ill: An alternative to institutional care.* Chicago: Aldine.

Family Resource Coalition (1983). *Program to strengthen families.* Bush Center for Child Development and Social Policy, Yale University, New Haven, CT.

Fanon, F. (1963). *The wretched of the earth.* New York: Grove.

Feldman, L. H. (1991). Evaluating the impact of intensive family preservation services in New Jersey. In K. Wells & D. E. Biegel (Eds.), *Family preservation services: Research and evaluation* (pp. 47–71). Newbury Park, CA: Sage.

Frankel, H. (1988). Family-centered, home-based services in child protection: A review of the research. *Social Service Review, 62*(March), 137–157.

Fraser, M. W., & Haapala, D. A. (1987–1988). Home-based family treatment: A quantitative-qualitative assessment. *Journal of Applied Social Sciences, 12,* 1–23.

Fraser, M. W., Pecora, P. J., & Haapala, D. A. (1989). *Families in crisis: Findings from the family-based intensive treatment project.* Social Research Institute, Graduate School of Social Work, University of Utah, Salt Lake City, and Behavioral Sciences Institute, Washington, August.

Fraser, M. W., Pecora, P. J., & Haapala, D. A. (1991). *Families in crisis: The impact of intensive family preservation services.* Hawthorne, NY: Aldine de Gruyter.

Freire, P. (1981). *Pedagogy of the oppressed.* New York: Continuum.

Froland, C., Pancoast, D., Chapman, N., & Kimboko, P. (1981). *Helping networks and human services.* Beverly Hills, CA: Sage.

Garbarino, J. (1983). Social support networks: Rx for the helping professionals. In J. K. Whittaker & J. Garbarino (Eds.), *Social support networks: Informal helping in the human services* (pp. 3–28). Hawthorne, NY: Aldine de Gruyter.

Garbarino, J., & Gilliam, G. (1980). *Understanding abusive families.* Lexington, MA: Lexington Books.

Garbarino, J., & Stocking, S. H. (Eds.) (1980). *Protecting children from abuse and neglect: Developing and maintaining effective support systems for families.* San Francisco: Jossey-Bass.

Gartner, A., & Riessman, F. (1977). *Self-help in the human services.* San Francisco: Jossey-Bass.

Gartner, A., & Riessman, F. (1984). *The self-help revolution.* New York: Human Sciences Press.

Gaudin, J. M. (1993). Effective intervention with neglectful families. *Criminal Justice and Behavior, 20,* 66–89.

Gaudin, J. M., Wodarski, J. S., Arkinson, M. K., & Avery, L. S. (1990–1991). Remedying child neglect: Effectiveness of social network interventions. *Journal of Applied Social Sciences, 15*(1), 97–123.

Geismar, L. L., & Ayres, B. (1958). *Patterns of change in program families.* St. Paul, MN: Family-Centered Project.

Geismar, L. L., & Krisberg, J. (1967). *The forgotten neighborhood: Site of an early skirmish in the war on poverty.* Metuchen, NJ: Scarecrow.

Giarretto, H. (1982). A comprehensive child sexual abuse treatment program. *Child Abuse and Neglect, 6,* 263–278.

Gottlieb, B. (1983). *Social support strategies: Guidelines for mental health practice.* Beverly Hill, CA: Sage.

Gottlieb, B. (1985). Combining lay and professional resources to promote human welfare: Projects and terrains. In J. A. Yoder, J. M. L. Jonker, & R. A. B. Leaper (Eds.), *Support networks in a caring community* (pp. 59–77). Dordrecht: Martinus Nijhoff.

Gray, J. D., Cutler, C. A., Dean, J. G., & Kempe, C. H. (1977). Prediction and prevention of child abuse and neglect. *Child Abuse and Neglect, 1,* 45–58.

Greenley, J. R., & Robitschek, C. G. (1991). Evaluation of a comprehensive program for youth with severe emotional disorders: An analysis of family experiences and satisfaction. *American Journal of Orthopsychiatry, 61,* 291–297.

Greenspan, M. (1982). *A new approach to women and therapy.* New York: McGraw-Hill.

Gutelis, M. F., Kirsch, A. D., MacDonald, S., Brooks, M. R., & McErlean, T. (1977). Controlled study of child health supervision: Behavioural results. *Pediatrics, 60,* 294–304.

Haapala, D., & Kinney, J. (1988). Avoiding out-of-home placement of high-risk status offenders through the use of intensive home-based family preservation services. *Criminal Justice and Behavior, 15,* 334–348.

Hall, A., & Wellman, B. (1985). Social networks and social support. In S. Cohen & L. S. Syme (Eds.), *Social support and health* (pp. 23–41). New York: Academic Press.

Halper, G. &, Jones, M. A. (1981). *Serving families at risk of dissolution: Public preventive services in New York City* (Grant #90-C-1269). New York: Children's Bureau of the Administration for Children, Youth and Families, Department of Health and Human Services.

Halpern, R., & Covey, L. (1983). Community support for adolescent parents and their children: The parent-to-parent program in Vermont. *Journal of Primary Prevention, 3*(3), 160–173.

Halpern, R., & Larner, M. (1987). Lay family support during pregnancy and infancy: The child survival/fair start initiative. *Infant Mental Health Journal, 8*(2) 130–143.

Harnett, J. (1989). An intergenerational support system for child welfare families. *Child Welfare, 68*(3), 347–353.

Hattie, J. A., Sharpley, C. F., & Rogers, H. J. (1984). Comparative effectiveness of professional and paraprofessional helpers. *Psychological Bulletin, 95*(3), 534–541.

Hawkins, J. D., & Fraser, M. W. (1983). Social support networks in delinquency prevention and treatment. In J. K. Whittaker & J. Garbarino (Eds.), *Social support networks: Informal helping in the human services* (pp. 333–352). Hawthorne, NY: Aldine de Gruyter.

Hawkins, R. (1979). Developing comprehensive emergency services. In S. May-banks & M. Bryce (Eds.), *Home-based services for children and families: Policy, practice, and research* (pp. 103–111). Springfield, IL: Charles C. Thomas.

Hayward, K., & Cameron, G. (1993). *Intensive family preservation services: A review of the literature.* Waterloo, Ontario: Wilfrid Laurier University, Centre for Social Welfare Studies.

Hayward, K., Cameron, G., & Peirson, L. (1995). *A different approach: Program development and service delivery in Intensive Family Preservation Services.* Waterloo, ON: Centre for Social Welfare Studies, Wilfrid Laurier University.

Heinicke, C. M., Beckwith, L., & Thompson, A. (1988). Early intervention in the family system: A framework and review. *Infant Mental Health Journal, 9*(2), 111–141.

Heins, H. C., Nance, N. W., & Ferguson, J. E. (1987). Social support in improving perinatal outcome: The resource mothers program. *Obstetrics and Gynecology, 70*(2, August), 263–266.

Helfer, R. E. (1982). A review of the literature on the prevention of child abuse and neglect. *Child Abuse and Neglect: The International Journal, 6*(3), 251–261.

Heller, K., & Lakey, B. (1985). Perceived support and social interaction among friends and confidants. In I. G. Sarason & B. R. Sarason (Eds.), *Social support: Theory, research, and applications* (pp. 287–300). Dordrecht: Martinus Nijhoff.

Heying, K. R. (1985). Family-based, in-home services for the severely emotionally disturbed child. *Child Welfare, 64,* 519–527.

Hinckley, E. C., & Ellis, W. F. (1985). An effective alternative to residential place-ment: Home-based services. *Journal of Consulting and Clinical Psychology, 14,* 209–213.

Hirsch, B. J. (1980). Systems and coping with major life changes. *American Journal of Community Psychology, 8*(2), 159–172.

Hobfoll, S. E. (1985). Limitations of social support in the stress process. In I. G. Sarason & B. R. Sarason (Eds.), *Social support: Theory, research, and applications* (pp. 391–414). Dordrecht: Martinus Nijhoff.

Hooyman, N. (1983). Social support networks in service to the elderly. In J. K. Whittaker & J. Garbarino (Eds.), *Social support networks: Informal helping in the human services* (pp. 133–164). Hawthorne, NY: Aldine de Gruyter.

Hornick, J. P., & Clarke, M. E. (1986). A cost/effectiveness evaluation of lay therapy treatment for child abusing and high risk parents. *Child Abuse and Neglect, 10,* 309–318.

House, J. S., & Kahn, R. L. (1985). Measures and concepts of social support. In S. Cohen & L. S. Syme (Eds.), *Social support and health* (pp. 83–108). New York: Academic Press.

Howze, D., & Kotch, J. (1984). Disentangling life events, stress and social support: Implications for the primary prevention of child abuse and neglect. *Child Abuse and Neglect, 8,* 401–409.

Hughes, J. (1977). Adolescent children of alcoholic parents and the relationship of Alateen to these children. *Journal of Consulting and Clinical Psychology, 45*(5), 946–947.

Hurd, G. S., Pattison, E. M., & Llamas, R. (1981). Models of social network intervention. *International Journal of Family Therapy, 3,* 246–257.

Huston, T. L., & Burgess, R. L. (1979). Social exchange in developing relationships: An overview. In R. Burgess & T. L. Huston (Eds.), *Social exchange in developing relationships* (pp.3–28). Hillsdale, NJ: Lawrence Erlbaum Associates.

Illich, I., et al. (1977). *Disabling professions.* Don Mills, Ontario: Burns & Mac-Eachern.

Irueste-Montes, A. M., & Montes, F. (1988). Court-ordered vs. voluntary treatment of abusive and neglectful parents. *Child Abuse and Neglect, 12,* 33–39.

Jones, M. A., Magura, S., & Shyne, A. (1981). Effective practice with families in protective and preventive services: What works? *Child Welfare, 60*(1), 67–80.

Jones, M. A., Neuman, R., & Shyne, A. W. (1976). *A second chance for families: Evaluation of a program to reduce foster care.* New York: Child Welfare League of America.

Jones, W. H. (1985). The psychology of loneliness: Some personality issues in the study of social support. In I. G. Sarason & B. R. Sarason (Eds.), *Social support: Theory, research, and applications* (pp. 225–241). Dordrecht: Martinus Nijhoff.

Kahn, R. L., & Antonucci, T. C. (1980). Convoys over the life course: Attachment, roles, and social support. *Life-Span Development and Behavior, 3,* 253–286.

Kasl, S. V., & Wells, J. A. (1985). Social support and health in the middle years: Work and the family. In S. Cohen & L. S. Syme (Eds.), *Social support and health* (pp. 175–198). New York: Academic Press.

Kempe, C. H., & Helfer, R. E. (Eds.) (1972). *Helping the battered child and his family.* Philadelphia: J. P. Lippincott.

Kessler, R. C., & McLeod, J. D. (1985). Social support and mental health in community samples. In S. Cohen & L. S. Syme (Eds.), *Social support and health* (pp. 219–240). New York: Academic Press.

Kessler, R. C., McLeod, J. D., & Wethington, E. (1985). The costs of caring: A perspective on the relationship between sex and psychological distress. In I. G. Sarason & B. R. Sarason (Eds.), *Social support: Theory, research, and applications* (pp. 491–506). Dordrecht: Martinus Nijhoff.

Kinney, J., Haapala, D., Booth, C., & Leavitt, S. (1990). The homebuilders model. In J. K. Whittaker, J. Kenney, E. M. Tracy, & C. Booth (Eds.), *Reaching high-risk families: Intensive family preservation in human services* (pp. 31–64). Hawthorne, NY: Aldine de Gruyter.

Kinney, J., Madsen, B., Fleming, T., & Haapala, D. A. (1977). Homebuilders: Keeping families together. *Journal of Consulting and Clinical Psychology, 45*(4), 667–673.

Lally, J. R., Mangione, P. L., & Honig, A. S. (1988). The Syracuse University family development research program: Long-range impact of an early intervention with low-income children and their families. In D. R. Powell (Ed.), *Parent education as early childhood intervention* (pp. 79–104). Norwood, NJ: Ablex.

Larson, C. P. (1980). Efficacy of prenatal and postpartum home visits on child health and development. *Pediatrics, 66*(2, August), 191–197.

Lefcourt, H. M. (1985). Intimacy, social support, and locus of control as moderators of stress. In I. G. Sarason & B. R. Sarason (Eds.), *Social support: Theory, research, and applications* (pp. 155–171). Dordrecht: Martinus Nijhoff.

Levens, H. (1968). Organizational affiliation and powerlessness: A case study of the welfare poor. *Social Problems, 16*(1), 18–32.

Lewis, M. (1978). *The culture of inequality.* New York: New American Library.

Lewis, R. E. (1990). *Service-related correlates of treatment success in intensive family preservation services for child welfare.* Unpublished doctoral dissertation. Ann Arbor, MI: UMI Dissertation Information Service.

Lieber, L. L. (1984). Parents Anonymous: The use of self-help in the treatment and prevention of family violence. In A. Gartner & F. Riessman (Eds.), *The self-help revolution* (Vol. 10) (pp. 53–64). New York: Human Sciences Press.

Lieber, L. L. & Baker, J. M. (1977). Parents Anonymous, self-help treatment for child abusing parents: A review and an evaluation. *Child Abuse and Neglect, 1,* 132–148.

Lieberman, M., & Borman, L. D. (1976). Special issue/self-help group. *The Journal of Applied Behavioral Science, 12*(July/August/September).

Lieberman, M., & Gourach, N. (1979). Effects of change groups on the elderly. In M. Lieberman & L. Borman (Eds.), *Self-help groups for coping with crisis* (pp. 387–405). San Francisco: Jossey-Bass.

Lines, D. (1987). The effectiveness of parent aides in the tertiary prevention of child abuse in South Australia. *Child Abuse & Neglect, 11,* 507–512.

Litwak, E. (1985). *Helping the elderly: The complementary roles of informal networks and formal systems.* New York: Guilford.

Lutzker, J. R., & Rice, J. M. (1984). Project 12-Ways: Measuring outcome of a large in-home service for treatment and prevention of child abuse and neglect. *Child Abuse and Neglect, 8,* 519–524.

Lutzker, J. R., Wesch, D., & Rice, J. M. (1984). A review of project "12-ways": An ecobehavioral approach to the treatment and prevention of child abuse and neglect. *Advances in Behavioral Research and Therapy, 6,* 63–73.

Madden, J., O'Hara, J., & Levenstein, P. (1984). Home again: Effects of the mother-child home program on mother and child. *Child Development, 55,* 636–647.

Magura, S. (1981). Are services to prevent foster care effective? *Children and Youth Services Review, 3*(2), 193–212.

Magura, S., & Moses, B. (1986). *Outcome measures for child welfare services: Theory and applications.* New York: Child Welfare League of America.

Magura, S., Moses, B., & Jones, M. A. (1987). *Assessing risk and measuring change in families: The family risk scales.* Washington, DC: Child Welfare League of America.

Mamatis, D., & Morrison, S. M. (1991). *Home visiting: A model of prevention and health promotion.* Unpublished paper presented at the Crossing Boundaries: Helping Disadvantaged Populations Conference, Wilfrid Laurier University, Centre for Social Welfare Studies, Faculty of Social Work, Waterloo, Ontario, October.

Maybanks, S., & Bryce, M. (1979). *Home-based services for children and families: Policy, practice, and research.* Springfield, IL: Charles C. Thomas.

McCall, G. J., & Simmons, J. L. (1966). *Identities and interactions.* New York: Free Press.

McCarthy, D. (1976). Parents anonymous self-help groups for abusive parents: A safe place to talk. *Challenge, 19*(2), 13–15.

McDonald, W. R., & Associates, Inc. (1990). *Evaluation of AB 1562 in-home care demonstration projects.* Sacramento, CA: Office of Child Abuse Prevention, Department of Social Services.

McKey, Candelli, Barrett, McConkey, & Plantz (1985). *The impact of Head Start in children, families, and communities.* Final report of the Head Start evaluator, Synthesis and Utilization Project, Washington, DC

McKnight, J. (1977). Professionalized service and disabling help. In J. Illich et al., *Disabling professions.* Don Mills, Ontario: Burns & MacEachern.

Metzl, M. (1980). Teaching parents a strategy for enhancing child development. *Child Development, 51,* 583–586.

Meyers, M., & Bernier, J. (1990). *Preventing child abuse: A resource for policymakers and advocates.* Boston: Massachusetts Committee for Children and Youth.

Milardo, R. M. (1983). Social networks and pair relationships: A review of substantive and measurement issues. *Sociology and Social Research, 68*(1), 1–18.

Miller, J. L., & Whittaker, J. K. (1988). Social services and social support: Blended programs for families at risk of child maltreatment. *Child Welfare, 67,* 161–174.

Miller, K., Fein, E., Howe, G. W., Gaudieo, C. P., & Bishop, G. U. (1984). Time-limited, goal-focused, parent aide service. *Social Casework, 65*(October), 472–477.

Ministry of Community and Social Services (1986). *Ontario child health study: Summary of initial finding.* Ontario: Queen's Printer of Ontario.

Ministry of Community and Social Services (1990a). *Better beginnings, better futures: An integrated model of primary prevention of emotional and behavioural problems.* Toronto: Queen's Printer for Ontario.

Ministry of Community and Social Services (1990b). *Children first: Report of the advisory committee on children's services.* Ontario: Queen's Printer for Ontario.

Mitchell, C., Tovar, P., & Knitzer, J. (1989). *The Bronx homebuilders program: An evaluation of the first 45 families.* New York: Bank Street College of Education, Division of Research, Demonstration and Policy.

Mitchell, R. E. (1982). Social networks and psychiatric clients: The personal and environmental context. *American Journal of Community Psychology, 10*(4), 387–401.

Mitchell, R. E., & Trickett, E. J. (1980). Task force report: Social networks as mediators of social support: An analysis of the effects and determinants of social networks. *Community Mental Health Journal, 16*(1), 27–45.

Monroe, S. M. (1983). Social support and disorder: Toward on untangling of cause and effect. *American Journal of Community Psychology, 11*(1), 81–97.

Moos, R. H. (1976). *Evaluating treatment environments: A social ecological approach.* New York: John Wiley.

Murphy, A. D. (1980). The perceptions of family environment by couples who are members of Parents Anonymous. *Dissertation Abstracts International, 41*(6), 2389–2413.

Nelson, K. (1990). How do we know family-based services are effective? *Prevention Report.* Oakdale, Iowa: National Resource Center on Family Based Services.

Nelson, K. (1991). Populations and outcomes in five family preservation programs. In K. Wells & D. E. Biegel (Eds.), *Family preservation services: Research and evaluation* (pp. 72–91). Newbury Park, CA: Sage.

Nix, H. (1980). Why Parents Anonymous? *Journal of Psychiatric Nursing and Mental Health Services, 18*(10), 23–28.

Nurcombe, B., Howell, D. C., Rauh, V. A., Teti., D. M., Ruoff, P., Brennan, J., & Murphy, B. (1984). An intervention program for mothers of low birth weight babies: Preliminary results. *Journal of the American Academy of Child Psychiatry, 23,* 319–325.

Olds, D. L., Henderson, C. R., Chamberlin, R., & Tatelbaum, R. (1986a). Preventing child abuse and neglect: A randomized trial of nurse home visitation. *Pediatrics, 78,* 65–78.

Olds, D. L., Henderson, C. R., Tatelbaum, R., & Chamberlin, R. (1986b). Improving the delivery of prenatal care and outcomes of pregnancy: A randomized trial of nurse home visitation. *Pediatrics, 77*(1), 16–28.

Olds, D. L., Henderson, C. R., Tatelbaum, R., & Chamberlin, R. (1988). Improving the life-course development of socially disadvantaged mothers: A randomized trial of nurse home visitation. *American Journal of Public Health, 78*(11), 1436–1445.

Olson, D. H., Portner, J., & Lavee, Y. (1985). *FACES III.* St. Paul: University of Minnesota, Department of Family Social Services.

Oostenbrink, A., Mathieson, L., Blase, K., Fixsen, D., Jaeger, D., & Olivier, K. (1990). *In-home treatment and support with multi-problem families.* Calgary, Alberta: Hull Community Services.

Pallone, S. R., & Malkemes, L. C. (1984). *Helping parents who abuse their children: A comprehensive approach for intervention.* Springfield, IL: Charles C. Thomas.

Paybel, E. S. (1985). Life events, social support and clinical psychiatric disorder. In I. G. Sarason & B. R. Sarason (Eds.), *Social support: Theory, research, and applications* (pp. 321–347). Dordrecht: Martinus Nijhoff.

Pearlin, L. I. (1985). Social structure and processes of social support. In S. Cohen &

L. S. Syme (Eds.), *Social support and health* (pp. 43–60). New York: Academic Press.

Pearson, C. L., & King, P. A. (undated). *Intensive family services: Evaluation of foster care prevention in Maryland, final report.* Baltimore: Maryland Department of Human Resources, Social Services Administration.

Pecora, P. J. (1991). Family-based and intensive family preservation services: A select literature review. In M. W. Fraser, P. J. Pecora, & D. A. Haapala, *Families in crisis: The impact of intensive family preservation services* (pp. 17–47). Hawthorne, NY: Aldine de Gruyter.

Pecora, P. J., Fraser, M. W., & Haapala, D.A. (1990). *Intensive home-based family preservation services: Client outcomes and issues for program design.* Revision of a paper presented at the NATO Advanced Research Workshop: State Intervention on Behalf of Children and Youth, Acquafredda di Maratea, Italy, February 23, 1989.

Pelton, L. H. (1981). *The social context of child abuse and neglect.* New York: Human Sciences Press.

Pepleau, L. A. (1985). Loneliness research: Basic concepts and findings. In I. G. Sarason & B. R. Sarason (Eds.), *Social support: Theory, research, and applications* (pp. 269–286). Dordrecht: Martinus Nijhoff.

Pilisuk, M., & Parks, S. H. (1986). *The healing web: Social networks and human survival.* Hanover and London: University Press of New England.

Polansky, N., Chalmer, M. A., Buttenweiser, E. W., & Williams, D. P. (1979). Isolation of the neglectful family. *American Journal of Orthopsychiatry, 49,* 149–152.

Powell, T. J. (1979). Comparisons between self-help groups and professional services. *Social Casework, 60*(9), 561–565.

Pressman, B., Cameron, G., & Rothery, M. (1989). *Intervening with assaulted women: Current theory, research and practice.* Hillsdale, NJ: Lawrence Erlbaum Associates.

Raiff, N. R. (1984). Some health related outcomes of self-help participation: Recovery Inc. as a case example of a self-help organization in mental health. In A. Gartner & F. Riessman (Eds.), *The self-help revolution* (pp. 183–193). New York: Human Services Press.

Rappaport, J. (1977). *Community psychology: Values, research and action.* New York: Holt, Rinehart and Winston.

Reid, J., Taplin, P., & Lorber, R. (1981). A social interactional approach to the treatment of abusive families. In R. B. Stuart (Ed.), *Violent behavior: Social learning approaches to prediction, management and treatment* (pp. 83–101). New York: Brunner/Mazel.

Rescarla, L. A., Provence, S., & Naylor, A. (1982). The Yale child welfare research program: Description and results. In E. F. Zigler & E. W. Gordon (Eds.), *Day care: Scientific and social policy issues* (pp. 183–199). Boston: Auburn House.

Richardson, R., & Pfeiffenberger, C. (1983). Social support networks for divorced and stepfamilies. In J. K. Whittaker & J. Garbarino (Eds.), *Social support networks: Informal helping in the human services* (pp. 219–247). Hawthorne, NY: Aldine de Gruyter.

Rivera, V. R., & Kutash, K. (1994). *Components of a system of care: What does the research say?* Tampa: University of South Florida, Florida Mental Health Institute, Research and Training Center for Children's Mental Health.

Rook, K. S., & Dooley, D. (1985). Applying social support research: Theoretical problems and future directions. *Journal of Social Issues, 41*(1), 5–28.

Rosenstein, P. J. (1978). Family outreach: A program for the prevention of child neglect and abuse. *Child Welfare, 57*(8), 519–526.

Rossi, P. H. (1991). *Evaluating family preservation programs: A report to the Edna McConnell Clark Foundation.* Amherst, MA: Social and Demographic Research Institute.

Rossi, P. H. (1992). Strategies for evaluation. *Children and Youth Services Review, 14*, 167–191.

Rothery, M. (1990a). Child maltreatment and the front-line worker. In M. Rothery & G. Cameron (Eds.), *Child maltreatment: Expanding our concept of helping* (pp. 1–9). Hillsdale, NJ: Lawrence Erlbaum Associates.

Rothery, M. (1990b). Family therapy with multiproblem families. In M. Rothery & G. Cameron (Eds.), *Child maltreatment: Expanding our concept of helping* (pp. 13–32). Hillsdale, NJ: Lawrence Erlbaum Associates.

Rothery, M., & Cameron, G. (1985). *Understanding family support in child welfare: A summary report.* Toronto: Ontario Ministry of Community and Social Services.

Rothery, M., & Cameron, G. (Eds.) (1990). *Child maltreatment: Expanding our concept of helping.* Hillsdale, NJ: Lawrence Erlbaum Associates.

Ryan, W. (1976). *Blaming the victim.* New York: Vintage.

Sarabin, T. R., & Scheibe, K. E. (Eds.) (1983). *Studies in social identity.* New York: Praeger.

Sarason, I. G., & Sarason, B. R. (1985). Social support—insights from experimentation. In I. G. Sarason & B. R. Sarason (Eds.), *Social support: Theory, research, and applications* (pp. 39–50). Dordrecht: Martinus Nijhoff.

Saulnier, K. (1982). Networks, change and crisis: The web of support. *Canadian Journal of Community Mental Health, 1*(1, March), 5–23.

Scarr-Salapatek, S., & Williams, M. L. (1973). The effect of early stimulation on low birth-weight infants. *Child Development, 44*, 94–101.

Schinke, S. P., Schilling, R. F., Kirkham, M. A., & Gilchrist, L. D. (1986). Stress management skills for parent. *Journal of Child and Adolescent Psychotherapy, 3*(4), 293–298.

Schorr, L. B. (1988). *Within our reach: Breaking the cycle of disadvantage.* New York: Anchor.

Schulz, R., & Rau, M. T. (1985). Social support through the life course. In S. Cohen & L. S. Syme (Eds.), *Social support and health* (pp. 129–149). New York: Academic Press.

Schwartz, I. M., AuClaire, P., & Harris, L. (1990). *Family-preservation service as an alternative to the out-of-home placement of seriously emotionally disturbed adolescents: The Hennepin County experience.* Mimeograph, March, University of Michigan, Center for the Study of Youth Policy, School of Social Work.

Seagull, E. A. (1987). Social support and child maltreatment: A review of the evidence. *Child Abuse and Neglect, 11*, 41–52.

Seitz, V., Rosenbaum, L. K., & Apfel, N. H. (1985). Effects of family support intervention: A ten-year follow-up. *Child Development, 56*, 376–391.

Sennett, R., & Cobb, J. (1972). *The hidden injuries of class.* New York: Vintage Books.

Sheehan, L. (1984). *The care and treatment program, Seattle Day Nursery.* Notes from presentation to American Psychological Association Convention, August.

Shumaker, S. A., & Brownell, A. (1984). Toward a theory of social support: Closing conceptual gaps. *Journal of Social Issues, 40*(4), 11–36.

Siegel, E., Bauman, K. E., Schaefer, E. S., Saunders, M. M., & Ingram, D. D. (1980). Hospital and home support during infancy: Impact on maternal attachment, child abuse, and neglect and health care utilization. *Pediatrics, 66,* 183–190.

Silverman, P.R., & Smith, D. (1984). "Helping" in mutual help groups for the physically disabled. In A. Gartner & F. Riessman (Eds.), *The self-help revolution* (pp. 73–93). New York: Human Sciences Press.

Sinanoglu, P. A. (1981). Working with parents. In A. N. Maluccio & P. A. Sinanoglu (Eds.), *The challenge of partnership: Working with parents of children in foster care.* New York: Child Welfare League of America.

Snider, G. E., & Skoretz, A. N. (1983). *Social indicators as predictors for child maltreatment.* Unpublished master's research project, Wilfrid Laurier University, Faculty of Social Work, Waterloo, Ontario.

Spaid, W. M., Fraser, M. W., & Lewis, R. E. (1991). Changes in family functioning: Is participation in intensive family preservation services correlated with changes in attitudes or behaviors? In M. W. Fraser, P. J. Pecora & D. A. Haapala (Eds.), *Families in crisis: The impact of intensive family preservation services* (pp. 131–148). Hawthorne, NY: Aldine de Gruyter.

Specht, H. (1986). Social support, social networks, social exchange, and social work practice. *Social Service Review, 60,* 218–240.

Stavrakaki, C. (1985). Peer groups and parent groups. In Ministry of National Health and Welfare, *Mental health treatment services to abused children.* Ottawa: Health and Welfare Canada.

Stephens, D. (1979). In-home family support services: An ecological systems approach. In S. Maybanks & M. Bryce (Eds.), *Home-based services for children and families: Policy, practice, and research* (pp. 283–295). Springfield, IL: Charles C. Thomas.

Szykula, S. A., & Fleischman, M. J. (1985). Reducing out-of-home placements of abused children: Two controlled field studies. *Child Abuse and Neglect, 9,* 277–283.

Thoits, P. A. (1982). Conceptual, methodological, and theoretical problems in studying social support as a buffer against life stress. *Journal of Health and Social Behavior, 23*(June), 145–159.

Thoits, P. A. (1983). Multiple identities and psychological well-being: A reformulation and test of the social isolation hypothesis. *American Sociological Review, 48*(April), 174–187.

Thoits, P. A. (1985). Social support and psychological well-being: Theoretical possibilities. In I. G. Sarason & B. R. Sarason (Eds.), *Social support: Theory, research, and applications* (pp. 49–72). Dordrecht: Martinus Nijhoff.

Thomlison, R. J. (1990). Uses of skill development and behavior modification-techniques in working with abusing/neglecting parents. In M. Rothery & G.

Cameron (Eds.), *Child maltreatment: Expanding our concept of helping* (pp. 127–143). Hillsdale, NJ: Lawrence Erlbaum Associates.

Todres, R. (1982). *Self-help groups: An annotated bibliography*. New York: National Self-Help Clearinghouse, Graduate School and University Center of the City University of New York.

Tracy, J., Ballard, C., & Clark, E. (1975). Child abuse project: A follow-up. *Social Work, 20*(5), 398–399.

Trickett, P. K., Apfel, N. H., Rosenbaum, L. K., & Zigler, E. F. (1982). A five-year follow-up of participants in the Yale child welfare research program. In E. F. Zigler & E. W. Gordon (Eds.), *Day care: Scientific and social policy issues* (pp. 200–222). Boston: Auburn House.

Turner, R. J., Frankel, B. G., & Levin, D. (1982). *Social support: Conceptualization, measurement and implications for mental health*. London, Ontario: University of Western Ontario, Health Care Research Unit.

Unger, D. G., & Wandersman, A. (1985). The importance of neighbors: The social, cognitive, and affective components of neighboring. *American Journal of Community Psychology, 13*(2), 139–169.

Unger, D. G., & Wandersman, L. P. (1985). Social support and adolescent mothers: Action research contributions to theory and application. *Journal of Social Issues, 41*(1), 29–45.

Vachon, M. L. S., Lyall, W., Rogers, J., Friedman-Letafsky, K., & Freeman, S. (1980). A controlled study of self-help interventions for widows. *American Journal of Psychiatry, 137*(11), 1380–1384.

Vaux, A. (1988). *Social support: Theory, research, and intervention*. New York: Praeger.

Wahler, R. G. (1980a). The insular mother: Her problems in parent-child treatment. *Journal of Applied Behavior Analysis, 13*(2), 207–219.

Wahler, R. G. (1980b). The multiply entrapped parent: Obstacles to change in parent-child problems. In J. P. Vincent (Ed.), *Advances in family intervention, assessment and theory* (Vol. 1) (pp. 29–52). Greenwich, CT: JAI.

Wahler, R. G., & Moore, D. M. (1975). *School-home behavior change procedures for oppositional children*. Paper presented at the Association for the Advancement of Behavior Theory, San Francisco.

Wald, M. S., Carlsmith, J. M., & Leiderman, P. H. (1988). *Protecting abused and neglected children*. Stanford, CA: Stanford University Press.

Weigert, A. J., Smith Teitge, J., & Teitge, D. W. (1986). *Society and identity: Towards a sociological psychology*. Cambridge: Cambridge University Press.

Weiss, H. B., & Jacobs, F. H. (1988). *Evaluating family programs*. Hawthorne, NY: Aldine de Gruyter.

White, E. H. (1981). *Evaluation of service improvement grants: Analysis of client case reports* (DHHS, under Contract HEW 105-78-1107). Washington, DC: National Center for Child Abuse and Neglect, Office of Human Development Services.

Whiteman, M., Fanshel, D., & Grundy, J. F. (1987). Cognitive-behavioral interventions aimed at anger of parents at risk of child abuse. *Social Work, 32*, 469–474.

Whittaker, J. K. (1983). Social support networks in child welfare. In J. K. Whittaker & J. Garbarino (Eds.), *Social support networks strategies: Informal helping in the human services* (pp. 167–187). Hawthorne, NY: Aldine de Gruyter.

Whittaker, J. K. (1986). Formal and informal helping in child welfare services: Implications for management and practice. *Child Welfare, 55*(1), 17–25.

Whittaker, J. K. & Garbarino, J. (1983). *Social support networks: Informal helping in the human services*. Hawthorne, NY: Aldine de Gruyter.

Wieder, S., Poisson, S., Lourie, R. S., & Greenspan, S. I. (1988). Enduring gains: A five-year follow-up on the clinical infant development program. *Zero to Three, 8*(4), 6–12.

Wilcox, B. L. (1981). Social support, life stress and psychological adjustment: A test of the buffering hypothesis. *American Journal of Community Psychology, 9*(4), 371–386.

Wilcox, B. L., & Vernberg, E. M. (1985). Conceptual and theoretical dilemmas facing social support research. In I. G. Sarason & B. R. Sarason (Eds.), *Social support: Theory, research, and applications* (pp. 3–20). Dordrecht: Martinus Nijhoff.

Wills, T. A. (1985). Supportive function of interpersonal relationships. In S. Cohen & L. S. Syme (Eds.), *Social support and health* (pp. 61–82). New York: Academic Press.

Withorn, A. (1984). *Serving the people: Social services and social change*. New York: Columbia University Press.

Wodarski, J. S. (1981a). Comprehensive treatment of parents who abuse their children. *Adolescence, 16*, 959–972.

Wodarski, J. S. (1981b). Treatment of parents who abuse their children: A literature review and implications for professionals. *Child Abuse and Neglect, 5*, 351–360.

Wolfe, D. A., Edwards, B., Manion, I., & Koverola, C. (1988). Early intervention for parents at risk of child abuse and neglect: A preliminary investigation. *Journal of Consulting and Clinical Psychology, 56*(1), 40–47.

Wolfe, D. A., & Sandler, J. (1981). Training abusive parents in effective child management. *Behavior Modification, 5*(3), 320–335.

Wolfe, D. A., Sandler, J., & Kaufman, K. (1981). A competency-based parent training program for child abusers. *Journal of Consulting and Clinical Psychology, 49*(5), 633–640.

Woodhead, M. (1988). When psychology informs public policy: The case of early childhood intervention. *American Psychologist, 43*(6), 443–454.

Wortman, C. B., & Conway, T. L. (1985). The role of social support in adaptation and recovery from physical illness. In S. Cohen & L. S. Syme (Eds.), *Social support and health* (pp. 281–302). New York: Academic Press.

Yuan, Y. Y. T., & Struckman-Johnson, D. L. (1991). Placement outcomes for neglected children with prior placements in family preservation programs. In K. Wells & D. E. Biegel (Eds.), *Family preservation services: Research and evaluation* (pp. 92–118). Newbury Park, CA: Sage.

Zigler, E., & Valentine, J. (Eds.) (1979). Project Head Start: A legacy of the war on poverty. New York: Free Press.

Zimrim, H. (1984). Do nothing but do something: The effect of human contact with the parent on abusive behaviour. *British Journal of Social Work, 14*, 475–485.

Additional References

Alexander, J., & Parsons, B. (1973). Short-term intervention with delinquent families: Impact on family process and recidivism. *Journal of Abnormal Psychology, 81*(3), 219–224.

Anderson, S., & Lauderdale, M. (1982). Characteristics of abusive parents: A look at self-esteem. *Child Abuse and Neglect, 6*(3, November), 285–294.

Andrews, D. A., & Robinson, D. (1983). *Sharing the parenting: An outcome evaluation*. Report to the Children's Aid Society of Ottawa-Carleton, April.

Armstrong, K. (1981). A treatment and education program for parents and children who are at-risk of abuse and neglect. *Child Abuse and Neglect, 5*, 167–175.

Armstrong, K. (1983). Economic analysis of a child abuse and neglect program. *Child Welfare, 67*, 3–13.

Asp, E., & Garbarino, J. (1983). Social support networks and the schools. In J. K. Whittaker & J. Garbarino (Eds.), *Social support networks: Informal helping in the human services* (pp. 251–297). Hawthorne, NY: Aldine de Gruyter.

Athay, M., & Darley, J. M. (1981). Toward an interaction-centered theory of personality. In N. Cantor & J. F. Kiffstrom (Eds.), *Personality, cognition, and social interaction* (pp. 281–307). Hillsdale, NJ: Lawrence Erlbaum Associates.

AuClaire, P., & Schwartz, I. M. (1987). *Home-based services as an alternative to placement for adolescents and their families: A follow-up study of placement resource utilization*. Minneapolis, MN: Hubert H. Humphrey Institute of Public Affairs, University of Minnesota.

AuClaire, P., & Schwartz, I. M. (1987). Are home-based services effective? *Children Today* (May/June) 6–9.

Bailey, M. B. (1965). Al-Anon family groups as an aid to wives of alcoholics. *Social Work, 10*(1), 68–74.

Baker, N. (1981). Social work through an interpreter. *Social Work, 26*(5), 391–397.

Bankoff, E. A. (1979). Widow groups as an alternative to informal social support. In M. Lieberman & L. Borman (Eds.), *Self-help groups for coping with crisis* (pp.181–193). San Francisco: Jossey-Bass.

Barozzi, R. L., Park, D. Jr., & Watson, E. L. (1982). A family agency integrates advocacy, counselling, and FLE. *Social Casework, 63*(4), 227–232.

Barrera, M., Jr., & Ainlay, S. A. (1983). The structure of social support: A conceptual and empirical analysis. *Journal of Community Psychology, 11*(April), 133–143.

Barth, R. (1983). Social support networks in services for adolescents and their families. In J. K. Whittaker & J. Garbarino (Eds.), *Social support networks: Informal helping in the human services* (pp. 229–331). Hawthorne, NY: Aldine de Gruyter.

Barth, R., & Berry, M. (1987). Outcomes of child welfare services under permanency planning. *Social Services Review, 61*, 71–90.

263

Beitchman, J. H., Hood, J., Zucker, K. J., da Costa, G., & Akman, D. (1988). *A review of the short- and long-term effects of child sexual abuse* (Grant No. 6606-3440-CSA). Ottawa, Ontario: Health and Welfare Canada, February.

Berger, P. L., & Luckman, T. (1967). *The social construction of reality.* Garden City, LI: Anchor Books.

Bernard, S. E. (1964). *Fatherless families: Their economic and social adjustment* (Papers in Social Welfare #7). Waltham, MA: F. G. Heller Graduate School for Advanced Studies in Social Welfare, Brandeis University.

Biegel, D., & Naparstek, A. J. (1982). The neighborhood and family services project: An empowerment model linking clergy, agency professionals, and community residents. In A. M. Jeger & R. S. Slotrich (Eds.), *Community mental health and behavioral-ecology.* New York and London: Plenum.

Biegel, D., Stone, B. K., & Gordon, E. (1984). *Building support networks for the elderly.* Beverly Hills, CA: Sage.

Biklen, D. P., & Reffucci, N. D. (1983). Social networks, information-seeking, and the utilization of services. *American Journal of Community Psychology, 11*(2), 185–205.

Black, R., & Mayer, J. (1980). Parents with special problems: Alcoholism and opiate addictions. *Child Abuse and Neglect, 4*(1), 45–54.

Blanchard, E., & Barsh, R. (1980). What is best for tribal children? A response to Fischler. *Social Work, 25*(5), 350–357.

Blumberg, M. L. (1974). Psychopathology of the abusing parent. *American Journal of Psychotherapy, 28,* 21–29.

Blythe, B. (1983). Social support networks in health care and health promotion. In J. K. Whittaker & J. Garbarino (Eds.), *Social support networks: Informal helping in the human services* (pp. 107–131). Hawthorne, NY: Aldine de Gruyter.

Boehm, R. G., & Larsen, R. P. (1978). *An evaluation of peer group counselling in Berrien County, Michigan.* Berrien County, MI: Berrien County Probate and Juvenile Court Services.

Boem, B. (1962). An assessment of family adequacy in protective cases. *Child Welfare, 41*(1), 10–16.

Borkman, T. (1976). Experiential knowledge: A new concept for the analysis of self-help groups. *Social Service Review, 50*(September), 445–456.

Borkman, T. (1990). Experiential, professional, and lay frames of reference. In T. J. Powell (Ed.), *Working with self-help.* Silver Spring, MD: National Association of Social Workers.

Borman, L. D. (1992). Introduction: Self-help/mutual aid groups in strategies for health. In A. H. Katz, H. L. Hedrick, D. H. Isenberg, L. M. Thompson, T. Goodrich, & A. H. Kutscher (Eds.), *Self-help: Concepts and applications* (pp. xix/xxvii). Philadelphia: Charles Press.

Borman, L. D., Birch, L. E., Hess, R., & Pasquale, F. L. (1982). Helping people help themselves: Self-help and prevention. *Prevention in Human Services, 1*(3), 1–129.

Borman, L. D., & Lieberman, M. (1981). Impact of self-help groups in widows' mental health. *National Reporter, 4*(7), 2–5.

Bradley, R., & Caldwell, B. (1976). Early home environment and changes in mental test performance in children 6 to 36 months. *Developmental Psychology, 12,* 93–97.

Breckenridge, C. C., & Arderson, C. T. (1981). The special care program: Exploring a future of prevention. In M. Bryce & J. C. Lloyd (Eds.), *Treating families in the home: An alternative to placement* (pp. 286–294). Springfield, IL: Charles C. Thomas.

Briar, S. (1963). Clinical judgment in foster care placement. *Child Welfare, 42*(3), 161–169.

Bribitzer, M. P., & Verdieck, M. J. (1988). Home-based, family-centered foster care prevention program. *Child Welfare, 67*, 255–267.

Brody, E. M. (1981). Women in the middle and family help to older people. *Gerontologist, 21*, 471–480.

Bronfenbrenner, U. (1974). Developmental research, public policy and the ecology of childhood. *Child Development, 45*(1), 1–5.

Bross, A. (1982). *Family therapy.* Toronto: Methuen.

Brown, H. F. (1981). Effective use of caretakers as an alternative to placement. In M. Bryce & J. C. Lloyd (Eds.), *Treating families in the home: An alternative to placement* (pp. 205–221). Springfield, IL: Charles C. Thomas.

Brown, J., & Daniels, R. (1968). Some observations of abusive parents. *Child Welfare, 47*, 89–94.

Bryce, M., & Lloyd, J. C. (1981). *Treating families in the home: An alternative to placement.* Springfield, IL: Charles C. Thomas.

Buck, S., & Dabrowska, M. (1981). An introduction to the work of the parent self-help groups in the United Kingdom. *Child Abuse and Neglect, 5*, 375–382.

Burt, M. (1976). Final results of the Nashville comprehensive emergency services project. *Child Welfare, 60*, 661–664.

Burt, M., & Balyeat, R. R. (1977). *A comprehensive emergency services system for neglected and abused children.* New York: Vantage.

Callard, E. D., & Morin, P. E. (1979). Parents and children together. In S. Maybanks & M. Bryce (Eds.), *Home-based services for children and families: Policy, practice, and research.* Springfield, IL: Charles C. Thomas.

Callister, J. P., Mitchell, L., & Tolley, G. (1986). Profiling family preservation efforts in Utah. *Children Today, 23*–25(November/December), 36–37.

Canzona, L., & McEachern, C. (1982). We asked . . . and they told us. *OACAS Journal, 26*(8), 1–6.

Caplan, G. (1974). *Support systems and community mental health.* New York: Behavioral Publications.

Caplan, G., & Killilea, M. (1976). *Support systems and mutual help: Multidisciplinary expectations.* New York: Grune & Stratton.

Caplan, R. (1979). Patient, provider and organization: Hypothesized determinants of adherence. In S. J. Cohen (Ed.), *New directions in patient compliance* (pp. 75–110). Lexington, MA: Lexington Books.

Caplan, R. (1979). Social support, person-environment fit and coping. In L. A. Ferman & J. P. Gordus (Eds.), *Mental health and the economy* (pp. 89–137). Kalamazoo, MI: Upjohn Institute.

Cardinal, J., & Farquharson, A. (1991). *The self-help resource kit.* Victoria, British Columbia: University of Victoria.

Carroll, C. (1978). The social worker's evaluation. In B. Schmitt (Ed.), *The child protection team handbook* (pp. 83–108). New York: Garland STPM.

Cartoof, V. (1978). Postpartum services for adolescent mothers. *Child Welfare, 57*(12), 660–666.

Chapman, N. J., & Pancoast, D. L. (1985). Working with the informal helping networks of the elderly: The experience of three programs. *Journal of Social Issues, 41*(1), 47–63.

Chiriboga, D. (1979). Divorce, stress and social supports: A study in help-seeking behaviors. *Journal of Divorce, 3*(1).

Clark, M. S., & Mills, J. (1979). Interpersonal attention in exchange and commercial relationships. *Journal of Personality and Social Psychology, 37*, 12–24.

Clayton, P. N. (1971). Meeting the needs of the single parent family. *Family Coordinator, 20*(4), 327–336.

Clayton-Fechtmann, K. A., & Siebold, J. I. (1981). Community and home-based treatment planning for adolescents and their families. In M. Bryce & J. C. Lloyd (Eds.), *Treating families in the home: An alternative to placement* (pp. 273–285). Springfield, IL: Charles C. Thomas.

Cobb, S. (1976). Social support as a moderator of life stress. *Psychosomatic Medicine, 38*(5), 300–314.

Cochran, M., & Brassard, J. A. (1979). Child development and personal social networks. *Child Development, 50*, 601–616.

Cohen, C. I., & Alder, A. (1984). Network interventions: Do they work? *Gerontologist, 24*(1), 16–22.

Cohen, F., & Densen-Gerber, J. (1982). A study of the relationship between child abuse and drug addiction in 178 patients: Preliminary results. *Child Abuse and Neglect, 6*(4), 383–387.

Cohen, S., Kamarck, T., & Mermelstein, R. (1983). A global measure of perceived stress. *Journal of Health and Social Behavior, 24*, 385–396.

Cohen, S., & Syme, L. S. (1985). *Social support and health.* New York: Academic Press.

Cohn, A. (1979). Essential elements of successful child abuse and neglect treatment. *Child Abuse and Neglect, 3*(4).

Cohn, A. H. (1983). *An approach to preventing child abuse.* Chicago: National Committee for Prevention of Child Abuse.

Colletta, N. (1979). Support systems after divorce: Incidence and impact. *Journal of Marriage and the Family, 41*(4), 837–846.

Collins, A. (1980). Helping neighbors intervene in cases of maltreatment. In J. Garbarino & S. H. Stocking (Eds.), *Protecting children from abuse and neglect: Developing and maintaining effective support systems for families* (pp. 133–172). San Francisco: Jossey-Bass.

Collins, A., & Pancoast, D. (1976). *Natural helping networks.* Washington: National Association of Social Workers.

Collins, M. C. (1978). *Child abuser: A study of child abusers in self-help group therapy.* Littleton, MA: P.S.G.

Compher, J. V. (1983). Home services to families to prevent child placement. *Social Work, 28*(5, September/October), 360–364.

Conklin, C. (1980). Rural community care givers. *Social Work, 25*(6), 495–496.

Coombes, P., Chipley, M., & Archer, B. (1978). The incadex approach to identifying problems and evaluating impact in child protective services. *Child Welfare, 57*(1), 41.

Coombes, P., McCormack, M., Chipley, M., & Archer, B. (1980). Are we protecting children? An approach to measuring impact in protective services. *Child Abuse and Neglect, 4*(2), 105–113.

Coopersmith, S. (1987). *Self-esteem inventories.* Palo Alto, CA: Consulting Psychologists.

Coplon, J., & Strull, J. (1983). Roles of the professional in mutual aid groups. *Social Casework: Journal of Contemporary Social Work, 64,* 259–266.

Cornell Empowerment Group (1989). Empowerment through family support. *Networking Bulletin,* 1(1), 1–7.

Costa, P. T., Zonderman, A. B., & McCrae, R. R. (1985). Longitudinal course of social support among men in the Baltimore longitudinal study of aging. In I. G. Sarason & B. R. Sarason (Eds.), *Social support: Theory, research, and applications* (pp. 137–154). Dordrecht: Martinus Nijhoff.

Cowan, E. L. (1982). Help is where you find it: Four informal helping groups. *American Psychologist, 37*(4, April), 385–395.

Crnic, K. A., Greenberg, M. T., Ragozin, A. S., Robinson, N. M., & Basham, R. B. (1983). Effects of stress and social supports on mothers and premature and full-term infants. *Child Development, 54,* 209–217.

Crowe, B. (1979). Self-help group for childrearing parents. *Child Abuse and Neglect,* 3(1), 335–340.

Cutrona, C. E., & Russell, D. W. (1987). The provisions of social relationships and adaptation to stress. *Advances in Personal Relationships, 1,* 37–67.

D'Augelli, A., & Ehrlich, R. (1982). Evaluation of a community-based system for training natural helpers. *American Journal of Community Psychology, 10*(4), 447–456.

D'Augelli, A., & Vallance, T. R. (1982). The helping community: Issues in the evaluation of a preventive intervention to promote informal helpers. *Journal of Community Psychology, 10,* 199–209.

Davenport, J., & Davenport, J., III. (1982). Utilizing the social network in rural communities. *Social Casework, 63*(2), 106–113.

David, P., & Kelly, T. (1982). An innovative approach to parenting in a rural community. *OACAS Journal, 26*(8), 11–16.

Davies, B., & Challis, D. (1986). *Matching resources to needs in community care.* Aldershot: Gover.

De-Nour, A., & Czaczkes, J. (1976). The influence of patient's personality on adjustment to chronic dialysis: A predictive study. *Journal of Nervous and Mental Disease, 162*(5), 323–333.

Dean, S. R. (1977). Self-help group psychology: Mental patients rediscover will power. *International Journal of Social Psychology, 17*(1), 72–78.

Defares, P. B., Brandes, M., Nass, C. H. Th., & van der Ploeg, J. D. (1985). Coping styles, social support and sex differences. In I. G. Sarason & B. R. Sarason (Eds.), *Social support: Theory, research, and applications* (pp. 173–186). Dordrecht: Martinus Nijhoff.

Depaulo, B. M., Nadler, A., & Fisher, J. D. (1983). *New directions in helping: Help seeking* (Vol. 2). New York: Academic Press.

Depue, R. A., & Monroe, S. M. (1985). Life stress and human disorder: Conceptualization and measurement of the disorder group. In I. G. Sarason & B. R. Sarason (Eds.), *Social support: Theory, research, and applications* (pp. 303–320). Dordrecht: Martinus Nijhoff.

Derdeyn, A. P. (1977). Child abuse and neglect: The rights of parents and the needs of their children. *American Journal of Orthopsychiatry, 43,* 377–387.

DiMatteo, M. R., & Hays, R. (1981). Social support and serious illness. In B. Gottlieb (Ed.), *Social networks and social support* (pp. 117–148). Beverly Hills, CA: Sage.

Dohrenwend, B., & Dohrenwend, B. (1974). Social and cultural influences on psychopathology. *Annual Review of Psychology, 25*(4), 417–452.

Dohrenwend, B., & Dohrenwend, B. (1976). *Social status and psychological disorder.* New York: Wiley-Interscience.

Dooley, D. (1985). Causal inference in the study of social support. In S. Cohen & L. S. Syme (Eds.), *Social support and health* (pp. 109–125). New York: Academic Press.

Dougherty, N. (1983). The holding environment: Breaking the cycle of abuse. *Journal of Contemporary Social Work, 64,* 283–290.

Downs, S., & Taylor, C. (Eds.) (1978). *Permanent planning in foster care: Resources for training.* Portland, OR: Regional Institute for Human Services.

Driedger, W. (1981). Social networks in family therapy. In D. Freeman & B. Trute (Eds.), *Treating families with special needs* (pp. 151–164). Ottawa: Alberta Association of Social Workers and Canadian Association of Social Workers.

Dunst, C. J., & Trivette, C. M. (1987). Enabling and empowering families: Conceptual and intervention issues. *School Psychology, 4,* 443–456.

Earp, J., & Ory, M. (1980). The influence of early parenting on child maltreatment. *Child Abuse and Neglect, 4*(4), 237–245.

Eckenrode, J., & Gore, S. (1981). Social support and life stress. In B. Gottlieb (Ed.), *Social networks and social support* (pp. 43–68). Beverly Hills, CA: Sage.

Egeland, B., & Sroufe, L. (1981). Attachment and early maltreatment. *Child Development, 52*(4), 44–52.

Egeland, B., Breitenbucker, M., & Rosenberg, D. (1980). Prospective study of the significance of life stress in the etiology of child abuse. *Journal of Consulting and Clinical Psychology, 48*(2), 195–205.

Ehrlich, R. P., D'Augelli, A. R., & Conter, K. R. (1981). Evaluation of a community-based system for training natural helpers. *American Journal of Community Psychology, 9*(3), 321–337.

Elmer, E. (1981). Traumatized children, chronic illness, and poverty. In L. H. Pelton (Ed.), *The social context of child abuse and neglect* (pp. 185–227). New York: Human Sciences Press.

Emlem, A. (1978). If you care about children, then care about families. In S. Downs & C. Taylor (Eds.), *Permanent planning in foster care: Resources for training* (pp. 2.1.27–2.2.3). Portland, OR: Regional Research Institute for Human Services.

Engler, A., & Shneewind, K. (1982). Causes and consequences of harsh parental punishment. *Child Abuse and Neglect, 6*(2), 129–139.

Equal Opportunities Commission. (1980). *The experience of caring for elderly and handicapped dependents.* Manchester, UK: Equal Opportunities Commission.

Erickson, G. (1975). The concept of personal network in clinical practice. *Family Process, 14*(4), 487–498.

Erickson, G. D. (1984). A framework and themes for social support intervention. *Family Process, 23*(June), 187–204.

Eyde, D. R., & Willig, S. (1981). Home support for families with disturbed children. In M. Bryce & J. C. Lloyd (Eds.), *Treating families in the home: An alternative to placement* (pp. 260–272). Springfield, IL: Charles C. Thomas.

Famularo, R., Stone, K., Barnum, R., & Wharton, R. (1986). Alcoholism and severe child maltreatment. *American Journal of Orthopsychiatry, 56,* 481–485.

Fandetti, D., & Gelfand, D. (1978). Attitudes towards symptoms and services in the ethnic family and neighborhood. *American Journal of Orthopsychiatry, 48*(3), 477–486.

Fellin, P. (1987). *The community and the social worker.* Itasca, IL: F. E. Peacock.

Finkelhor, D. (1980). Risk factors in the sexual victimization of children. *Child Abuse and Neglect, 4*(3), 265–273.

Fischbuch, M. (1985). *Preventing child abuse: A review of recent programs.* Thorold, Ontario: Niagara Children's Services Committee.

Fischer, J. (1978). *Effective casework practice: An eclectic approach.* New York: McGraw-Hill.

Fischler, R. (1980). Protecting Indian children. *Social Work, 25*(5), 341–349.

Fisher, B., & Berdie, J. (1978). Adolescent abuse and neglect: Issues of incidence, intervention and social delivery. *Child Abuse and Neglect, 2*(3), 173–192.

Fitch, M. (1977). *Prospective study in child abuse: The child study program.* Denver, CO: Developmental Education Center.

Fixsen, D. L., Olivier, K. A., Adams, K., Blase, K. A., Geake, R., Lander, L., & Oostenbrink, A. (1989). *Alberta family support systems annual report.* Calgary, Alberta: Hull Community Services.

Fixsen, D. L., Olivier, K. A., & Blase, K. A. (undated). *Home-based, family-centred treatment for children.* Calgary, Alberta: Hull Community Services.

Fleming, R., Baum, A., & Singer, J. E. (1985). Social support and the physical environment. In S. Cohen & L. S. Syme (Eds.), *Social support and health* (pp. 327–345). New York: Academic Press.

Friedman, R. (1976). Child abuse: A review of the psychosocial research. In Herner & Company (Eds.), *Four perspectives on the status of child abuse and neglect research.* Washington: National Centre on Child Abuse & Neglect.

Froland, C. (1980). Formal and informal care: Discontinuation in a continuum. *Social Service Review, 54*(December), 572–587.

Froland, C., Brodsky, G., Olson, M., & Stewart, L. (1979). Social support and social adjustment: Implications for mental health professionals. *Community Mental Health Journal, 15*(2), 82–92.

Furstenberg, F., & Crawford, A. G. (1978). Family support: Helping teenage mothers to cope. *Family Planning Perspectives, 10*(6, November/December), 322–333.

Gambrill, E., & Stein, T. (1981). Decision making and case management: Achieving continuity of care for children in out-of-home placement. In A. N. Maluccio & P. A. Sinanoglu (Eds.), *The challenge of partnership: Working with parents of children in foster care.* New York: Child Welfare League of America.

Garbarino, J. (1977). The human ecology of child maltreatment. *Journal of Marriage and the Family, 39*(4), 721–735.

Garbarino, J. (1979). The role of the school in the human ecology of child maltreatment. *School Review, 87*(2).

Garbarino, J. (1980). Changing hospital childbirth practices: A developmental perspective on prevention of child maltreatment. *American Journal of Orthopsychiatry, 50*(4), 588–597.

Garbarino, J. (1980). What kind of society permits child abuse? *Infant Metal Health Journal, 1*(2).

Garbarino, J. (1981). *Children and families in the social environment.* Hawthorne, NY: Aldine de Gruyter.

Garbarino, J., & Carson, B. (1979). *Mistreated youth in one community.* Boys Town, NE: Center for the Study of Youth Development.

Garbarino, J., & Crouter, A. (1978). Defining the community context for parent-child relations: The correlates of child maltreatment. *Child Development, 49*(6), 604–616.

Garbarino, J., & Ebata, A. (1982). *On the significance of cultural differences in child maltreatment.* Unpublished study.

Garbarino, J., & Sherman, D. (1980). High-risk neighbourhoods and high-risk families: The human ecology of child maltreatment. *Child Development, 51*(2), 188–198.

Gatti, F., & Colman, C. (1976). Community network therapy: An approach to aiding families with troubled children. *American Journal of Orthopsychiatry, 46*(4, October), 608–617.

Gaudin, J., Jr., & Polansky, N. A. (1986). Social distancing of the neglectful family: Sex, race and social class influences. *Children & Youth Services Review, 8*(1), 1–12.

Gaudin, J., Jr., & Pollane, L. (1983). Social networks, stress and child abuse. *Children & Youth Services Review, 5,* 91–102.

Gaudin, J. M. (1979). *Mothers' perceived strength of primary group networks and maternal child abuse.* Unpublished doctoral dissertation, Florida State University.

Geismar, L. L. (1971). *Family and community functioning.* Metuchen, NJ: Scarecrow.

Gelles, R. (1973). Child abuse and psychopathology: A sociological critique and reformulation. *American Journal of Orthopsychiatry, 43,* 611–621.

General Accounting Office (1979). *Early childhood and family development programs improve quality of life for low-income families.* Washington, DC: USGPO.

Gergen, K. J., Greenberg, M. S., & Willis, R. H. (1980). *Social exchange: Advances in theory and research.* New York: Plenum.

Giblin, P., Starr, R., & Agronow, S. (in press). A comparison of abused and control children. *Child Development.*

Gil, D. (1970). *Violence against children: Physical child abuse in the United States.* Cambridge, MA: Harvard University Press.

Gilman, S. (1983). Self-help groups untapped resource in preventing family violence. *Health Education, 21*(4), 2–7.

Giovannoni, J. (1982). Prevention of child abuse and neglect: Research and policy issues. *Social Work Research and Abstracts, 18*(3, Spring).

Gitterman, A., & Shulman, L. (1986). *Mutual aid groups and the life cycle.* Itasca, IL: F. E. Peacock.

Goetzel, R., Fein, E., Maluccio, A., Bishop, G., & Armstrong, B. (1982). *Reunification of families: A study of services and supports.* Hartford, CT: Child & Family Services.

Goldstein, H. (1981). Home-based services and the worker. In M. Bryce & J. C. Lloyd (Eds.), *Treating families in the home: An alternative to placement* (pp. 127–134). Springfield, IL: Charles C. Thomas.

Goldstein, J., Freud, A., & Solnit, A. (1973). *Beyond the best interests of the child.* New York: Free Press.

Goodluck, C., & Short, D. (1980). Working with American Indian parents. *Social Casework, 61*(8), 472–475.

Goodwin, J., McCarthy, T., & DiVasto, P. (1981). Prior incest in mothers of abused children. *Child Abuse and Neglect, 5*(2), 87–95.

Gordon, R. E., Edmunson, E., Bedell, J., & Goldstein, N. (1979). Peer mutual aid networks reduce rehospitalization of mental patients. *Self-Help Reporter, 3*(2, March/April).

Gore, S. (1985). Social support and styles of coping with stress. In S. Cohen & L. S. Syme (Eds.), *Social support and health* (pp. 263–278). New York: Academic Press.

Gottlieb, B. (1978). The development and application of a classification scheme of informal helping behaviours. *Canadian Journal of Behavioural Science, 10*(1), 105–115.

Gottlieb, B. (Ed.) (1981). *Social networks and social support.* Beverly Hills, CA: Sage.

Gottlieb, B. (1982). Mutual-help groups: Members' views of their benefits and of roles for professionals. In L. D. Borman, L. E. Borck, R. Hess, & F. L. Pasquale (Eds.), *Helping people to help themselves: Self-help and prevention* (pp. 55–67). New York: Haworth.

Gottlieb, B. (1985). Theory into practice: Issues that surface in planning interventions which mobilize support. In I. G. Sarason & B. R. Sarason (Eds.), *Social support: Theory, research, and applications* (pp. 417–437). Dordrecht: Martinus Nijhoff.

Gottlieb, B. (1985). Social support and community mental health. In S. Cohen & L. S. Syme (Eds.), *Social support and health* (pp. 303–326). New York: Academic Press.

Gottlieb, B., & Hall, A. (1980). Social networks and the utilization of preventive health services. In R. H. Price, R. F. Ketterer, B. C. Bader, & J. Monahan (Eds.), *Prevention in mental health* (pp. 167–194). Beverly Hills, CA: Sage.

Gray, S. W., & Ruttle, K. (1980). The family-oriented home visiting program: A longitudinal study. *Genetic Psychology Monographs, 102,* 299–316.

Gray, S. W., & Wandersman, L. P. (1980). The methodology of home-based intervention studies: Problems and promising strategies. *Child Development, 51,* 993–1009.

Green, A. (1978). Psychopathology of abused children. *American Journal of Psychiatry, 17,* 92–103.

Greer, T. V., & Greer, J. G. (1982). Problems in evaluating costs and benefits of social programs. *Public Administration Review, 42*(2), 151–156.

Griest, D. L., & Farehand, R. (1982). How can I get any parent training done with all these other problems going on? *Child & Family Behavior Therapy, 4,* 73–80.

Gwyn, F., & Kilpatrick, A. (1981). A family therapy with low income blacks: Tool or turn-off? *Social Casework, 65*(5, May), 259–266.

Haapala, D. (1983). *Perceived helpfulness, attributed critical incident responsibility, and a discrimination of home-based family therapy treatment outcomes: Homebuilders model.* Federal Way, WA: Behavioral Sciences Institute.

Haapala, D., Johnston, B., & McDade, K. (1990). *The homebuilders family reunification project.* Federal Way, WA: Behavioural Sciences Institute.

Haapala, D., & Kinney, J. (1979). Homebuilders' approach to the training of in-home therapists. In S. Maybanks & M. Bryce (Eds.), *Home-based services for children and families: Policy, practice, and research* (pp. 248–259). Springfield, IL: Charles C. Thomas.

Hall, J. A. (1984). Empirically based treatment for parent-adolescent conflict. *Social Casework: Journal of Contemporary Social Work, 65,* 487–495.

Halpern, R. (1984). Lack of effects for home-based early intervention? Some possible explanations. *American Journal of Orthopsychiatry, 54,* 33–42.

Halpern, R. (1986). Home-based early intervention: Dimensions of current practice. *Child Welfare, 65,* 386–399.

Hanvohan, P., & Reid, W. J. (1984). Choosing effective interventions. *Social Service Review, 58*(June), 244–258.

Harrison, M. (1981). Home start: A voluntary home-visiting scheme for young families. *Child Abuse and Neglect, 5,* 441–447.

Hartman, A., & Laird, J. (1983). *Family-centered social work practice.* New York: Free Press.

Haugaard, J., & Hokanson, B. (1983). *Measuring the cost-effectiveness of family-based services and out-of-home care.* Baltimore: Maryland Department of Human Resources.

Hayes, J. R., & Joseph, J.A. (1985). *Home-based family centered project evaluation.* Columbus, OH: Metropolitan Human Services Commission.

Hedrick, H. L., Isenberg, D. H., & Martini, C. J. M. (1992). Self-help groups: Empowerment through policy and partnership. In A. H. Katz, H. L. Hedrick, D. H. Isenberg, L. M. Thompson, T. Goodrich, & A. H. Kutscher (Eds.), *Self-help: Concepts and applications* (pp. 3–55). Philadelphia: Charles Press.

Heller, K. (1979). The effects of social support: Prevention and treatment implications. In A. P. Goldstein & F. H. Kanfer (Eds.), *Maximizing treatment gains: Transfer enhancement in psychology* (pp. 353–382). New York: Academic Press.

Hemley van der Velden, E., Halevy-Martini, J., Ruhf, L., & Schoenfeld, P. (1984). Conceptual issues in network therapy. *International Journal of Family Therapy, 6*(2, Summer), 68–81.

Henry, S. (1977). Self-help: Sometimes the best medicine is hardest to swallow. *Health and Social Service Journal, 87,* 892–893.

Herberg, E. (1980). *West Indians in Toronto, Ontario: Implications for helping professionals.* Toronto: Family Service Association of Metro Toronto.

Hinckley, E. C. (1984). Homebuilders: The Maine experience. *Children Today* (September/October), 14–18.

Hirsch, B. J. (1985). Social networks and the ecology of human development: Theory, research, and applications. In I. G. Sarason & B. R. Sarason (Eds.), *Social support: Theory, research, and applications* (pp. 287–300). Dordrecht: Martinus Nijhoff.

Hirsch, B. J., & Rapkin, B. D. (1986). Social networks and adult social identities: Profiles and correlates of support and rejection. *American Journal of Community Psychology, 14*(4), 395–412.

Horejsi, C. R. (1981). The St. Paul family-centered project revisited: Exploring an old gold mine. In M. Bryce & J. C. Lloyd (Eds.), *Treating families in the home: An alternative to placement* (pp.12–23). Springfield, IL: Charles C. Thomas.

Hornick, J., et al. (1982). *Alternate care, community child care, family caring and sharing, and group work programs study* (interim report). Toronto: Children's Aid Society of Metropolitan Toronto.

Hornick, J., et al. (1983). *Alternate care and community child care programs: Objectives, service and cost.* Toronto: Children's Aid Society of Metropolitan Toronto.

Horowitz, A. (1978). Family, kin and friend networks in psychiatric help-seeking. *Social Science and Medicine, 12*(4), 297–304.

Horowitz, B., & Wolock, I. (1981). Material deprivation, child maltreatment, and agency interventions among poor families. In L. H. Pelton (Ed.), *The social context of child abuse and neglect* (pp. 137–184). New York: Human Sciences Press.

Hudson, W. W. (1982). *The clinical assessment package: A field manual.* Chicago: Dorsey.

Hull, G. (1982). Child welfare services to Native Americans. *Social Casework, 63*(6), 340–347.

Hunter, R. S., & Kilstrom, N. (1979). Breaking the cycle in abusive families. *American Journal of Psychiatry, 136*, 1320–1322.

Hutchinson, J. R. (1986). Progress towards changes: The National Resource Center on Family-Based Services. *Children Today* (November/December), 6–7.

Irizarry, C., & Appel, Y. H. (1986). Growing up: Work with preteens in the neighborhood. In A. Gitterman & L. Shulman (Eds.), *Mutual aid groups and the life cycle* (pp. 111–140). Itasca, IL: F. E. Peacock.

Issacs, C. D. (1982). Treatment of child abuse: A review of the behavioral intervention. *Journal of Applied Behavior Analysis, 15*, 273–294.

Jansen, C., & Harris, O. (1980). *Family treatment in social work practice.* Itasca, IL: F. E. Peacock.

Jeger, A. M., & Slotrich, R. S. (Eds.) (1982). *Community mental health and behavioral-ecology.* New York and London: Plenum.

Jenkins, L., & Cook, A. (1981). The rural hospice: Integrating formal and informal helping systems. *Social Work, 26*(5), 414–416.

Jenkins, S. (1980). The ethnic agency defined. *Social Service Review, 54*(4), 249–261.

Jenkins, S., Schroeder, A., & Burgdorf, K. (1981). *Beyond intake: The first ninety days.* Washington, DC: Department of Health and Human Services.

Johnson, W., & L'Esperence, J. I. (1984). Predicting the recurrence of child abuse. *Social Work Research and Abstracts, 20*, 21–26.

Jones, J. M., & McNeely, R. L. (1980). Mothers who neglect and those who do not: A comparative study. *Social Casework, 61*(9), 559–567.

Jones, M. A. (1985). *A second chance for families-five years later: Follow-up of a program to prevent foster care.* New York: Child Welfare League of America.

Justice, B., & Justice, R. (1976). *The abusing family.* New York: Human Sciences Press.

Kadushin, A. (1979). *Child welfare services.* Toronto: MacMillan.

Kadushin, A., & Martin, J. (1981). *Child abuse: An international event.* New York: Columbia University Press.

Kagey, R., Vivace, J., & Lutz, W. (1981). Mental health primary prevention: The role of parent mutual support groups. *American Journal of Public Health, 71*(21), 166–167.

Kalisch, B. (1978). *Child abuse and neglect: An annotated bibliography*. Westport, CT: Greenwood.

Kaplan, R. M. (1985). Social support and social health. In I. G. Sarason & B. R. Sarason (Eds.), *Social support: Theory, research, and applications* (pp. 95–113). Dordrecht: Martinus Nijhoff.

Katz, A., & Bender, E. (1976). *The strength in us*. New York: Franklin.

Kelley, V. R., Kelley, P. L., Gauron, E. F., & Rawlings, E. I. (1977). Training helpers in rural mental health delivery. *Social Work, 22*(3), 229–232.

Kempe, H., Franklin, A., & Cooper, C. (Eds.) (1980). *The abused child in the family and in the community* (Vol. 1). London: Pergamon.

Kempe, R., & Kempe, H. (1976). Assessing family pathology. In R. Helfer & C. Kempe (Eds.), *Child abuse and neglect* (pp. 115–126). Cambridge, MA: Ballinger.

Kinney, J. (1978). Homebuilders: An in-home crisis intervention program. *Children Today* (January/February), 15–35.

Knight, B., Wollert, R. W., Levy, L. H., Frame, C. L., & Padgett, V. P. (1980). Self-help groups: The members' perspectives. *American Journal of Community Psychology, 8*(1), 53–65.

Koverola, C., Elliot-Faust, D., & Wolfe, D. A. (1984). Clinical issues in the behavioural treatment of a child abusive mother experiencing multiple life stress. *Journal of Clinical Child Psychology, 13*(2), 187–191.

Lahti, J., & Dvorak, J. (1981). Coming home from foster care. In A. N. Maluccio & P. A. Sinanoglu, *The challenge of partnership: Working with parents of children in foster care*. New York: Child Welfare League of America.

Lahti, J., Green, K., Einlen, A., Zendry, J., Clarkson, Q., Kuehnel, M., & Casciato, J. (1978). *A follow-up study of the Oregon project*. Portland, Oregon: Portland State University, Regional Research for Human Services.

Lamb, M., & Sternberg, K. (1992). Establishing the design. *Children and Youth Services Review, 14*, 157–165.

Lavoie, F. (1990). Evaluating self-help groups. In J. M. Romeder (Ed.), *The self-help way: Mutual aid and health* (pp. 75–96). Ottawa: Canadian Council on Social Development.

Lee, B. (1982). Three models of child welfare services to native communities. *OACAS Journal, 26*(8), 7–10.

Lee, J. A. B. (1986). No place to go: Homeless women. In A. Gitterman & L. Shulman (Eds.), *Mutual aid groups and the life cycle* (pp. 245–262). Itasca, IL: F. E. Peacock.

Lee, J. A. B., & Swenson, C. R. (1985). The concept of mutual aid. In A. Gitterman & L. Shulman (Eds.), *Mutual aid groups and the life cycle* (pp. 361–380). Itasca, IL: F. E. Peacock.

Leler, H. (1981). Program approaches designed to enhance parental strengths and self-concepts. In M. Bryce & J. C. Lloyd (Eds.), *Treating families in the home: An alternative to placement* (pp. 238–248). Springfield, IL: Charles C. Thomas.

Levine, M., & Perkins, D. (1980). Social setting intervention and primary prevention. *American Journal of Community Psychology, 8*(2), 147–157.

Levine, T., & McDaid, E. (1979). Services to children in their own homes: A family-based approach. In S. Maybanks & M. Bryce (Eds.), *Home-based services for children and families: Policy, practice, and research* (pp. 260–271). Springfield, IL: Charles C. Thomas.

Levy, L. H. (1976). Self-help groups: Types and psychological processes. *Journal of Applied Behavioral Science, 12*(3), 310–322.

Libbey, P., & Bybee, R. (1979). The physical abuse of adolescents. *Journal of Social Issues, 35*(2), 101–126.

Lickoff, L., Beaver, L., & West, D. (1983). *Informal supports: A summary of federally funded research and demonstrations.* Washington, DC: National Council on the Aging.

Lieber, L. L. (1983). The self-help approach: Parents anonymous. *Journal of Clinical Child Psychology, 12*(3), 288–291.

Lieberman, M., & Bond, G. (1979). Problems in studying outcomes. In M. Lieberman & L. Borman (Eds.), *Self-help groups for coping with crisis* (pp. 323–340). San Francisco: Jossey-Bass.

Lieberman, M., & Bond, G. (1979). Women's consciousness raising as an alternative to psychotherapy. In M. Lieberman & L. Borman (Eds.), *Self-help groups for coping with crisis* (pp. 150–163). San Francisco: Jossey-Bass.

Lieberman, M., Bond, G., Solow, N., & Reibstein, J. (1975). Effectiveness of women's consciousness raising. In M. Lieberman & L. Borman (Eds.), *Self-help groups for coping with crisis* (pp. 341–361). San Francisco: Jossey-Bass.

Lieberman, M., & Borman, L. D. (1976). Self-help and social research. *Journal of Applied Behavioral Science, 12*(3), 455–463.

Lieberman, M., & Borman, L. D. (1979). *Self-help groups for coping with crisis.* San Francisco: Jossey-Bass.

Lieberman, M., & Glidewell, J. (1978). Overview: Special issue on the helping process. *American Journal of Community Psychology, 6*(5), 405–411.

Lieberman, R. P., Kuehnel, T. G., Kuehnel, J. M., Eckman, T., & Rosenstein, J. (1982). The behavioral analysis and modification project for community mental health: From conception to dissemination. In A. M. Jeger & R. S. Slotnick (Eds.), *Community mental health and behavioral-ecology* (pp. 95–112). New York and London: Plenum.

Lieberman, M., & Mullan, J. (1978). Does help help? The adaptive consequences of obtaining help from professionals and social networks. *American Journal of Community Psychology, 6*(5), 499–517.

Lindsey, D. (1993). Our hopes and dreams for children. *Children and Youth Services Review, 15*, 1–7.

Lipson, J. G. (1982). Effects of a support group on the emotional impact of cesarean childbirth. In L. D. Borman, L. E. Borck, R. Hess, & F. L. Pasquale (Eds.), *Helping people to help themselves: Self-help and prevention* (pp. 17–29). New York: Haworth.

Litwak, E. (1978). Agency and family linkages in providing neighborhood services. In D. Thursz & J. L. Vigilante (Eds.), *Reaching people: The structure of neighborhood services* (pp. 59–94). Beverly Hills, CA: Sage.

Lloyd, C. (1986). The process of goal setting using goal attainment scaling in a therapeutic community. *Occupational Therapy in Mental Health, 6*, 19–30.

Loewe, B., & Hannahan, T. E. (1975). Five-day foster care. *Child Welfare, 54*(January), 7–18.

Londsdale, S., Flowers, J., & Saunders, B. (1980). *Long term psychiatric patients: A study in community care.* London: Personal Social Services Council.

Lourie, I. (1979). Family dynamics and the abuse of adolescents. *Child Abuse and Neglect, 3*(4), 967–974.

Lusky, R. A., & Irgman, S. R. (1979). The pros, cons and pitfalls of "self-help" rehabilitation programs. *Social Science and Medicine, 13A,* 113–121.

Mace, D. R. (1983). *Prevention in family services.* Beverly Hills, CA: Sage.

Madara, E. J. (1986). How-to ideas for developing groups. In E. J. Madara & A. Meese (Eds.), *The self-help sourcebook* (pp. 101–103). Denville, NJ: St. Clares/Riverside Medical Center.

Magura, S., & Moses, B. (1980). Outcome measurement in child welfare. *Child Welfare, 59,* 595–606.

Malcom, P., & Young, I. (1978). *Evaluation: Positive peer culture, instructional research report #1977-3.* Omaha, NE: Omaha Public Schools.

Maluccio, A. N., & Sinanoglu, P. A. (Eds.) (1981). *The challenge of partnership: Working with parents of children in foster care.* New York: Child Welfare League of America.

Martin, H. P., & Berzley, P. (1977). Behavioral observations of abused children. *Developmental Medicine and Child Neurology, 19*(2), 373–387.

Maton, K. I. (1988). Social support, organizational characteristics, psychological well-being, and group appraisal in three self-help group populations. *American Journal of Community Psychology, 16,* 53–77.

McCleave Kinney, J., Madsen, B., Fleming, D., & Haapala, D. (1977). Homebuilders: Keeping families together. *Journal of Consulting and Clinical Psychology, 45,* 667–673.

McCord, J. (1983). A forty year perspective on effects of child abuse and neglect. *Child Abuse and Neglect, 7,* 265–270.

McHenry, S. (1980). Sister to sister: We're about navigating systems. *Ms. Magazine* (June).

McLuire, L. (1983). *Understanding social networks.* Beverly Hills, CA: Sage.

Melnick, B., & Hurley, J. R. (1969). Distinctive personality attributes of child abusing mothers. *Journal of Consulting and Clinical Psychology, 33,* 746–749.

Menaghan, E. (1978). Seeking help for parental concerns in the middle years. *American Journal of Community Psychology. 6*(5), 477–488.

Milner, J. S., & Ayoub, C. (1980). Evaluation of "at-risk" parents using the child abuse potential inventory. *Journal of Clinical Psychology, 36,* 945–948.

Ministry of Community and Social Services (1979). *The state of the art: A background paper on prevention.* Toronto: Government of Ontario.

Ministry of Community and Social Services (1982). *Key elements of a family support/case management model.* Toronto: Government of Ontario.

Ministry of Community and Social Services (1982). *Funding of community-based family response services.* Toronto: Government of Ontario.

Ministry of Community and Social Services (1982). *Evaluation report: Ontario family support worker program.* Toronto: Government of Ontario.

Minkler, M. (1985). Social support and health of the elderly. In S. Cohen & L. S. Syme (Eds.), *Social support and health* (pp. 199–216). New York: Academic Press.

Minuchin, S., & Montalvo, B. (1967). Techniques for working with disorganized low socioeconomic families. *American Journal of Orthopsychiatry, 37,* 880–887.

Mitchell, R., Billings, A., & Moos, R. H. (1982). Social support and well-being: Implications for prevention programs. *Journal of Primary Prevention, 3,* 77–98.

Mitchell, R., & Hurley, D., Jr. (1981). Collaboration with natural helping networks: Lessons from studying paraprofessionals. In B. Gottlieb (Ed.), *Social networks and social support* (pp. 277–298). Beverly Hills, CA: Sage.

Morin, P. (1981). The extended family model: Increasing service effectiveness. In M. Bryce & J. C. Lloyd (Eds.), *Treating families in the home: An alternative to placement.* Springfield, IL: Charles C. Thomas.

National Resource Center on Family Based Services (1983). *Family-centered social services: A model for child welfare agencies.* Oakdale, Iowa: University of Iowa School of Social Work, Oakdale Campus, National Resource Center on Family Based Services.

Nelson, D. (1990). Recognizing and realizing the potential of family preservation. In J. K. Whittaker, J. Kenney, E. M. Tracy, & C. Booth (Eds.), *Reaching high-risk families: Intensive family preservation in human services* (pp. 13–30). Hawthorne, NY: Aldine de Gruyter.

Nicholaichuk, T. P., & Wollert, R. (1989). The effects of self-help on health status and health-services utilization. *Canadian Journal of Community Mental Health, 8,* 17–29.

Oxley, D., Barrera, M., Jr., & Sadalla, E. K. (1981). Relationships among community size, mediators, and social support variables: A path analytic approach. *American Journal of Community Psychology, 9*(6), 637–651.

Palley, H. A., & Fisher, J. (1991). Societal deprivation, the underclass and family deterioration in Baltimore: A structural analysis. *Children and Youth Services Review, 13,* 183–197.

Pancer, S. M., & Cameron, G. (1994). Resident participation in the Better Beginnings, Better Futures prevention project: Part I—The impacts of involvement. *Canadian Journal of Community Mental Health, 13,* 197–211.

Patterson, C. (1979). Support staff to help abusing families. *OACAS Journal, 22*(October), 6–10.

Patterson, G., Cobb, J., & Ray, R. (1973). A social engineering technology for retraining the families of aggressive boys. In H. Adams & I. Unikel (Eds.), *Issues and trends in behavior therapy* (pp. 139–210). Springfield, IL: Charles C. Thomas.

Pattison, E. M., Llamas, R., & Hard, G. (1979). Social network mediation of anxiety. *Psychiatric Annals, 9*(9), 56–67.

Pearson, R. E. (1983). Support groups: A conceptualization. *Personnel and Guidance Journal, 62,* 361–364.

Pecora, P. J. (1994). Assessing the impact of family-based services. In B. Galaway & J. Hudson (Eds.), *Research on the child welfare system.* Toronto: Thompson Educational Publishing.

Pecora, P. J., Fraser, M. W., Haapala, D. A., & Bartlome, J. A. (1987). *Defining family preservation services: Three intensive home-based treatment programs.* Salt Lake City: Social Research Institute, University of Utah.

Plas, J. M., Hoover-Dempsey, K. U., & Strudler Wallston, B. (1985). A conceptualization of professional women's interpersonal fields: Social support, reference groups, and persons-to-be-reckoned-with. In I. G. Sarason & B. R. Sarason (Eds.), *Social support: Theory, research, and applications* (pp. 187–204). Dordrecht: Martinus Nijhoff.

Polansky, N. (1981). *Damaged parents: An anatomy of child neglect*. Chicago: University of Chicago Press.

Polansky, N., & Gaudin, J. M. (1983). Social distancing of the neglectful family. *Social Service Review, 57*, 196–208.

Polster, R. A., & Pinkston, E. M. (1979). A delivery system for the treatment of underachievement. *Social Science Review, 53*, 35–55.

Powell, T. J. (1979). Interpreting Parents Anonymous as a source of help with those with child abuse problems. *Child Welfare, 58*(2), 105–113.

Powell, T. J. (1987). *Self-help organizations and professional practice*. Silver Spring, MD: National Association of Social Workers.

Powell, T. J. (1990). *Working with self-help*. Silver Spring, MD: National Association of Social Workers.

Pressman, B. (1984). *Family violence: Origins and treatment*. Guelph, Ontario: University of Guelph, Office of Educational Practice.

Price, R. H., Cowen, E. L., Lorion, R. P., & Ramos-McKay, J. (1989). The search for effective prevention programs: What we learned along the way. *American Journal of Orthopsychiatry, 59*, 49–58.

Raiff, N. R. (1982). Self-help participation and quality of life: A study of the staff of Recovery, Inc. In L. D. Borman, L. E. Brock, R. Hess, & F. L. Pasquale (Eds.), *Helping people to help themselves: Self-help and prevention* (pp. 183–193). New York: Haworth.

Raschke, H. (1977). The role of social participation in postseparation and post-divorce adjustment. *Journal of Divorce, 1*(2), 129–140.

Reid, W., & Hanrahan, P. (1982). Recent evaluations of social work: Grounds for optimism. *Social Work, 27*(July), 328–340.

Reid, W., Kagan, R. M., & Schlosberg, S. B. (1988). Prevention of placement: Critical factors in program success. *Child Welfare, 67*, 25–36.

Riessman, F. (1965). The "helper" therapy principle. *Social Work, 10*, 27–32.

Riessman, F. (1976). How does self-help work. *Social Policy, 7*(2, September/October), 41–45.

Robin, A. L., & Foster, S. L. (1984). Problem-solving communication training: A behavioural-family systems approach to parent-adolescent conflict. In P. Koroly & J. J. Steffar (Eds.), *Adolescent behavior disorders: Foundations and contemporary concerns* (pp. 195–240). Lexington, MA: D. C. Heath.

Rogers, S. (1980). Enforced social isolation as a contributory factor in child abuse. *Child Abuse and Neglect, 4*(1), 39–44.

Romeder, J. M. (1990). *The self-help way: Mutual aid and health*. Ottawa: Canadian Council on Social Development.

Rook, K. S. (1985). The functions of social bonds: Perspectives from research on social support, loneliness and social isolation. In I. G. Sarason & B. R. Sarason (Eds.), *Social support: Theory, research, and applications* (pp. 243–267). Dordrecht: Martinus Nijhoff.

Rosenberg, P. P. (1984). Support groups: A special therapeutic entity. *Small Group Behavior, 15*, 173–186.

Rossi, P. H. (1992). Assessing family preservation programs. *Children and Youth Services Review, 14*, 77–97.

Rothery, M. (1983). Intervention with maltreating families: The CAS worker's role in family support. In G. Cameron, R. Holmberg, & M. Rothery (Canadian Sociofamily support. In G. Cameron, R. Holmberg, & M. Rothery (Canadian Socio-telic Limited), *The nature and effectiveness of family support measures in child welfare* (pp. 110–138). Toronto: Ontario Ministry of Community and Social Services.

Rubin, A. (1984). Practice effectiveness: More grounds for optimism, *Social Work, 29*, 469–476.

Russell, D., Cutrona, C. E., Rose, J., & Yurko, K. (1984). Social and emotional loneliness: An examination of Weiss' typology of loneliness. *Journal of Personality and Social Psychology, 46*, 1313–1321.

Rzepnicki, T. L. (1987). Recidivism of foster children returned to their own homes: A review and new directions for research. *Social Service Review, 61*, 56–70.

Sandler, I. N. (1980). Social support resources, stress, and maladjustment of poor children. *American Journal of Community Psychology, 8*(1), 41–52.

Sandler, I. N., & Barrera, M. (1984). Toward a multi-method approach to assessing the effects of social support. *American Journal of Community Psychology, 12*, 37–51.

Sandler, I. N., Wolchich, S., & Brower, S. (1985). Social support and children of deviance. In I. G. Sarason & B. R. Sarason (Eds.), *Social support: Theory, research, and applications* (pp. 371–389). Dordrecht: Martinus Nijhoff.

Sarabin, T. R., & Scheibe, K. E. (1983). A model of social identity. In T. R. Sarabin & K. E. Scheibe (Eds.), *Studies in social identity* (pp. 5–28). New York: Praeger.

Sarason, I. G., & Sarason, B. R. (Eds.) (1985). *Social support: Theory, research, and applications*. Dordrecht: Martinus Nijhoff.

Schilling, R. F., & Schinke, S. P. (1983). Social support networks in developmental disabilities. In J. K. Whittaker & J. Garbarino (Eds.), *Social support networks: Informal helping in the human services* (pp. 383–404). Hawthorne, NY: Aldine de Gruyter.

Schreiber, S., & Glidewell, J. (1978). Social norms and helping in a community of limited liability. *American Journal of Community Psychology, 6*(5), 441– 453.

Seekins, T., Mathews, R. M., & Fawcett, S. B. (1984). Enhancing leadership skills for community self-help organizations through behavioral instruction. *Journal of Community Psychology, 12*, 155–163.

Sefcik, T., & Ormsby, N. (1978). Establishing a rural child abuse/neglect treatment program. *Child Welfare, 57*(3), 187–195.

Selig, A. (1979). Research and evaluation in community-oriented primary prevention programs. *Canada's Mental Health, 27*(2), 19–23.

Shapiro, D. (1976). *Agencies and foster children*. New York: Columbia University Press.

Shapiro, D. (1979). *Parents and protectors: A study of child abuse and neglect*. New York: Child Welfare League of America.

Shearer, D. (1979). Parents as educators: The portage project. In S. Maybanks & M. Bryce (Eds.), *Home-based services for children and families: Policy, practice, and research* (pp. 125–135). Springfield, IL: Charles C. Thomas.

Sheda, M., & Winger, J. (1978). *Peer dynamics 1977–78 evaluation report*. Lincoln: Nebraska Department of Health.

Sherman, E., Phillips, M., Haring, B., & Shyne, A. (1973). *Service to children in their own homes: Its nature and outcome*. New York: Child Welfare League of America.

Shinn, M., Lehmann, S., & Wong, N. W. (1984). Social interaction and social support. *Journal of Social Issues, 40*(4), 55–76.

Shumaker, S. A., & Brownell, A. (1985). Introduction: Social support intervention. *Journal of Social Issues, 41*(4), 1–4.

Silverman, P. R. (1980). *Mutual aid groups: Organization and development.* Beverly Hills, CA: Sage.

Silverman, P. R. (1992). Critical aspects of the mutual help experience. In A. H. Katz, H. L. Hedrick, D. H. Isenberg, L. M. Thompson, T. Goodrich, & A. H. Kutscher (Eds.), *Self-help: Concepts and applications* (pp. 76–89). Philadelphia: Charles Press.

Simeonsson, R. J., Cooper, D. H., & Scheiner, A. P. (1982). A review and analysis of the effectiveness of early intervention programs. *Pediatrics, 69*, 635–641.

Skoretz, A. N., & Snider, G. E. (1983). *Social indicators as predictors for child maltreatment.* Unpublished master's research project, Wilfrid Laurier University, Waterloo, Ontario.

Smith, C., Farrant, M., & Marchant, M. (1972). *The Wincroft youth project: A social work program in a slum area.* London: Tavistock.

Smith, J., & Hocking, E. (1981). Index of concern: An instrument for use in treatment of cases of physical abuse of children. *Child Abuse and Neglect, 5*(3), 275–279.

Smith, M., Glass, C., & Miller, T. (1980). *The benefits of psychotherapy.* Baltimore, MD: Johns Hopkins University Press.

Smith, S., Hanson, R., & Noble, S. (1974). Social aspects of the battered baby syndrome. *British Journal of Psychiatry, 125*, 568–582.

Smyth, P. J. (1986). *The impact of social group work on social isolation.* Unpublished master's thesis, York University, Toronto.

Snyder, M. (1981). On the influence of individuals on situations. In N. Cantor & J. F. Kihlstrom (Eds.), *Personality, cognition, and social interaction* (pp. 309–329). Hillsdale, NJ: Lawrence Erlbaum Associates.

Speck, R., & Attneave, C. (1973). *Family networks: A way toward retribalization and healing in family crises.* New York: Pantheon.

Steger, C., & Kotler, T. (1979). Contrasting resources in disturbed and non-disturbed family systems. *British Journal of Medical Psychology, 52*, 243–251.

Stein, T. J. (1985). Projects to prevent out-of-home placement. *Children and Youth Services Review, 7*, 109–121.

Stein, T. J., & Gambrill, E. D. (1974). Foster care: The use of contracts. *Public Welfare, 32*(1), 20-25.

Stein, T. J., & Gambrill, E. D. (1977). Facilitating decision making in foster care: The Alameda project. *Social Service Review, 51*(4), 502–513.

Stein, T. J., & Gambrill, E. D. (1980). The Alameda project: A two year report and one year follow-up. In G. H. Kempe, A. Franklin, & C. Cooper (Eds.), *The abused child in the family and in the community* (Vol. 1) (pp. 521–528). Oxford: Pergamon.

Stein, T. J., & Gambrill, E. D. (1985). Permanency planning for children: The past and present. *Children and Youth Services Review, 7*, 83–94.

Stein, T. J., Gambrill, E. D., & Wiltse, K. (1977). Contracts and outcome in foster care. *Social Work, 22*(2), 148–149.

Stein, T. J., Gambrill, E. D., Wiltse, K., Gilbert, N., & Specht, H. (1978). *Children in foster homes—Achieving continuity of care.* New York: Praeger.

Stein, T. J., & Rzepnick, T. (undated). *Decision making at child welfare intake: A training manual.* Unpublished manuscript, University of Illinois, Jane Adams School of Social Work, Chicago.

Steinman, R., & Traunstein, D. (1976). Redefining deviance: The self-help challenge to the human sciences. *Journal of Applied Behavioral Science, 12*(3), 347–361.

Stevenson, D. G., & Grauerholz, E. (1993). The role of crisis centers in defining and reporting child abuse. *Families in Society, 74,* 221–225.

Stewart, M. J. (1983). Supportive group action for women: A self-help strategy. *Canada's Mental Health, 31*(3), 11–13.

Stewart, M. J. (1990). Professional interface with mutual aid self-help groups: A review. *Social Science and Medicine, 31*(10), 1143–1158.

Stinnett, N., Clesser, B., & DeFrain, J. (1979). *Building family strengths: Blueprints for action.* Omaha: University of Nebraska Press.

Straus, M., Gelles, R., & Steinmetz, S. (1980). *Behind closed doors.* New York: Doubleday.

Stroebe, M. S., & Stroebe, W. (1985). Social support and the alleviation of loss. In I. G. Sarason & B. R. Sarason (Eds.), *Social support: Theory, research, and applications* (pp. 440–462). Dordrecht: Martinus Nijhoff.

Sudia, C. (1981). What services do abusive and neglecting families need? In L. Pelton (Ed.), *The social context of abuse and neglect* (pp. 268–290). New York: Human Sciences Press.

Sudia, C. (1982). Family-based services: A conference report. *Children Today* (September/October), 12–13.

Sudia, C. (1986). Preventing out-of-home placement of children. *Children Today* (November/December), 4–5.

Summit, R., & Kryso, J. (1978). Sexual abuse of children: A clinical spectrum. *American Journal of Orthopsychiatry, 48*(2), 237–251.

Thomlison, R. J. (1984). Something works: Evidence from practice effectiveness studies. *Social Work, 29*(January/February), 51–56.

Tomatzby, L. G., & Fergus, E. O. (1982). Innovation and diffusion in mental health: The community lodge. In A. M. Jeger and R. S. Slotnick (Eds.), *Community mental health and behavior-ecology* (pp. 113–126). New York and London: Plenum.

Toseland, R. W., & Hacker, L. (1982). Self-help groups and professional involvement. *Social Work, 27*(4), 341–347.

Tracy, J. J., & Clark, E. H. (1974). Treatment of child abusers. *Social Work, 19,* 338–343.

Tremble, D., & Kliman, J. (undated). Community network therapy: Strengthening the networks of chronic patients. *International Journal of Family Psychiatry, 2,* 3–4.

Triplett, B., Preston, I., Henry, A., & Thompson, M. (1986). Moving toward family preservation services in Kentucky. *Children Today* (November/December), 8–11.

Turner, R. J. (1981). Social support as a contingency in psychological well-being. *Journal of Health and Social Behavior, 22*(4), 357–367.

Tuszynski, A., & Dowd, J. (1979). Home-based services to protective services families. In S. Maybanks & M. Bryce (Eds.), *Home-based services for children and families: Policy, practice, and research* (pp. 296–307). Springfield, IL: Charles C. Thomas.

Tweraser, G., & Waddle, J. (1981). Every parent's birthright: Bonding as the key to effective lay therapy. In M. Bryce & J. C. Lloyd (Eds.), *Treating families in the home: An alternative to placement* (pp. 191–204). Springfield, IL: Charles C. Thomas.

Unger, D. G., & Powell, D. R. (1980). Supporting families under stress: The role of social networks. *Family Relations, 29*(4, October), 566–574.

Van Meter, M. J. S. (1986). An alternative to foster care for victims of child abuse/neglect: A university-based program. *Child Abuse and Neglect, 10,* 79–84.

Videka, L. M. (1979). Psychosocial adaptation in a medical self-help group. In M. Lieberman & L. Borman (Eds.), *Self-help groups for coping with crisis* (pp. 362–386). San Francisco: Jossey-Bass.

Videka-Sherman, L. (1982). Effects of participation in a self-help group for bereaved parents: Compassionate friends. *Prevention in Human Services, 1*(3), 69–77.

Videka-Sherman, L. (1985). *Harriett M. Bartlett practice effectiveness project: Report to NASW board of directors.* Silver Springs, MD: National Association of Social Workers.

Videka-Sherman, L., & Lieberman, M. (1985). The effects of self-help and psychotherapy intervention on child loss: The limits of recovery. *American Journal of Orthopsychiatry, 55*(1), 70–82.

Von Stolk, M. (1973). *The battered child in Canada.* Toronto: McClelland & Stewart.

Wahler, R. G. (1983). Predictors of treatment outcome in parent training: Mother insularity and socioeconomic disadvantage. *Behavioral Assessment, 5,* 301–313.

Wahler, R. G., Afton, A. D., & Fox, J. J. (1979). The multiply entrapped parent: Some new problems in parent training. *Education and Treatment of Children, 2*(4), 279–286.

Wald, M. S. (1982). State intervention on behalf of endangered children—A proposed legal response. *Child Abuse and Neglect, 6*(1), 3–45.

Wald, M. S. (1988). Family preservation: Are we moving too fast? *Public Welfare, 3,* 33–38.

Warren, D. I. (1980). Support systems in different types of neighborhoods. In J. Garbarino & S. H. Stocking (Eds.), *Protecting children from abuse and neglect: Developing and maintaining effective support systems for families* (pp. 61–93). San Francisco: Jossey-Bass.

Warren, D. I. (1981). *Helping networks: How people cope with problems in the urban community.* Notre Dame, IN: Notre Dame University Press.

Weinraul, M., & Woef, B. M. (1983). Effects of stress and social supports on mother-child interactions in single- and two-parent families. *Child Development, 54,* 1297–1311.

Weiss, H. B. (1989). State family support and education programs: Lessons from the pioneers. *American Journal of Orthopsychiatry, 59*(January), 32–48.

Weiss, R. S. (1975). *Marital separation.* New York: Basic Books.

Weiss, R. S. (1979). *Doing it alone.* New York: Basic Books.

Weiss, R. S. (1973). The contributions of an organization of single parents to the well-being of its members. *Family Coordinator, 22*(July), 321–326.

Weissbourd, B., & Kagan, S. L. (1989). Family support programs: Catalysts for change. *American Journal of Orthopsychiatry, 59,* 20–31.

Wellman, B. (1979). The community question: The intimate networks of East Yorkers. *American Journal of Sociology, 84*(8), 1201–1231.

Wellman, B. (1985). From social support to social network. In I. G. Sarason & B. R. Sarason (Eds.), *Social support: Theory, research, and applications* (pp. 205–222). Dordrecht: Martinus Nijhoff.

Wells, K., & Biegel, D. E. (1992). Intensive family preservation services research: Current status and future agenda. *Social Work Research and Abstracts, 28,* 21–27.

White, K. R. (1988). Cost analyses in family support programs. In H. B. Weiss & F. C. Jacobs (Eds.), *Evaluating family programs* (pp. 429–443). Hawthorne, NY: Aldine de Gruyter.

Whittaker, J. K. (1981). *Community supports for troubled children and youth: A project summary.* Seattle: University of Washington, School of Social Work.

Whittaker, J. K., Kinney, J., Tracy, E. M., & Booth, C. (1990). *Reaching high-risk families: Intensive family preservation in human services.* Hawthorne, NY: Aldine de Gruyter.

Whittaker, J. K., & Tracy, E. M. (1990). Family preservation services and education for social work practice: Stimulus and response. In J. K. Whittaker, J. Kinney, E. M. Tracy, & C. Booth (Eds.), *Reaching high-risk families: Intensive family preservation in human services* (pp. 1–11). Hawthorne, NY: Aldine de Gruyter.

Wichlacz, C. R., Lane, J. M., & Kempe, C. H. (1978). Indian child welfare: A community team approach to protective services. *Child Abuse and Neglect, 2*(1), 29–35.

Willen, M. L. (1984). Parents Anonymous: The professional's role as sponsor. In A. Gartner & F. Riessman (Eds.), *The self-help revolution* (pp. 109–119). New York: Human Sciences Press.

Wilson, M. (1979). Home and school: Partners in learning. In S. Maybanks & M. Bryce (Eds.), *Home-based services for children and families: Policy, practice, and research* (pp. 145–153). Springfield, IL: Charles C. Thomas.

Wolfe, D. A., & Koverola, C. (1984). Multimodal assessment of child abusive families: Research and clinical findings. Paper presented at the Association for Advancement of Behavior Therapy Annual Convention, Philadelphia, Pennsylvania.

Wolfe, D. A., & Marion, I. G. (1984). Impediments to child abuse prevention issues and directions. *Advanced Behavioral Research and Therapy, 6,* 47–62.

Wolfender Report. (1978). *The future of voluntary organization.* London: Croom Helm.

Wollert, R. W. (1986). Psychosocial helping processes in a heterogeneous sample of self-help groups. *Canadian Journal of Community Mental Health, 5,* 63–76.

Wollert, R. W., Barron, N., & Bob, M. (1982). Parents United of Oregon: A natural history of a self-help group for sexually abusive families. *Prevention in Human Services, 1*(3), 99–109.

Wollert, R. W., Levy, L. H., & Knight, B. G. (1982). Help-giving in behavioral central and stress coping self-help groups. *Small Group Behavior, 13*(2), 204–218.

Wolock, I. (1981). Child health and developmental problems and child maltreatment among AFDC families. *Journal of Sociology and Social Welfare, 8,* 83–96.

Wolock, I. (1982). Community characteristics and staff judgments in child abuse and neglect cases. *Social Work Research and Abstracts, 18*(2), 9–15.

Wolve, D. A. (1984). Treatment of abusive parents: A reply to the special issue. *Journal of Clinical Child Psychology, 13*(2), 142–194.

Wortman, C. B., & Lehman, D. R. (1985). Reactions to victims of life crisis: Support attempts that fail. In I. G. Sarason & B. R. Sarason (Eds.), *Social support: Theory, research, and applications* (pp. 462–489). Dordrecht: Martinus Nijhoff.

Yamamoto, J. (1967). Racial factors in patient selection. *American Journal of Psychiatry, 124*(May), 630–636.

Yoder, J. A., Jonker, J. M. L., & Leaper, R. A. B. (1985). *Support networks in a caring community.* Dordrecht: Martinus Nijhoff.

Young, C. E., Giles, D. E., Jr., & Plantz, M. C. (1982). Natural networks: Help-giving and help-seeking in two rural communities. *American Journal of Community Psychology, 10*(4), 457–469.

Young, G., & Gately, T. (1988). Neighborhood impoverishment and child maltreatment: An analysis from the ecological perspective. *Journal of Family Issues, 9,* 240–254.

Young, L. (1964). *Wednesday's children.* New York: McGraw-Hill.

Young, R. D., & McEachern, W. D. C. (1983). *Family formation and marital status of client families.* London, Ontario: Family and Children's Services of London and Middlesex.

Zigler, E., & Black, K. B. (1989). America's family support movement: Strengths and limitations. *American Journal of Orthopsychiatry, 59,* 6–19.

Zuckler, J., & Brondstadt, W. (1975). *The teenage pregnant girl.* Springfield, IL: Charles C. Thomas.

Index

DATE DUE

APR 06 1996		
NOV 13 2005		
28th Nov '05 DEC 17 2012		
GAYLORD		PRINTED IN U.S.A.